Encounters

Encounters

JARVIS ASTAIRE

Robson Books

First published in Great Britain in 1999 by Robson Books, 10 Blenheim Court, Brewery Road, London N7 9NT

Copyright © 1999 Jarvis Astaire
The right of Jarvis Astaire to be identified as author of this work has been asserted by him in accordance with the Copyright, Designs and Patents Act 1988.

British Library Cataloguing in Publication Data
A catalogue record for this title is available from the British Library

ISBN 1 86105 248 0

Typeset in Janson by SX Composing DTP, Rayleigh, Essex
Printed and bound in Great Britain by
Creative Print and Design, (Wales).

Contents

1	Beginnings	8
2	The Greatest	24
3	Movie Star Manager	38
4	The Trouble with Hoffman	51
5	Business Genius	73
6	Wilson and the Honours List	89
7	Lew and I	104
8	That's Entertainment	116
9	Sport on the Screen	131
10	The Fight Game	142
11	Frank and Mike	157
12	Bookies and Horses	169
13	Wembley, Venue of Legends	181
14	Variety and Other Clubs	211
15	All the Way	222

Acknowledgements

I would like to thank Mihir Bose for his help, Chris Dighton for his research, Ken Follett for his valuable advice and Andrew Freeman who motivated me to write this book.

All of us can point to a day or a moment which had a major impact on our lives. I am no different. My seminal moment came on a dank, cold October morning in 1964.

For days I had been in a lather, not knowing what to do. I had arranged for Terry Downes to fight Willie Pastrano for the world light-heavyweight boxing championship. In those days you booked a venue making sure it was big enough to accommodate everyone. There was little or no television and hardly anyone not physically present saw the fight live.

A London venue was a must for Downes. He was a London boy, this was where his fans were. But we couldn't get a London venue. Manchester was the only place where we could stage the fight and even there we had to opt for a smaller arena, the King's Hall at Belle Vue. Not only was that nowhere near big enough to satisfy the massive demand, it was more than 200 miles from Downes' army of supporters.

I wrestled with this dilemma. That October morning, having spent a restless night worrying about it, I woke up at six o'clock and thought to myself this is absurd. Terry's fans would have to take a day off work, travel all the way to Manchester and somehow find a ticket. Yet, if I could show it on closed-circuit television in a cinema in London, it would solve all our problems.

But to the powers-that-be in Britain that was totally unacceptable. The Post Office, who controlled the lines which would be used for beaming the action back to a cinema, had consistently refused to sanction any such arrangement. Since 1959 I had been writing and pleading with them for a change of heart, yet the civil servants running the Post Office would not even grant me a meeting.

That morning, I decided to write again to the Post Office, explaining the situation and asking if just as an experiment I could have the line. I made much in my letter of Downes' fans having to travel to Manchester and how they would have to miss a day's work. It was a time of change. Only the week before, Labour, led by Harold Wilson, had come to power ending 'thirteen wasted years' of Conservative rule, to use the phrase made popular by Wilson. There was change in the undergrowth as well. Although nobody had yet invented the term, we were in the middle of what is now called the Sixties revolution. Despite all this, I still expected the Post Office civil servants to say no. Instead a letter came back agreeing to the experiment on a trial basis. To this day, I don't know what changed their minds.

But wonderful as this unexpected green light from the Post Office was, it did not solve all my problems. I still had to find a London theatre willing to stage the show. Eventually I managed to book the Phoenix in Charing Cross Road. Then I had to solve the technical problems of showing the fight from Manchester. The BBC would not give me any help; I could not rent their equipment, although I did persuade David Coleman to be the commentator.

My search led me to two men in West London, Trevor Wallace and Michael Style. From their garage in Ealing they were running a company called Intertel Services which provided makeshift TV facilities. They had cameras and some experience of working in television, and in Manchester they did just the job that was needed.

The trouble I had in putting on what was the first closed-circuit sporting event proved worthwhile. The Downes fight, and particularly the screening of it at the Phoenix Theatre, was a great success and it began to make people sit up. The very next day Rank offered me their cinemas and although the BBC cut up rough and would no longer let me use David Coleman – it meant chances for Reg Gutteridge, who had had several trials with ITV but had not been taken on, and later on also Desmond Lynam, whose work had been confined to radio – closed-circuit television had arrived. At the age of forty-one, I had managed to change the viewing contour of this country.

Writing this in 1999, when Sky and pay-per-view are as much part of our television world as the BBC or ITV, the idea that some thirty years ago the powers-that-be resisted closed-circuit television in the cinemas seems strange. It almost sounds prehistoric. But then we in this country have always resisted change and only accepted it grudgingly and often too late. It was not always so; after all, we led the world in the industrial revolution and Britain was where television was invented in the first place.

I have always been a believer that in life you keep on going. Life has a way of throwing up unexpected challenges and you will always meet awkward people, but the trick is to make sure you are not overwhelmed by surprise, that you surprise other people as well. Prime Minister Harold Macmillan was once asked what concerned him most. He replied, 'Events, dear boy, events.' I know exactly what he meant. You never know what is round the next corner.

Perhaps the most surprising event of my life, certainly the most frightening, happened one Saturday evening in 1968 as my wife Phyllis and I were dressing to go to see the show 'A Funny Thing Happened on the Way to the Forum'. Just as we were about to go out of the door, the phone rang. Phyllis answered. Without saying a word and looking very pale and frightened, she handed the receiver to me.

The man's voice on the other end sounded very menacing and he spoke very clearly, using phrases like 'justice will be done'. He then told me I would be dead within seven days of the phone conversation. The person appeared to be referring to a 'Mr X' story in the *People* newspaper – a story about which

I shall have more to say later – and although I tried hard to persuade him that he was obviously being put up to something by people who were deceiving him, he would not be deterred and said he would phone again.

I was obviously concerned but for the moment there was nothing I could do. Phyllis and I, together with two friends, went on to the show which, remarkably under the circumstances, I greatly enjoyed. When afterwards we got to the Savoy for dinner, I rang Chief Superintendent Jack Manning, head of the Murder Squad at Scotland Yard, who was also a personal friend. Jack tried to reassure me but said the matter clearly needed to be looked into.

The following Monday, a young and very bright detective, Inspector David Dilley, came to see me. I was hoping Dilley would say it was just a crank call but he took the threat seriously, which did nothing to calm my fears. However, when he promised he would make sure the threat was not carried out, I was reassured. He arranged to have me watched at the office and at home and have my telephone tapped. (This had the unintentional, if somewhat comical effect of prompting calls from neighbours warning us our house was being watched.) That evening the man rang again and I got the impression he was a professional gangster who was not only intent on carrying out his threat but also enjoying turning the screw and making me squirm.

Despite Dilley saying my phone would be tapped, that conversation was not overheard. The problem once again, as I discovered the next day, was the Post Office, who told Dilley they had too few facilities for such procedures. In some fury I rang the head of the London Telecommunications Division. I had great difficulty getting through to him and finally did so after pretending I was calling from the Home Office.

This particular official confirmed my worst suspicions of civil servants. He made it quite clear that it was not so much that they did not have the facilities to tap my phone, but that they did not think my life was important enough to be worth bothering about! When I asked what they would do if the life of Reginald Bevins, the then Postmaster General, was threatened, the official calmly said, 'In those circumstances, we would have to provide the facilities.'

That answer shook me. I have never been so furious in my life and I fairly barked into the phone, 'Let me tell you, my life is as important to me as Mr Bevins' life is to him or, for that matter, the life of the man who is cleaning my window at this very moment is to him. We all value our lives and have every right to hold them dear, so you'd better start tapping my phone as Scotland Yard has requested.' I don't know whether it was what I said or the way I said it, but within twenty minutes the same official had rung to say the tapping arrangements would be in place by that evening. As it happened, no-one was cleaning my windows when I spoke to the official, but the story had clearly served its purpose.

That evening there was no phone call from the mystery man, although I learnt that the *Daily Express* had been rung up by him and told I was being threatened with murder. Curiously, the *Express* did not bother to inform the police. The next phone call came on Wednesday evening at about 8pm. I knew I had to keep the man on the line long enough for the call to be traced and I did everything I could to keep him talking. He was clearly enjoying baiting me but on at least three occasions he nearly hung up. By now I had begun to feel the man was crazy but this was not exactly reassuring for, as Dilley had explained, crazy people were even more difficult to deal with. I had managed to keep him talking for an hour, by the end of which I was soaked in sweat, when he suddenly said, 'I have got to go,' and put the phone down. I felt sick with frustration, convinced the opportunity to nab him had gone, but then I heard a voice on the other end of the line saying, 'It's alright, sir, we've got him.'

The mystery was soon solved. The call had eventually been traced to a phone box in Feltham in Middlesex and the reason the man had put the phone down so suddenly was because the police had arrived to pick him up. He turned out to be a Mr Prince, a former employee of the Hurst Park Syndicate, a public company where I was a shareholder and non-executive director. Prince appeared to be involved with an accomplice in stealing some money from the company. The accomplice was charged and convicted. Prince claimed the company owed him money, something like £160, and on the day his friend was convicted he had come close to running down Sam Burns, the company's managing director. Burns had actually warned me that he was a little scared of what this man would do, as he felt he was unstable.

The police investigation also reminded me of a phone conversation I had had with Prince some ten months earlier, although at the time I did not know his name and the conversation had made no impression on me. What had happened was that he had rung me at my office. He had been told I was a director of the company and wanted me to try and get him the money he claimed was his. He had then proceeded to tell me that Sam Burns and his colleagues were robbing me and the other directors. I tried to tell him I could not interfere because I was not involved in the day-to-day running of the company. He was phoning from a call box and his money ran out before our conversation could be concluded, but I told my telephone operator that if he rang again he was to be told I had nothing more to say to him.

I had forgotten all about that call by the time Prince rang me at home that Saturday night threatening to kill me. He was charged with making threatening calls and Phyllis and I gave evidence at the magistrates' court near Feltham. We were subjected to a pretty rigorous cross-examination by Prince's counsel but he could not shake our story. Nor did he impress the judge when he said that I looked very calm while giving evidence and did not look like a man who could be frightened. The judge tartly pointed out to him that I was unlikely to have been quite so calm when I received Prince's death threats.

Prince, of course, was anything but calm. As Phyllis was

leaving the witness box he ran out of the dock and the court and had to be chased by a police car. They caught up with him a mile or so down the road. This only emphasized his unstable character and his counsel quickly changed his plea to guilty, albeit with mitigation. Prince was put on probation for two years on the condition that he receive psychiatric treatment. Ironically, his escapade of running from court probably kept him from jail, as it convinced the judge that he was mentally unstable.

If that was one of the times when I have come close to physical danger, there have been many other moments of excitement and drama, all of which have made me feel greatly privileged and fortunate to have been born when I was. For in many ways, my life story has been a chronicle of the vast changes that have come to the worlds of sport and entertainment – two worlds with which I have been intimately associated. It has brought me into contact with an extraordinary cast of people and it is amazing to reflect on the changes that have taken place during those seventy-five years.

I was born when this country still had an empire, and nobody doubted that it would, like the Roman empire, last 1,000 years. It was a mere five years after the end of the Great War, as the First World War was known, and the sense of grief, desolation and waste it produced was something of which I was quickly made aware. Many people had expected simply to return to the pre-1914 days, to the natural order of things. Little did they realize that world was gone for ever. As for the twists and turns that the century has since brought, they were surely beyond even the wildest imagination and confined to the fertile minds of science fiction writers.

Growing up then in England between the wars, I could not have anticipated how my life would have turned out although my upbringing did, in many ways, prepare me to cope with the changes that came – and even take advantage of them.

1

Beginnings

I was born on 6 October 1923 in Bromhead Street in Stepney, East London, at my grandmother's house. My mother was only just twenty at the time and had come to her mother's house to have me, a decision influenced by the fact that she quite liked the young doctor there, Dr Philip Steinberg. For my grandmother his charm mattered not a jot. When he came she hustled him unceremoniously into the room where my mother was having her labour pains, locked him in and wouldn't let him out until I was safely delivered.

The experience terrified the doctor, who left the house vowing he would never do another delivery again. But he did. Nearly seven years later my brother Edgar was born and my mother again went home to Bromhead Street, where Dr Steinberg once more took charge.

The doctor was not the only one to fall under the spell of my grandmother, Rebecca. I had a great deal to do with her and I both loved and respected her. It was due to her intense desire to learn English that I ended up learning Yiddish. I was about twelve years old and my school, Kilburn Grammar, was much nearer to her house than mine, so I used to go to her home in Willesden for lunch. She craved reading English and wanted me to give her an English reading lesson every day. So I would buy the racing paper, that being the only newspaper around when I left school at lunchtime, and read to her from a small section of general news on the front page.

She had told me she would give me three pennies for doing

it, but I said: 'Don't give me three pennies. You teach me in return to read the Yiddish paper.' She used to get the *Jewish Times*, which was the Yiddish paper, and the American paper called *The Forward*, which still exists. The deal worked out better for me than for my grandmother. I learned to understand Yiddish by reading the serial every day, but my grandmother only learnt to read English rather falteringly. Many years later when I travelled to the lands that brought my grandparents here, I was grateful for her determination.

My grandmother had come to this country from the Ukraine part of Russia, a town called Chotin, very near Chernobyl on the borders of Romania, Ukraine and Moldova. The family had a background of learning and some wealth. My mother's father was a cantor, leading synagogue services, and my grandmother's family had orchards. This was the end of the nineteenth century and it was a time of pogroms in eastern Europe. Jews were fleeing persecution and my mother's father was brought over from the Ukraine to be a cantor in the East End of London, where there was a growing Jewish population. It was in England that my mother was born and given the name Esther.

The people who had brought my mother's family over had a cap-making business and they gave my grandfather a part-time job, because he couldn't support his family out of his wages as a cantor. Eventually, he set up, with his elder sons, his own cap-making factory. By coincidence, it was very near where my father's father had a furniture factory. My father's family had made a similar journey from eastern Europe to the East End, the only difference being that while my mother was born here, my father was three years old when he arrived in England. His family had come from Pinsk, which alternated over the centuries between being part of Russia and Poland.

Many years later, accompanied by my eldest grandson Daniel, I visited Pinsk, my father's birthplace, which is now part of Belarus. I also travelled to Stollin, a small town forty-five kilometres further away, where my grandfather grew up

before he went to Pinsk and married my grandmother. In
Stollin the last Jew had died about six months before Daniel
and I went there, but I found the synagogue where my grandfather – a very pious man – used to pray. It was exactly as he
described it. There was a chilling experience to follow when
we were driven five kilometres into a forest near Stollin to be
shown a clearing where 600 Jews were massacred on one night
and put into a huge open grave. There were impressive
memorials provided by both the Soviet government and the
World Jewish Congress. I thought of my grandfather and the
words 'There but for the grace of God' had a special meaning.

We flew on to Minsk to meet the chief Rabbi of Minsk and
Belarus, Rabbi Isaac Wolpin, an American dynamo who was
successfully restoring the presence of the Jewish community in
Belarus, where around 125,000 remained. He in turn put me
in touch with Isaac Kliner, the leader of the community in
Pinsk (which now has just a thousand Jews), who proudly
showed me pictures of himself as a paratrooper in the Russian
army during the war. He spoke Yiddish and it was then that
the lessons I had with my grandmother all those years ago
came back to me and stood me in good stead.

I also had a very close relationship with my paternal grandmother Leah, who spoiled me with gifts and money and if I
had eaten everything she offered me I would have ended up as
some sort of giant. She was different from Rebecca in that if I
tried to speak to her in Yiddish, she would simply answer me,
very elegantly, in English.

It was, perhaps, inevitable that the two families should have
been joined in a marriage alliance. They were both from very
pious Orthodox backgrounds and both my grandfathers used
to go to their own synagogue every day. My mother was a very
attractive woman and my father became friendly with her
brother, who worked nearby. One day he saw her out with her
brother and asked if he could take her out. Whether it was love
at first sight I do not know, but it was a deep, abiding love and
they were married in December 1922. Ten months later I was

born. I was named in memory of my great-grandfather Joseph and my mother added the name Jarvis. She thought it had the right ring to it.

Although my grandparents' journey to this country was duplicated by many other Jewish families, mine is not a rags to riches story. My parents had gone into the millinery business and I always say I grew up in the manner to which I became accustomed. My mother made sure the house was always managed perfectly, and before the war she went to Paris every few weeks to look at designs for hats. It was a time when all ladies wore hats, as did a lot of men, and my parents were quick to sense the business opportunities available.

My mother, who had trained as a milliner, opened her first shop around the time I was born in Fulham, where we lived for a while above the shop. Then she opened a second shop in Upton Park, best known as the home of West Ham United. We moved there while that business was established, then went back to Fulham and on to a house in nearby Putney. By the early 1930s my parents had progressed from running shops that sold hats to manufacturing hats, as more sophisticated machinery was invented and mass production became the thing. By the time the war started, they had a hundred girls working for them in a factory in the Barbican making ladies' hats. I sometimes used to sit and watch the girls at work. They were of various ages and they made a tremendous fuss of me. I liked it best when they told me about the films they had seen the night before. This was their favourite pastime and I would sit fascinated as they talked about the movie stars.

My father ran the business side of things while my mother looked after the design and making of the hats. She could be a very masterful woman, very articulate with a powerful turn of phrase. For example, if she thought I was going over the top she would say, 'Jarvis, always remember one thing. I'll stand for too much, but never three much.' It says a lot for her character that she drove a car in 1922.

My mother worked hard and played hard and her greatest

pleasure was to go to the cinema and music hall. I remember her taking me to see Al Jolson in 'The Jazz Singer', the first talking picture, at the Piccadilly Theatre. My parents were also very keen on variety shows and they used to take me to theatres all over London. They spent hours telling me about the stars, comedians and singers they had seen in earlier years. They were big fans of the music halls and we would go to the Holborn Empire or the Finsbury Park Empire or the Hackney Empire to see all manner of acts, including some top name Americans who came over to Britain. Through my parents' love of the stage I saw Gracie Fields, Tommy Trinder, Max Miller, the street singer Arthur Tracey, Eddie Cantor, Stéphane Grappelly, Owen McGiven, Jimmy Wheeler, Florence Desmond, the xylophone player Teddy Brown and Jack Hylton & His Band.

Because my parents were still very young – my father was only twenty-three when I was born – in a sense we all grew up together. When we went out it was as friends. I suppose I was always precocious and being very tall even at fourteen, I mixed with older people and was quite comfortable in their company. By the time Edgar was born I was almost seven and there was never any sibling rivalry. My brother grew up with three parents – I was the third one. I used to teach him nursery rhymes and read him bedtime stories. In photos of us as children you will always see me with my hands over my brother's shoulder. I was his protector.

We were, I suppose, no different from most other pre-war middle-class families. We always had the *Daily Express* and the *Sunday Express* at home, this being the heyday of those papers, then owned by Lord Beaverbrook. I quickly joined that wonderful class of people who start reading the newspapers from the back – with the sports pages. My interest in sport had been kindled early. My father liked all sport but particularly football and cricket, and I had uncles also interested in boxing. One of them bought me some boxing gloves when I was about ten years old and my mother said, 'Don't start him on boxing!'

She hated boxing and wasn't at all interested in sport.

Although my name has become associated with boxing, I am actually more knowledgeable about football and during the early years of the *Rothmans Football Yearbook*, now the sport's bible, I was on the advisory panel. I always say, with tongue in cheek, 'I'm not a supporter of any team because no club has ever supported me,' but I'm a fan and Chelsea was the first club for me. I have been asked on several occasions to become a director of a football club but have refused principally because I am convinced it would spoil my enjoyment of the game. I did, however, help found Wingate FC, a club which was formed to bring together the best players from Jewish Youth Clubs' into higher-grade football. It later merged with Finchley and the club plays in the Ryman League. As a result of this involvement with them, in 1951 I arranged for the Israeli club side Hapoel Tel Aviv to come over to Britain for a three-month tour and play matches against Manchester United, Leeds and Arsenal. The Arsenal fixture was the first senior football match ever to be played under floodlights – although underneath a large picture on display today at Highbury the caption still claims, despite my regular protests, that the first such game was against Rangers! The tour was a great inspiration to Israeli football and many friendships formed on it have lasted to this day.

When I was six years old I lived less than a mile from Chelsea's ground. My father was then working on Saturday afternoons and couldn't take me to football, and he certainly wouldn't give me the money to go on my own at that age. But I found a way of getting in. I followed a lot of other boys and slid on my back under the exit turnstile at Stamford Bridge. I did that for a whole season until I eventually got caught. One day my small cousin, a year younger than me, came with me. He was just about to slide under the turnstile when he saw a policeman, took fright and ran away. Fortunately, he remembered where we lived and the policeman took him back, but when I got home I had some explaining to do. The result was my father gave me a smack, but the one good thing to come out of it was that he did buy me a ticket for the next season.

In 1989, when Chelsea won promotion to the then First Division, we had a boxing dinner at the National Sporting Club in aid of the Variety Club, and the Chelsea team and staff were the guests of honour. I was asked to propose the toast to Chelsea, so when I got up to speak I said, 'When the committee asked me to propose this toast this evening, they couldn't have known how eminently qualified I am.' I went on to tell the story of how I had a free season at the Bridge, and finished by saying, 'I couldn't have come here this evening with a clear conscience. I've had my office calculate how much I owe Chelsea FC for all those tickets at 6d, with interest, and I have a cheque here for £89.50 for the Chelsea chairman, Mr Ken Bates.' As he took the cheque, Ken said, 'Is this straight interest or compound?'

My father did eventually take me to football but that was to White Hart Lane. He had been a Spurs supporter since 1912 and my journeys to matches with my father meant every Saturday I combined religion and football – literally. By then, having moved to manufacturing hats, my father no longer worked on Saturday afternoons but he did work on Saturday mornings, which meant going to the City. That is when I had my dose of religion as my paternal grandfather took me to the synagogue on Saturday mornings. In the afternoon I met up with my father and we would go by train from Liverpool Street to White Hart Lane.

I had other sporting experiences besides football. My favourite game was, and still is, cricket and we used to go to Lord's and The Oval. I can remember watching Stan Squires of Surrey score over 250 in a day against Nottinghamshire. I saw Don Bradman and Jack Hobbs play and I remember a visit to Hobbs' sports shop in Fleet Street. Later on Bill Edrich and Denis Compton were my Middlesex favourites at Lord's, and Denis became a good friend.

My first school was a prep school in Fulham, Heathfield

House. When I was ten we moved to Dollis Hill, so I went to Kilburn Grammar School. It was a typical red-brick grammar which produced High Court judges as well as successful businessmen. I think it was a terrible error to get rid of so many of those schools and I am glad to see the Labour Government is thinking of preserving those that remain. I only wish they would go further and open up a few more. The school motto was *Pasce Agnos Meos* – Feed My Lambs. You had to pass an entrance exam and the students came from a very mixed background.

In the summer, because my mother was so busy with work, I went to a summer school in Hampstead. The people who ran it, the Schindlers, would take us away to Bognor and Bexhill and try to make school life varied and interesting. While I enjoyed school and did well in languages – I speak French well and enough German and was good at Latin – my main interest was playing football and cricket.

But I was really shaped by the Boys' Clubs. As a child I was tall for my age and mixed with boys older than me, and they were constantly talking about the local Boys' Club – something I was desperate to join. You had to be thirteen and the minute I reached that age I was off to the North West Jewish Boys' Club. It lived up to all my expectations. I learnt more from it than I did at school; this was where my character and leadership skills were formed and I have been associated with Boys' Clubs ever since. I have been a Vice President and the treasurer of the London Federation of Clubs for Young People for sixteen years, and for many years President of the Lion Club in Shoreditch. I am still a Vice-President of my own Boys' Club, which merged with the Kingsbury Club and is known as Kinnor, and for some years have been a member of the Council of the National Association of Clubs for Young People.

School gave me the basics, but the Boys' Club was my education. While I could do school work, I was somewhat lazy and if I scored low marks in some subjects it didn't worry me.

If something didn't interest me then that was it, and that has been true of everything in my life: I'm either totally involved or indifferent. The Boys' Club allowed the extrovert side of me to come out and I was secretary of the cricket eleven and captain of both cricket and football teams. Not that I was the best player by a long chalk, but I impressed with my skill for organizing and getting things done.

By then, of course, the long shadow of the Second World War had begun to fall on us. I knew all about the terrible sufferings Hitler's Nazi regime was inflicting on people, especially the Jews, because we had started taking in refugee Jewish girls from Germany. The brains behind the scheme was my maternal grandmother. She engaged new maids about every three weeks and that way she helped a lot of girls. She used to take me to a domestic staff agency to fill in the forms and we got them into the country that way. Some of them were beautiful, well-educated girls, whose parents were spiriting them out of Germany.

I often wonder what happened to them all. They probably never saw their families again but then they were, of course, the lucky ones. Millions of others perished in the terrible death camps which we only heard about after the war. When I think of the Jewish girls my grandmother helped, I cannot but give thanks that my grandparents migrated to Britain not Germany when fleeing from persecution in eastern Europe. I shudder to think what would have happened to us had they, like millions of others, gone to Germany.

The war changed my life as well. Before it began I wanted to be a lawyer. By the time it was over, given the disruption it had caused to my education, or more accurately my hopes for further education, there was no chance of that.

Two days before the war started, I was in the Royal Northern Hospital having had ingrown toenails removed and my feet were all bound up. My mother came in our car, a Wolseley, and took me and my brother to Brighton. That was where she had gone with her parents towards the end of the

First World War and she was determined that should there be another such conflict, she would move me and my brother to Brighton straight away. I remember the trip to the south coast clearly. I was helped into the car and we drove straight to Brighton, where we stayed in an hotel. Soon after, Neville Chamberlain came on the radio and announced war had broken out, and my mother and other women started crying. I couldn't understand her tears because to me it was exciting, and I retained this feeling of war being fun and glamorous even when the bombs started falling.

We were to spend almost the first year of the war in Brighton, with both my parents returning to London on a regular basis to keep their business ticking over. We lived in a nice house in Preston Park but eventually left because my father found it difficult to commute, especially in the winter. He became ill with pneumonia and soon after that we returned to London and took a flat in Park West, near Marble Arch. I can remember standing outside the Cumberland Hotel at Marble Arch as the Battle of Britain raged overhead and seeing men dropping out of the sky with parachutes opening behind them as they fell to the earth. In the Blitz, I didn't think about my own safety in spite of the falling bombs and the only real concession to the danger came at night when we slept in the shelters under the block of flats where we lived. By day we got on with life as best we could. I remember going to see Tommy Trinder at the London Palladium on the night the Blitz started. I was with a friend, Ronnie Specterman, and afterwards we walked down from Oxford Circus to Marble Arch as the bombs blasted out windows and the night sky turned red from the fires the German bombs had lit in the City of London. To my young eyes, it represented not danger but something out of a movie.

By this time, not much more than seventeen, I had started working – my pre-war dreams to become a lawyer having been shattered – for a firm making surgical instruments. I had an uncle who had been a polio victim in the First World War and he used to have to wear callipers made by a Mr Becket, who was the head of the Surgical Instrument Manufacturers Association. In 1937 my uncle, a very resourceful man, built himself a car with hand controls only, a Morris Minor which he adapted. I remember Mr Becket telling him that, with the advent of war, there would be a need for people to go into the hospital equipment business. My uncle suggested me and so I went for an interview. Mr Becket did not have a job for me at that time but introduced me to another major supplier, Allen & Hanbury's, just round the corner from his company.

Initially, I worked in the department supplying artificial arms and legs. I got on very well there and by the age of nineteen I was the manager of the electro-medical department, going to hospitals all over the country. The company played a big part in the war effort, being contracted to the Ministry of War and the Royal Army Medical Corps, and I was on call twenty-four hours a day. I had to be available all the time, so much so that I wasn't allowed to leave London. As a result I was never called up for military service. My company would not even allow me to join the Home Guard, although I did do some fire watches, which were formed to deal with incendiary bombs. My chance to leave London did not come until towards the end of the war and then it involved me in a cloak and dagger operation straight out of a John Le Carré thriller.

The war had entered its fifth year, I was twenty-one and I suddenly found myself working with Tito's partisans. It was a clandestine thing, involving Winston Churchill, his son Randolph and Fitzroy McLean, the man sent by Churchill to Marshal Tito to act as British liaison to the Yugoslav partisans. Some of these partisans came to London and stayed in an anonymous house near Hyde Park. I was always good at languages and one day I was sent for. Two men were there, one speaking French and the other German. They were in Britain to buy medical equipment and I had been asked to come along because of my knowledge of the products they needed to acquire, and being able to converse with them. Soon I was going round the country with them buying equipment.

That sounds simple enough, except that the whole operation was shrouded in secrecy. It had to be. At Churchill's invitation, Tito's partisans had set up a secret office in London, but this had to be completely unofficial because Britain had recognized the exiled Yugoslavian government of King Peter. However, Tito's partisans were providing the most effective opposition to the Nazis and although they were communists, Churchill's attitude was that he would make a pact with the devil if necessary to defeat Hitler. But it would have been embarrassing if it had emerged that Tito's men were in London buying supplies behind King Peter's back, so these partisans had no bank account. Instead I went round the country with them carrying bundles of cash, stuffed in brief-cases and suitcases, and paying for most purchases with those big white £5 notes of the time.

I was originally expecting to go overseas to military hospitals, but we didn't suffer as many casualties as had been envisaged. Then I was meant to be going to Yugoslavia, but I didn't go there either. For suddenly the war was over and on VE-Day I was in London pressed up against the gates of Buckingham Palace as thousands of people thronged the streets and headed down The Mall to celebrate the end of this long, exhausting six-year war.

After the war I left Allen & Hanbury's and joined the medical equipment firm AC Daniels as their export manager. War had ended but things were tight and my business involved a lot of travelling in Britain. There were plenty of customers but not enough products. I made regular trips to Birmingham and Sheffield to seek out supplies and proved to be quite successful. I had already made, through the Yugoslavs, con-tacts and was able to buy syringes, scissors and scalpels, all items that were in short supply. I was to stay with AC Daniels, run by Alfred and Sidney Daniels, until 1948. The firm, which had set up a modern showroom in London, was eventually bought out by a big American corporation called HJ Searle.

THE war, for all the upheaval it produced, had not interfered with my continuing love affair with the Boys' Clubs. I had switched from the North West Jewish Boys' Club to the Maccabi Youth Club in Hampstead where, apart from my interest in football and cricket, I had become the boxing secretary, my fascination with the sport having already taken hold. The first fight posters that caught my imagination were for bantamweight fights featuring Johnny Ryan of Kilburn and middleweight contests featuring George Davis of Notting Hill. Soon I was on my way to the Vale Hall at Kilburn to find out more. At fifteen I was, by a mile, the youngest person there, but I was hooked.

After that I went to the Paddington Baths on a Monday night, probably a dozen times, to see, among others, Gateshead's Billy Charlton take on Dick Corbett from Bethnal Green. Other names that spring to mind from that period are Billy Hardy, a Leicester fighter, and Tommy Martin from Manchester. But it was Davis and Ryan who were the house favourites. Aware of how much my mother loathed the game, I kept my interest in boxing from my parents. On Monday evenings I would tell them I was going to the Boys' Club but instead I would catch the 52 bus from Dollis Hill. At the price of a shilling and nine pence, I would get to watch the boxing and pick up a colourful vocabulary.

Somerset Maugham once wrote, 'There is no thrill in gambling for less than you can afford to lose.' From personal experience I would disagree with Maugham because for many years I have enjoyed betting and gambling for considerably less than I could afford to lose – and that's because I was 'cured' at a very early age. I was only seventeen when I heard David Fisher, with whom many years later I had an association in the stallion Virginia Boy, telling his brother he had a tip that a dog called Tamarisk, running in a heat of the Greyhound Derby the following evening, was 'sure to win'. With some difficulty, I persuaded David and his brother Jack to take me with them to the dogs at White City and as luck would have it, Tamarisk won with consummate ease from trap six at 33-1 and I won £100, a fortune in 1940. I backed other winners and came out of the track winning £165 altogether. Then I proceeded to lose it all.

The scene of seduction followed by ruin can easily be pictured. I spent the next three weeks at every greyhound track in London losing not only the £165 but also the £350 which I had in the Post Office. Even worse, I incurred a debt with a Covent Garden bookmaker for £50, and bookies in those days pursued anyone who owed them vigorously. There was no way I was going to tell my parents but luckily, a friend, Maurice Kinn, who would later own the *New Musical Express* and was then promoting band concerts and dances, loaned me the £50. The experience cured me of reckless gambling. Ironically, forty years later I became chairman of the Greyhound Racing Association, which operates six greyhound tracks, and am a director of the British Greyhound Racing Board, which controls the sport in this country.

But to return to boxing and the inevitable question: If I had such interest in boxing, why did I not box? I did. In the Boys' Club I was not only involved with running the boxing but stepped into the ring myself. However, by the time I was fourteen I was six foot tall and very thin, had outgrown my strength and knew I couldn't become a boxer. So instead I used to put the fights on.

I was barely twenty when I ran my first professional show. I had got to know Archie Shenburn, the owner of the Hammersmith Palace Theatre, and because of that my early shows were staged there. The very first one, held in aid of the Soldiers, Sailors and Airmen Family Association, was a double top-of-the-bill event featuring Al Phillips and Bobby Hinds and Dave Crowley and Syd Worgan from Wales. There was a dearth of promotions in London at the time so it was a success and all the profits went to the SSAFA. With friends, I arranged two or three of these shows but I never really thought of it as a career.

Then I had a stint as unofficial manager of a boxer called Billy Gunn, a sergeant in the Air Force at High Wycombe, where my friend Ronnie Specterman was also based. Ronnie introduced me to Gunn and the first professional fight I arranged for him was in 1942 at Watford Town Hall, where he took on the local man Pat Cubis and flattened him in round one. I thought I had a world beater and arranged another fight for Gunn at Hornsey Town Hall against a bearded sailor called Mickey Franks. Franks shattered my illusions by winning easily and then repeating the victory in a rematch at Oxford Town Hall.

Gunn was soon posted abroad and I didn't try management again for another three years, and then only after I was approached by Ben Beckwith and Harry Greenberg, two firemen I knew through the amateur circuit. They wanted me to have a look at a lightweight called Billy Thompson, who had just won the amateur championship of Great Britain. Thompson came from the Hickleton Main Colliery Boxing Club and I went to watch him in Yorkshire, then met him and his father afterwards. They wanted me to handle him because they felt that he needed to come to London to further his career.

Thompson was a good boxer and soon started to make an impact – and that led to my first brush with the British Boxing Board of Control. Other managers, jealous of the success I was having with Thompson, started complaining that I was unlicensed, and the autocratic secretary of the BBBC, Charles Donmall, told me I had to have a licence if I was arranging fights for Thompson. I had no problems with that, except there was quite a bit of opposition to me getting a licence, the argument being that I was too young – I was twenty-two. But in the end I got my licence and managing Billy Thompson became my first official professional involvement in the game.

I went to Jack King, a matchmaker I knew at the time, and

he put Thompson on the bill at Seymour Hall for a fight with Billy Cunningham from Kew. Thompson proved a big success and became the British and European lightweight champion. However, as he climbed the ladder it became clear he would need more and more of my time, which I could not give him, and in the end I sold his contract.

I turned my attention to business, but twenty years later I was not only back in the fight game, I had the pleasure and the privilege of promoting a boxer who was truly the greatest. A man of whom it can be said that he took boxing on to a different planet.

2

The Greatest

Pound for pound, Sugar Ray Robinson was the best boxer I've seen, but Muhammad Ali was 'The Greatest'. And that is no hype. It is the literal truth.

I had liked Muhammad Ali, or Cassius Clay as he then was, when I first saw him win a gold medal at the 1960 Rome Olympics. Four years later when he fought Sonny Liston for the heavyweight championship, I had £500 on him at 8-1 against, a colossal bet in those days and an uncharacteristically bold one for me. The price was a reflection of the lack of regard people had for Clay at that time – they thought he was just a hyped-up big mouth. I knew he was very much more than that and he proved it by easily beating Liston twice.

My first direct dealings with him took place in 1966. I was visiting New York with Harry Levene, with whom I was co-promoting at the time. Levene, like me, knew New York well, having lived there in the 1920s and worked as a boy in the circulation department of the *New York Times*. He had gone on to manage the Bagatelle Restaurant in London's Mayfair and had also been friendly with the legendary author Damon Runyon. Levene still had some of his New York ways and, apart from anything else, always impressed me as being the best-dressed man in boxing. The two of us went to see Arthur Grafton, the lawyer acting for the Louisville syndicate who were then managing Cassius Clay.

Clay was persona non grata in the United States because he had refused to go and fight in the Vietnam war. He had been outlawed from boxing in America and there was a huge anti-Ali feeling. That made the idea of him coming to London to defend his championship against Henry Cooper a viable and very attractive proposition. Cooper, of course, was a genuine challenger, primarily because he had put the young Cassius Clay on the floor in 1963 at Wembley.

When Harry and I met Grafton, he would not commit himself. There were other lucrative deals being dangled before Clay from various parts of the world, including Canada and South America. Grafton said he would ring us but I left the meeting with no great optimism that such a call would come, let alone that it would be a yes.

About two months later I did receive a telephone call, not from Grafton but from George Parnassus, a Greek-American living in Los Angeles. George was an unusual man – there can't be many boxing promoters whose son has taken up holy orders and ended up as a Bishop. I liked George enormously. Since our first meeting in California in 1956, when he was the promoter of a fight at the Hollywood Legion Stadium, he and I had struck up a fine rapport, so much so that I managed substantial investments for him in England. We did many deals involving hundreds of thousands of dollars for world championships without even having a written contract between us.

George's first words to me were, 'I hear you've got the Clay-Cooper bout?' I could barely contain my surprise and delight as George told me how the previous evening he had been rung by Grafton and asked for a reference about me. George told him, 'If Jarvis Astaire tells you something, you can go to sleep on it.' Grafton asking for a reference meant he had decided we could have the fight and with George's recommendation we had no problems.

Grafton and I soon agreed terms. Those being the days before faxes, we had to exchange cables and this created a problem of security. I didn't want the news to break, not before we were ready, and I certainly didn't want the people in the telegram offices to know how much we were paying for the fight. So I instructed a lawyer I knew in Boston called John Cronin and he sent the cables to Grafton.

Another reason for keeping the news quiet was that Harry Levene was then on holiday in Venice, a Venice so badly in flood that while I could talk to George in Los Angeles and Grafton in Louisville, there was no way I could reach Harry in Venice. For about a week it was impossible to get hold of a soul there. While I waited for the Venice waters to recede, I got the Arsenal football ground for the fight, swearing Ken Friar, the Arsenal club secretary, to secrecy.

But all my efforts to keep it a secret came to nought because Clay himself broke the story. The day before Harry Levene finally managed to escape the Venice floods, Clay announced he was fighting Henry Cooper. Not for nothing was he known as the Louisville Lip. Now the BBC decided it was such a big event that they sent David Coleman to interview Levene live as he stepped off the plane at London airport.

Just as telegrams still existed, so in those days you stepped out of an aeroplane on to stairs and faced the world, not like today where you walk out of the plane into the airport building in a seamless journey through what seems like test tubes. Had it been today's airport, I might have managed to get to Levene before Coleman did. But that summer Friday in 1966, Coleman was waiting on the tarmac and no sooner had Levene's foot hit the bottom step than Coleman asked him, 'Harry, how does it feel to be promoting a world heavyweight title fight in London?' A lesser man would have been flustered. Levene reacted as if he knew everything: 'It's the proudest moment of my life, something I've always wanted to do.'

But if publicity had gone right, we still needed a lot of planning and on-the-spot dealing to get things off the ground. I wanted the fight to be shown on closed-circuit television. I had thirty-two outlets available in cinemas throughout the country and they were vital to the promotion, the difference between talking about putting on a world heavyweight championship bout and actually putting it on.

The problem revolved around the pay-TV experiment then going on in South London, which I intended to combine with the closed-circuit coverage. The BBC and ITV, in one of their rare get-togethers, appealed to the Postmaster General, Anthony Wedgwood-Benn, claiming that it was in the public interest for the heavyweight championship to be made available to all. We were called to Wedgwood-Benn's Holland Park home on a Sunday morning where the case was put to him by both sides, although Benn seemed more interested in the media swarm around his house. Eventually, it was time for his verdict and this notorious left-wing socialist, amazingly, came down on our side, on the side of private enterprise. We offered the BBC and ITV a recording of the fight for £32,000 but they sneered at the offer and that opened the door for me to use it as a cinema film. We ended up clearing £100,000 for the film! My conflicts with the BBC and ITV were, in those days, very vicious, something that surprised me because the people marching into these wars were not using their own money to fight the battles.

There was one other problem I had to resolve before I could put the fight on: the money Henry Cooper wanted. Cooper was handled by Jim Wicks, who was very obstinate and was holding out for a straight £30,000 for his man rather than a percentage of the takings. But with the help of Mickey Duff, the matchmaker for the promotion, I persuaded Jim to accept a percentage deal, which in the end earned Cooper £43,000. Ali, of course, got a lot more. We guaranteed him $250,000 in a percentage deal and he ended up receiving $560,000. Although it may not sound much now, you have to remember that this was a great deal of money in those days – you can multiply the amounts by eleven to get some idea of how much this would have been in today's terms.

The fight, on the night of 21 May 1966, generated colossal interest. There were 43,000 people at Highbury, which was sold out completely and could have been sold many times over.

The feeling in the British camp was that Cooper might be able to repeat his heroics of three years previously when he had put Clay on his rump in their first clash at Wembley. That famous moment resulted in the saga of the ripped glove. With their man dazed on his stool, Clay's corner had to go in search of a new glove and the time between rounds was so extended that there was plenty of chance for Clay to regain his composure and go on to win the fight.

This time at Highbury there was no such drama, no such hope of a British victory. Ali, who didn't even go to the stadium until the night of the fight – the weigh-in being at Leicester Square – proved too quick for Cooper. It went to the sixth round, when Ali's speed of hand finally told. Up until that point he had been dancing well but, ever mindful of Cooper's main weapon, the left hook, he had not ventured too close. But a right and left combination opened Cooper up and, scenting blood, Ali moved in for the kill. In the end Cooper wasn't so much bleeding as leaking blood, slashed to ribbons above his eyes. He was later to say it was the worst cut he ever received in the ring. The game was up for 'Enry and his 'ammer.

After the fight, Ali went into the wilderness of Europe, involving himself in a very hectic schedule. He made five defences of his title between May and November that year and the gap between his fights with Brian London and Karl Mildenberger was just a month. It was great business for closed-circuit TV because there was no shortage of people wanting to see him fight and win. The deal I had done with Ali and his backers meant that I was given first crack and I was more than willing to show the fights. The only one I would not touch was the Brian London fight. It was plain to me that it was a mismatch. London was a big, lumbering boxer and there was no way he could live in the same ring as Ali, so I decided to give it a miss. Lew Grade took it up and it didn't surprise me when I learnt he had made a big loss on it. As for London, he was knocked out in the third round.

I soon realized that when it came to promoting himself and

his fights, Ali was a genius, an absolute joy. He had such a natural instinct for the job that you just let him get on with it and the ticket sales would follow. We had established from the outset that we would be meticulous in our accounting to him for his share of the receipts, plus we looked after him very well when he was in London. I immediately struck up a rapport with him. He did some advertising work here, for which he got paid £25,000. Ali said to me that as he was often coming to England, could I keep the money in an account for him and run it? It was through this arrangement that I got to see at first hand the generous nature of Muhammad Ali.

At that time an Irishman called Paddy Monahan was running Ali's British fan club and had got into financial difficulties. He got in touch with Ali, who told me to give Monahan £10,000. I told Ali I didn't want to pay out that much in one go and he agreed to pay Monahan £1,000 per month. From this account Ali also instructed me to give to the various charities that came knocking on his door. I continued to handle the money here until only a few years ago, winding up the account when Ali came over for the Variety Club tribute to Henry Cooper.

Ali's largesse extended to me as well. I was in Frankfurt in September 1966 when he was fighting Karl Mildenberger and Ali was wearing a watch, a fabulous thing with a dial surrounded by diamonds, which I said I liked very much. That was it, he wanted to buy me one and he marched me across to the jewellers in the hotel lobby. He insisted on me trying on watches but I wouldn't accept the gift and he really seemed quite put out.

Remarkably, he did not forget that incident. Five years later when he was back in Europe to fight Jurgen Blin, appropriately enough on Boxing Day in Zurich, Switzerland, he overheard my wife Phyllis talking about a watch she had seen and liked. It was quite expensive and I didn't have enough money with me so I asked Herbert Muhammad, Ali's mentor and the man who replaced the Louisville Group as his manager, if he had any cash on him. He didn't – but Ali did. I borrowed the money from Ali knowing I could pay him back the following week because he was going to be in London to do a milk commercial.

A week later I saw him at the Royal Lancaster Hotel and wanted to give the money back, but he wouldn't take it. It was a lot of money, around £4,000. He reminded me of the time he had tried and failed to buy me a watch in Frankfurt and it was clear it made him happy to be generous.

Ali had a large entourage, as one would expect, all of whom seemed to pull their weight, but by far the most fascinating individual was Dr Ferdie Pacheco, a brilliant man whose medical qualifications were almost overshadowed by his great ability and flair as a painter, as well as being a prolific writer of books and magazine articles. I remain great friends with Ferdie and his lovely wife Luisita, a former dancer. Ferdie, of course, was a very important contributor to Ali's career, although he withdrew from the Ali camp for the last few fights because, wisely, he thought that Ali was going on too long.

To me as a businessman, one of Ali's most endearing virtues was his willingness to see a project through. Prior to his famous fight with George Foreman, the 'Rumble in the Jungle' in Zaire in 1974, I did a deal through Herbert Muhammad for Ali to come to Europe afterwards and do a tour. If he lost to Foreman then it would be a sentimental farewell; and if he won, then that was a big bonus. It was all wrapped up, contracts sorted out and dates confirmed with Herbert. Ali was going to do some exhibitions and we were putting him on for his first appearance at the New Victoria in London. The plan was to run a film and then have a question and answer session.

However, unbeknown to me, Ali had accidentally double-booked himself. While in Zaire for the Foreman fight, he had promised the president that he would go back for their Independence Day celebrations. To get to Africa from London meant his flying over to Paris, a short stop-over, then another plane in the evening to Zaire. The first we knew of his plans was when Mickey Duff received a call from Herbert Muhammad, explaining that Ali had not realized the celebrations would be quite so soon. I arranged to meet Ali with Mickey at the airport in Paris. Ali arrived with his wife Belinda and Howard Bingham, the photographer who followed him everywhere. Also in the reception committee was a chap from the Zairean Embassy called Banda, and he had arranged a limousine to take Ali to his hotel for a rest.

Ali was all hugs and smiles when he saw me. As we made our way through the airport to the limousine, Banda suddenly turned round and told me and Mickey to get a taxi and follow them to the hotel. He said we couldn't travel in the car because of 'security problems'. Ali was having none of it. He told Banda that I was very important and had to travel in the car. So we ended up driving into central Paris with the Embassy official stuck up front next to the driver while Ali discovered why I'd come out to see him.

I was very nervous about his tour because I had the posters printed, the tickets sold, yet there was this nagging fear that he might not turn up. I explained my position to him and he realized he was working to a tight schedule and could see how much I had riding on him. So he suggested: 'Can I arrive on the morning of the show?' He was confident he could make it back from Zaire by then. I agreed, but it did little to ease my gut fears that he would fail to show. But come the big day I got a call from him: 'Don't worry, I'm here in Brussels and I'll be with you soon.'

That tour, which had him going all over Europe for three weeks, was a massive success. He was in and out of London, staying at the Royal Lancaster, and appearing all over. One trip was to Italy where he gave an exhibition in Genoa. On the same show there was a European title fight taking place and the referee was Teddy Waltham, previously secretary of the British Boxing Board of Control. Ali knew him because he had been the referee in Frankfurt when he fought Mildenberger in

1966. When Ali heard Waltham had been pickpocketed, losing all of his $3,000 fee for taking charge of the European title fight, he secretly gave him the money. And when Mickey Duff said to him, 'That was good of you,' Ali replied: 'The man earned his money, he was entitled to it.'

I have met Ali on many occasions since his retirement and he always greets me with a warm hug. His condition of Parkinson's Disease is very distressing to observe. I do recall that his father suffered from the same illness but whether or not boxing has contributed to Ali's problem who can tell? There are plenty of boxers who took many times the amount of punishment Ali did without seeming to be adversely affected. Maybe fortune simply dealt him a bad hand.

IF Ali was a dream to work with, the man he famously defeated, Sonny Liston, was a terror. I brought him to England when he was the world heavyweight champion to give exhibitions up and down the country. We met him at Heathrow and in the car back from the airport, sitting next to Liston, was a man I had working with me. Liston constantly cuffed my employee round the ear, not playfully but nastily, a constant stream of hard blows delivered with spite. Once we had him set up in a Mayfair hotel he demanded 'hot and cold running women'. He was a detestable bully, had a police record to go with it from his younger days and ended up dying alone in a room, his body undiscovered for something like six days.

As world champion, however, Liston had considerable appeal and the tour was sold on to other promoters. One of the places Liston was booked to appear was Newcastle. He had no sooner arrived in the North East than he was off out to a nightclub where he tried to pick up a woman. When he was rejected, he went absolutely mad. He stormed back to the hotel and demanded, in the middle of the night, a car back to London. He threatened Les Roberts, the road manager who was accompanying him everywhere, with physical damage if he didn't do as he was told. Roberts naturally gave him his return airline ticket and soon Liston was heading for Chicago.

I was not happy about this. I was not going to let a bully just walk out on a deal. I got in contact with Jack Green, an agent for ABC Booking in America, and he was immediately in touch with Liston's agent Joe Glaser, who had cornered the market in black American talent and also represented Louis Armstrong and Ella Fitzgerald. Liston was met at the airport but there was no chance of his being persuaded to return. I later called Glaser seeking compensation and after a lot of haggling we settled on $14,000, which he promised he would send to me. It didn't come. The only thing to do was to call round and collect the next time I was in New York. I went to the ABC Booking office, where Jack Green took me to see Glaser. He was a little old man sitting behind a big desk. I said to him, 'Where's my money? You've been promising it for months and months and I haven't seen a cent.'

'Well, it's like this, one or two problems. . .'

'Don't give me that rubbish,' I growled, picking up an ebony ruler and banging it down on Glaser's desk. This little old man gave Green a baleful look and said, 'Give him his money and get him the hell out of here,' or words to that effect.

We left Glaser's office and Jack wanted to give me a cheque, but I asked for cash as I was running short in expensive New York. This meant a trip to the bank and as we walked down the street I noticed Jack was very quiet, unusually so, so I asked him what the problem was. He said, 'I can't believe you got away with talking to Joe Glaser like that.'

'Why not? He's just a cantankerous old man.'

Jack smiled. 'Don't you know Joe Glaser's background?'

'No.'

'He was Al Capone's driver.'

Recalling that Capone was once America's most notorious gangster, I replied: 'Thank goodness you didn't tell me that before I asked for the money.'

The fighter that Ali did not meet in a real head-to-head

battle was Rocky Marciano although they did have a computer fight, a remarkable staged battle with the two of them going through set moves in a carefully choreographed routine. It was a brilliant idea from a man called Murray Woroner and meant that Ali was having his first 'fight' in the ring since being stripped of his title after his problems with the draft. At this stage Marciano hadn't fought for fourteen years, having retired as undefeated heavyweight world champion, and he needed to shake off some weight to look convincing in the part.

The two champions went off to make the film, five cameras covering the angles as they went through some seventy one-minute rounds with Marciano, twenty years older than Ali, wearing a wig to try and bridge the years. It worked really well, looked good and consisted of a number of different endings, some in which Ali won and others in which Marciano triumphed. The idea was to release the film simultaneously around the world. I was in America when Woroner got in touch with me to see if the fight could go out on closed-circuit TV. I thought about it but eventually sold the package on to the BBC. There was considerable doubt at the time that such a stunt could be pulled off. I remember asking Woroner about the ending.

'I suppose you know the result of the fight?' I said to him.

'Do you think I want to end up in a block of cement?' came the reply. There was big money riding on the outcome of this fight and quite a few underworld dealings in an attempt to prise open the sealed film canisters and discover the result – which had been reached by a panel of boxing experts who gave their verdict and were sworn to secrecy. The irony is that Marciano, who was given the decision, never lived to see the fight. He was killed in a plane crash a few weeks later.

Brilliant though it looked, I don't think Marciano would have beaten Ali, because he was too small. Interestingly, Marciano, a wild, almost animal brawler in the ring, was quiet and reserved out of it. He was also incredibly tight-fisted. We once held a dinner for him in Manchester where he was the guest of honour at the Anglo-American Sporting Club, yet he was so parsimonious that he turned up in a suit that was falling apart. It was so bad that Mickey Duff had to get one made for him before he could attend the function. It was said that after he died nobody could find any of his money, which must have been considerable and was kept in cash. Not even his wife knew where it was.

Marciano's manager had been a man called Al Weill, who belonged to the era of the old-time fight men when gangsters held a lot of influence. He had an English heavyweight called Dave Rent, whom he was building up in the States. Rent was from Liverpool and was not a bad fighter, but not great. I ran into Weill at Madison Square Garden one day and said to him that he would do better putting Rent on in Britain, where he had been a former amateur champion. I suggested he brought him over to fight in his old home town. He agreed and Rent came over to train in Liverpool, Weill arriving just a few days before the fight. We took the train north and on the way Weill discovered that in England the referee gave the decision and not the judges, at which point he said to me, 'You've got the ref, 'ain't ya?'

'What do you mean?' I asked. I had to explain to him that was not the way we worked in England, but he didn't believe me. If we didn't have the ref then according to Al, the other guy had him. In fact, his trip was quite eventful. On the night of the fight Weill was arrested for working in Britain without a labour permit. We sorted it out but I still suspect to this day that the authorities had been put up to it by a rival promoter, Jack Solomons.

Boxing in America has always had its scams and I was reminded of this at Christmas in 1980 when Harold Smith appeared from nowhere as a real big-time boxing promoter who also dabbled in the entertainment business. Smith was trying to buy his way into boxing promotions and had received Muhammad Ali's nod of approval for a youth sporting foundation to promote black athletes. Subsequently that organization carried Ali's name and Smith used it as a lever for his own ambitions. Smith also had very good connections at the Wells Fargo Bank.

As it happened, Mickey Duff, who by then had become my partner in boxing, was in Los Angeles negotiating with Smith for two British fighters, Jim Watt and John L Gardner, to meet Alex Arguello and Muhammad Ali respectively, under Smith's promotion. Eventually Mickey's negotiations reached the point where Smith offered to give him $350,000 for an option on Watt and Gardner on the understanding that Smith would forego the money if he could not deliver the agreed opponents in seven days.

Mickey told me about this and said he was going to pick up the cheque. I told him not to do that because cheques took so long to clear in America that by the time it was deposited and processed, the time for the option would have been virtually up. By then Smith could quite easily have cancelled the cheque. I told Mickey to get a banker's draft or, as the Americans call it, a cashier's cheque, and he agreed. He went off to see Smith with this in mind but was told that Smith couldn't manage a cashier's cheque. What he could do was produce the hard currency there and then, because, as he told Mickey, he had won a lot of money on his own horse in the big race at Hollywood Park and at the tables in Las Vegas.

Delighted as Mickey was to have the money like this, he was also slightly nervous about walking out of Smith's office with it. He called a friend to collect him and came over to my hotel – I had arrived in Los Angeles, on a trip concerned with the film business, a few days earlier. We decided to put the money in a hotel safe. We then went out to Robinsons department store in Beverly Hills and bought two large holdalls, transferred the money into them and the following day took a flight to New York and deposited the cash in the bank there.

Two weeks later, back in London I received a call at 1am from Mickey, who told me that Smith's involvement in a huge scam had been discovered. He had been arrested for stealing $21 million from Wells Fargo. I told Mickey the first thing he had to do was find out whether he had received stolen money and to get in touch with my Los Angeles lawyer, a man called Anthony Glassman, who had contacts in the Los Angeles District Attorney's office.

The next day Mickey went out to Los Angeles and met Glassman, who took him to see the District Attorney. There he was told he could keep the money because the DA's office had no way of knowing that Smith had not, as he said, won it. Amazingly, Smith had the nerve to phone Mickey and ask him to stand bail for him! In the end Mickey provided evidence for the Smith trial while Watt and Gardner did pretty well without raising a fist.

Smith received a five-year prison sentence and when he came out of jail, he applied for a renewal of his promoter's licence, saying: 'I had no trouble in boxing, my trouble was with banks.'

3

Movie Star Manager

THE cinema has always held a fascination for me. My generation was the first in England to be seduced by the magic of Hollywood. For me, as for all young people growing up in the pre-war and immediate post-war years, going to the movies was a weekly joy, the great source of entertainment and millions left Gaumonts and Odeons dreaming of emulating their heroes and becoming film stars. Like many teenagers I liked to think I had film-star looks, but had never thought of films as a career. Then, quite suddenly during the war, at the age of nineteen, the doors of the wonderful world of films opened in front of me.

I had been introduced to a lady called Irene Howard who was the casting director at Denham Film Studios, the main studios in England in those days, and was very flattered when she asked if I had ever thought about acting as a career. I had not, but I was not going to appear disinterested and my enthusiasm must have shown, for she offered me a part in the film 'English Without Tears', the Terence Rattigan follow-up to his 1939 hit, 'French Without Tears'.

Adapted from Rattigan's successful play, 'French Without Tears' was the story of some young English people at a French cramming course, where one of the party falls for the younger sister of one of the group. Paramount Studios bought the rights, originally as a vehicle for Marlene Dietrich. It astonishes me even today that Paramount could ever have thought she could have played any role in such a film but, even without her, probably because of her absence, the film was still a big enough hit for the studio to sanction another screenplay from Rattigan. This was 'English Without Tears', the one Irene Howard had in mind for my cinematic debut. Harold French was the director and the cast included Lilli Palmer, Michael Wilding, Margaret Rutherford, Penelope Dudley Ward, Claud Dauphin, Ronald Culver and myself. In this story of a rich ATS girl in the Second World War who falls for her butler, he having become a lieutenant during the war, I played a Belgian officer in a classroom. I had three lines of dialogue but they were never seen by the world, as they ended up on the cutting-room floor.

However, I must have made a good impression as Irene had another kind of role in mind for me. The actor James Mason was making a film at that time called 'Fanny By Gaslight', directed by Anthony Asquith, then a famous English film director. I went to see Asquith at Lime Grove Studios, in some apprehension, but all he did was look me up and down and say, 'Yes, fine. You'll do as a double for James Mason.'

Mason, then in his prime, had been contracted for another film before 'Fanny By Gaslight' had been completed and for good measure 'Fanny By Gaslight' was behind with its shooting. I was left to pick up the part in the few remaining scenes which could be completed by a double. Flattered though I was by all this, I kept my head and was far from star-struck by life in the studios. I quickly learned that the actual business of making films, as opposed to watching them, was very unexciting. Sitting in the Gaumont watching a film was one thing but behind the cameras, being involved in bringing all that excitement to the screen, it was deadly dull. The weeks I'd spent on 'English Without Tears' had meant hanging around endlessly, waiting for a scene to be shot, and it had left me bored to tears. 'Fanny By Gaslight' was admittedly much more interesting because in the two to three weeks I spent on the film I was out on location, but even that left a lot to be desired.

My principal involvement in 'Fanny By Gaslight' was a duel scene with Stewart Granger, where, as Mason's double, I was meant to be shot and fall to the ground. Anthony Asquith set up the cameras and we must have done the scene ten times at least. Could I fall to the ground as if I had been shot? Never! I was hopeless, so bad indeed that the crew were in stitches. Asquith remonstrated with his crew but to no avail, they just could not stop themselves laughing at my ham-fisted 'death'. He was so frustrated he finally decided to re-take the shot as a long-range scene of the duel, thus avoiding the hilarious close-ups of me being felled. I've got the film on videotape, but I rarely look at it and, not surprisingly, it marked the end of my film career, at least as far as appearing before the cameras was concerned.

'Fanny By Gaslight' had long been consigned to history when, many years later, I finally met Mason through Robin Dalton, an Australian literary agent. I was charmed by his easy-going style and he did some work for me, narrating a short documentary about Sadlers Wells Theatre called 'Celebration', which I produced. Not long after this I also caught up again with Stewart Granger but, compared to Mason, I found him a bitter, arrogant man who spoke excep-tionally badly of people. Hollywood had turned its back on him and Granger's swashbuckling career finished with him acting in low-budget Italian and German films.

My early involvement with films was to prove a prelude to the period in the 1970s when I got involved with Dustin Hoffman, as his manager and running his production com-pany, Sweetwall Productions.

My involvement with Dustin is the sort of story that if presented in fiction would be dismissed as too far-fetched. The story begins in the early 1960s, not with Hoffman, who was yet to explode on the world scene in Mike Nichols' 'The Graduate', but with another American called Walter Hyman, a great eccentric whose main business was the textile industry but who harboured a huge love for show business and had managed the singer Sally Blair.

Hyman also formed a partnership with a man called Sidney Bernstein and ran concerts at New York's Carnegie Hall on Sundays. The pair took The Beatles to America and in the same era they also put on Shirley Bassey at Carnegie Hall. I played a role in getting Shirley to America. I had taken Walter to The Talk of The Town in London to see Bassey and he was captivated by her. When he came back to my house, he immediately phoned Sid Bernstein to tell him about it, urging him to sign Shirley for the Carnegie Hall.

'Sid,' said Walter, 'she is sensational.'

'But nobody's ever heard of her,' said Sidney. 'Has she made any records?'

I had a copy of her singing 'I, Who Have Nothing'. So over the transatlantic lines I played Bernstein the record and he agreed with Walter's assessment. The result was Shirley played the Carnegie Hall and launched her American career.

Then Walter, together with Alan King, a famous American comedian who was his partner in theatrical productions and a producer in his own right, came up with the idea of putting on a Barbra Streisand concert in a big open-air stadium. The deal was finalized in my house. Jackie Green, an agent for Walter, and Barbra's manager Marty Erlichman were in London. They needed to thrash out a deal and keep in touch with Walter so the best place to do that was at my home.

From that sprang up a friendship between Walter and Barbra, whose husband at the time was the actor Elliott Gould. He, in turn, was friendly with Dustin, who had just become a big star with 'The Graduate'. Dustin was considering the offer he had been made for his next picture, 'John and Mary', but was not sure how good it was. Walter was sure the offer was not good enough and Dustin asked him to act as his intermediary and talk to Jane Oliver at the William Morris Agency. Jane, who represented Dustin at that time, had clearly thought the offer was a good one but Walter's intervention meant Jane had to go back and renegotiate. Dustin, impressed by Walter's success on his behalf, decided – wrongly in my opinion – to ask Walter to become his agent and Jane Oliver was dropped.

The problem was Walter. In spite of his love of show business and involvement with Alan King and Sally Blair, he did not really know much about the film business, in fact virtually nothing. Suddenly he was acting for one of Hollywood's hottest properties. Because he did not want to reveal his lack of knowledge at home, the only way out for Walter was to turn to me and make the most of the experience I had gained by that time. So, whenever major questions of Dustin's business came up, Walter would phone me from America. These calls would go on for as long as forty-five minutes as I advised him on Dustin's affairs. And when Dustin and his first wife Anne, a ballerina, came to London on honeymoon, Phyllis and I entertained them.

About eighteen months later Dustin came to England to make 'Straw Dogs'. He was accompanied by Anne and their children Jenna and Karina (who was from Anne's first marriage and was adopted by Dustin). I had met Dustin a few times in New York and the South of France while on holiday with Walter, so it was natural for my office to help him out. We sorted out things like schools for his children and some-where to live, and became quite close – and, inevitably, when things started to go wrong with the film, he turned to me.

Sam Peckinpah, the director, had gone on an alcoholic binge. In desperation, Dustin phoned me from St Ives in Cornwall and I sent my friend Dr David Sacks down there to straighten out Peckinpah. Then there were problems with Susan George, the film's leading lady, and Dustin ended up being in England much longer than expected, probably about nine months, so we got to know each other even better. His next film was 'Papillon', being shot in Spain with Steve McQueen and again there were problems, this time with the money, so Walter asked me about it and I said I would keep Dustin in England until the money came through. He stayed in London for a few weeks, where I fed him a diet of French films starring people like Jean Gabin and Michel Simon. It helped in his preparation for playing the part of the French counterfeiter Louis Dega in 'Papillon'.

My curious relationship with Dustin might have continued like this for ever had not Walter Hyman, who had suffered from angina for many years, suddenly dropped dead at the Roosevelt trotting track in New York in November 1973. It left Dustin without an agent or manager and he often turned to me for advice. He was involved in directing a play written by a friend of his, Murray Schisgal, called 'All Over Town'. Dustin asked me to invest some money in it, which I was happy to do.

About six weeks after Walter died, Dustin called me and asked me to manage him. It was not really a very attractive proposition. I explained: 'Dustin, I'm over here, you're in America, I've got my life here, it's just not practical.' He then told me that all the top agents, including Freddie Fields and Sue Mengers, were after him and said Walter had suggested I would be the ideal man.

Dustin was not the only Hoffman asking me to become his manager. In April 1974, Anne Hoffman, who was making a guest appearance in Birmingham with the Frankfurt Ballet, came to London and said, 'Dustin really needs you because he doesn't know which way to turn.' I told her I had already talked to Dustin about it but it really was impractical. Not long after this, Dustin's brother Ronald Hoffman, an academic working for the US government, passed through London on his way to Romania. I took him to the White Elephant Club for dinner and we were walking along Park Lane afterwards when he said, 'Dustin really needs you to manage him.'

By now my wife Phyllis, who had been suffering from cancer for some years, had died and this had so dramatically changed my life that it made me more receptive to the idea. I was in something of a vacuum and the thought of this challenge intrigued me. Three days after Ronald Hoffman's visit, I was sitting at my home in Hampstead when Dustin called: 'I hear you are going to manage me.' I said I wasn't sure about that but added that his brother had mentioned it. I thought about it some more. English actors working in America retained their UK agents and managers. Laurence Olivier did it, so with planes and easy access to America it suddenly seemed to me that there was no reason why I couldn't become a London-based manager for an American actor living in New York. But while I was prepared to be his manager, I was in no rush and I suggested we talk when I was next due in New York. Dustin couldn't wait. He said he was coming over to London because he wanted to see the Alan Ayckbourn plays, 'The Norman Conquests' with Tom Courtenay. Dustin said it had been suggested he could play the part on Broadway. Over he came, we talked for a long time and reached an agreement.

One of my first tasks was to agree on how and when the filming of 'All the President's Men' was going to take place, because Dustin had said to Robert Redford that he wanted to play Carl Bernstein to Redford's Bob Woodward but negotiations over the contract and a start date for the shooting were dragging on. Redford had also signed to make 'Three Days of the Condor' and because of that I wanted a contract for Dustin with a starting date and extra payments for any time that filming overran the agreed dates. Redford's interest in 'All the President's Men' was more than just appearing in it. His production company Wildwood was involved and because of that he wanted to meet me to discuss the problems.

I went to Redford's New York office with Dustin and was struck by his very western looks: denim trousers and denim cap. But far from proving a rough cowboy, he turned out to be sophisticated and business-like, impressively so. He made it clear he thought I was being unreasonable with my demands, but I made out the case that he was making another film while Dustin was being precluded from doing the same. I told Redford: 'You know as an actor yourself that you only have a certain length of time and can be involved in so many projects, it's like a taxi with the meter running – and I don't think it is fair or equitable that you can be involved in making another film and making money, which you are entitled to, and Dustin is not able to do so.' Redford listened attentively to what I said and accepted my argument. Then, turning round to Dustin, he said, 'I can see why you have this man around.'

I told Redford I hadn't enjoyed the meeting at all and he was surprised by this, asking me why. I said, 'In future when I meet women and tell them I have met Robert Redford, I wanted to say he is an idiot, but I can't now.'

Ironically, Dustin had tried to buy the film rights to 'All the President's Men' himself. When he realized Redford had beaten him to the punch, pride intervened and he refused to go and put himself forward for the role he wanted, Carl Bernstein. Luckily, Redford also wanted him for that role and went to the theatre where Dustin was working in the play, 'All Over Town'. There he asked Dustin to play Bernstein. As Redford walked in, Dustin said, 'What kept you?'

Even before I agreed to become his manager, Dustin had talked to me about playing the part of stand-up comic Lenny Bruce in the film about him. At this stage, in the months between Walter's death and my agreeing to act for Dustin, he was shooting 'Lenny' and was not sure whether he could go through with it. I told him I had seen Lenny Bruce and was convinced that Dustin, in that role, could be better than the real thing. Bruce, to my mind, was grossly overrated. I loathed his act and thought his crude humour was just not funny.

To my delight, Dustin turned out a remarkable performance. As he nearly always did, he got under the skin of the part, researching it back as far as he could, although in the process he gave the director Bob Fosse a hard time. To be fair to Dustin, Fosse was not the easiest man to work with either. He had Dustin performing Bruce's stage act before live audiences around Miami, homing in with the camera on Dustin as he went through the very real agonies of facing a live audience. The strain told on Fosse and he had a heart attack. Although he recovered to make 'All That Jazz' with Roy Scheider – which for Bob was very much an autobiographical picture – and had drastically altered his lifestyle, he was to die of another heart attack shortly after making that film.

Dustin came out of 'Lenny' with his usual response that it was 'a flawed work'. Yet it went down a storm at the Cannes Film Festival, where it had its European premiere. In the States the film received a very favourable reception and went on to become a box office hit. At the 1974 Oscar ceremony, it was nominated in four of the six main categories, including best film, best direction, best actor – Dustin – and best actress, Valerie Perrine. But it won nothing, and was not helped by the fact that Dustin didn't go to the Oscar ceremonies. He just did not like them and it took him years before he would attend one. He actually said to me that he couldn't stand having to sit there and look like a good loser. I pleaded with him to go to the award ceremony, but it was all in vain. Frank Sinatra, as compere, castigated Dustin for not being there and I believe his absence cost him the main prize that year. It went instead to Art Carney for 'Harry and Tonto', a fine enough per-formance but hardly of the calibre of Dustin's gripping portrayal of Lenny Bruce.

I was not the only one bewitched by Dustin's Lenny. Many years later, on a plane from Los Angeles to London, I sat next to the director Barry Levinson whose work is always very watchable (I particularly liked 'The Natural', which starred Robert Redford). Like me, he thought that Dustin's portrayal of Lenny Bruce was the best work he had ever done. Later on, Levinson directed 'Rain Man', which I think is the best thing Dustin has done.

One of the bonuses of managing Dustin, of course, was that I got to meet show business people I had always admired. I arranged for him to be in the Bette Midler Television Special, where he played the piano, which he is very good at, and Midler sang a song Dustin had written called 'Shooting the Breeze'. Burt Lancaster was also there, and I told him that I had seen him way back in 1948 at the Capitol Theatre in New York, where he had done a trapeze act. He had been the catcher and a man called Nick Cravat was the acrobat he caught. He was amazed that I remembered.

It was as if the magical world of Hollywood had opened up before me. Robert Evans was the sort of man who could have walked out of a real life 'Sunset Boulevard'. The producer of numerous films including Dustin's 'Marathon Man', he had a sumptuous and tasteful house in Hollywood and was famed as the giver of some great parties, with the major stars of the cinema as his guests. The house had a tennis court which Dustin, who was a very keen player, loved. Charlton Heston and Robert Duvall also liked tennis and were often to be found playing there. Evans' place also had a fabulous screening room and regular guests included Jack Nicholson, Anjelica Houston, the screenwriter and director Robert Towne and Warren Beatty. I was at one of Evans' parties on the night of the Presidential election of 1976, when the Republican President Gerald Ford lost to Jimmy Carter, the Democrat. The elections clearly fascinated Nicholson and Beatty and I was very impressed with Beatty's knowledge of American politics.

I must admit to having a soft spot for Beatty because he made one of my favourite films, a remake of 'Here Comes Mr Jordan' called 'Heaven Can Wait'. As for Nicholson, he is a huge sports fan and I meet him at a lot of the big events around the world. At the Los Angeles Olympics in 1984 I even managed to persuade him to do a half-hour interview for the BBC.

I also met an American TV star, Henry Winkler, the Fonz from the hit series 'Happy Days'. I had been offered a script by an experienced film man, David Picker, as a possible project for Dustin. It was about a young man who wants to be an actor but can't get a job. In desperation he becomes a wrestler, as a way of satisfying his acting bug. It was based on the life of the wrestler Gorgeous George – a big attraction in American wrestling in the 1950s, years before the days of Hulk Hogan.

He would preen himself and come into the ring with a valet.

Dustin was very interested in playing the part of Gorgeous George but backed away at the last moment, feeling he was just too old to play the main character, who was a newlywed and fresh out of college. At my instigation we still bought the screenplay, splitting the cost 50-50. Within a week of doing the deal I received a call from an agent who represented Henry Winkler.

'Henry Winkler?' I said. 'I've never heard of him.'

'What are you talking about?' said the bemused agent. 'He's the Fonz.'

'Well, why didn't you say that in the first place?' I laughed. 'I know who the Fonz is!'

Winkler, it appeared, was very interested in the role of Gorgeous George and we fixed a dinner appointment at La Scala in Beverly Hills, where Henry joined me and a couple of friends. I did not know what to expect but he quite mesmerized me and I came away convinced he would do a brilliant job. It turned out he was the first-generation son of German-Jewish refugees, who by chance were related to a lawyer who had acted for me in London. Dustin agreed that Henry would be good in the part. I got back to Henry and promised that if we had anything to do with it, he would be Gorgeous George.

After that I was approached by Sue Mengers, Ryan O'Neal's agent, who said MGM wanted to make the picture and they wanted O'Neal to be Gorgeous George. I told her we couldn't sell the screenplay on those terms because of the promise to Henry Winkler. As luck would have it, David Picker, the man who sold it to us, was appointed the studio chief at Paramount and we sold it back to him at a substantial profit, with the condition that Henry was the lead. The film did get made as 'The One and Only' and Henry did a good job in it, but he never made it as a movie star. This was not his first film – he had been in a Vietnam story called 'Heroes' before – but as is often the case, someone who makes it on television can't make it on the bigger screen. He took up directing instead, but I think it was a pity he did not get the film success he deserved.

Henry was grateful for my part in his film role. A little while later I visited Los Angeles with my daughter Susan, who was eighteen at the time. When I told her I had met Henry Winkler, she asked if I could fix it for her and a couple of friends to be in the audience for the taping of 'Happy Days'. I told her I could and we arranged to go to Henry's office at Paramount TV. On the big day, Susan was very worried that she would not get to meet Henry and would look a fool in front of her friends. I reassured her: We were going to see 'Happy Days' being filmed and we were going to meet the star.

When we reached the Paramount studios, the man on the gate recognized me from the many times I had visited the studios during the filming of 'Marathon Man' and let me through. Near the actual sound stage there was a huge line of people and again my daughter's doubts surfaced. She thought we would have to queue up behind them all. Again I soothed her worries. We were led through to the studio floor, where Henry was rehearsing with the director Jerry Parish. Henry suddenly caught my eye, excused himself from the rest of the cast and came running over and gave me a big hug. Over his shoulder, I saw my daughter's face wreathed with smiles.

My favourite Hollywood experience, though, was seeing the eventual success of a young lawyer whom I first met and became friendly with in 1969. Arnold Kopelson was brought up in Brooklyn, New York, the son of a piano teacher (and he has certainly inherited his father's musicianship and plays the piano beautifully). He worked his way through Law School partly by being a part-time waiter at hotels in the Catskill Mountains in New York State, otherwise known as the 'Borscht Belt' and the proving ground for many of the world's greatest entertainers.

Arnold's life changed dramatically when he joined Henry Bushkin, another young New York lawyer, when Henry became the lawyer for Johnny Carson, the host of 'The Tonight Show' on NBC. Henry and Arnold moved out to Los

Angeles when the show was relocated there. They set up a law firm and enjoyed some success, with Bushkin supervising Carson's various interests and Arnold, with his former secretary Anne, running an International Film Distribution business. I also had a slight involvement with Carson, supervising the twenty-six week run of 'The Tonight Show' on London Weekend Television.

Arnold became involved in one or two speculative business ventures, a small bank and a gold mine, both of which failed, and also the production of some 'B' movies which did not set the world on fire. But I am sure those films gave Arnold the first-hand experience of production which stood him in good stead for what was to come.

The change in fortune came about when he became the producer of 'Platoon', a film about the Vietnam War which deservedly won the Best Film Award at the Oscar ceremonies. I saw a preview screening in Hollywood at Arnold's invitation and told him I thought the film was a masterpiece, but that no-one was particularly interested in hearing about Vietnam any more. How wrong I was! 'Platoon' was a huge success, both critically and at the box office, and as success breeds success, other hits were to follow. The Harrison Ford film 'The Fugitive', based on the television series, was an instant hit, as was 'Seven', a disturbing thriller which really launched the career of Brad Pitt, one of the hottest current film stars. Arnold also made 'Triumph of the Spirit' starring Willem Dafoe, which was a sombre film based in Auschwitz, the notorious Nazi concentration camp. The film was actually shot at Auschwitz, where Arnold spent several weeks supervising production. I know it is a film he is particularly proud of. Arnold and Anne, whom he married after the death of his first wife Joy, are delightful people who have never changed despite their huge success, and we remain great friends.

But if being Dustin Hoffman's manager opened a door to Hollywood's magic kingdom, I also glimpsed past the other door that nearly led me to a kind of hell.

4

The Trouble with Hoffman

Until you live with someone, you don't really know what they are like – and the same applies in the working world. Until you have been close to someone in that environment, you never know the truth. And discovering the truth can be quite painful, exhausting and sometimes downright infuriating.

Dustin Hoffman is a fine actor, arguably the best of his generation, a man who is a genius at portraying various characters on film: sometimes funny, nice, innocent and endearing; at other times unpleasant, mean and twisted. But to reach the stage where he has the character under control can be trying and soul-destroying – maybe not for him, but without a doubt for those working with him.

I had my first glimpse of Dustin at work during the making of 'All the President's Men'. He had become friendly with the *Washington Post* journalist Carl Bernstein, the character he was playing in the film opposite Redford's Bob Woodward. For three months Dustin followed Bernstein everywhere, learning about the foibles of the man, the way he worked, talked and reacted. He even watched and learned the mechanics of newspaper production. It was painstaking to the point of obsessiveness.

While all this was going on there was still no director for the film. Dustin suggested John Schlesinger, the maker of the Oscar-winning 'Midnight Cowboy', the film in which Dustin played the down-and-out Ratso and for which he had been nominated in the Best Actor category for the second time.

This was a remarkable suggestion for him to make because he and Schlesinger had not spoken to each other for a year after the completion of the film and might never have done so again had they not bumped into each other in a New York department store.

Schlesinger was aware of the creative force driving Hoffman on but found that, of the twenty or so ideas Dustin would come up with, only a couple were worth following up. Yet when told this, Dustin would react as if each rejection by the director was some brutal insult. As a consequence there was considerable hysteria from Dustin and the crack in the relationship between him and Schlesinger over 'Midnight Cowboy' became a gulf when Dustin disagreed with the way the finished film had been edited.

In the event, 'All the President's Men' actually went to Alan J Pakula (who died recently in a freak car accident) who had a big hit with 'Klute' starring Donald Sutherland and Jane Fonda, the latter winning an Oscar for her portrayal of the call girl in the story. Pakula had also made 'The Parallax View', a political thriller starring Warren Beatty. His credentials for making 'All the President's Men' were in place. But the real question on everyone's lips, from the production team through to the Hollywood press, was how would Dustin and Redford get on?

Two huge star names in one film has been the recipe for disaster throughout the history of movie-making yet, sur-prisingly, they got on fine. They were wary of each other at first and had very differing approaches to their jobs – much like Woodward and Bernstein, in fact – but they gelled before the cameras. Redford was very easy-going, laid back between scenes and when he was called upon, got up and jumped straight into the role. When it was 'Cut', he was relaxed again. Dustin, on the other hand, was the caged beast on the prowl, always tense and tormented about every single aspect of his performance, a strange paradox of professional assurance mixed with insecurity. He could see at least twenty ways to do each scene and would have to explore every single one of them before he was content.

In spite of this, shooting of the film went well. The storm wasn't to blow up until the project was in the can and Dustin saw a rough cut in the Warner Brothers viewing theatre in Burbank, Los Angeles. The rough form of the film was far too long, to the point of being boring and self-indulgent, and had far too many shots of Redford, as Woodward, climbing in and out of taxis on the way to a car park for his clandestine meetings with Deep Throat. There was also a confusing plethora of names in the dialogue. It wrecked the pace, the drama and the tension of the work. There were even times when Dustin, as Bernstein, would be talking on film yet all we saw was Redford's face.

As the showing ended, Dustin, who had been watching with Anne, leapt up and sprinted out into the street and into his car. I followed him to the house where he was staying. 'What a terrible film!' he yelled. 'I don't give a damn about that movie. No wonder Redford is the number one box office star – he gets himself all over the screen, the film is full of him.' I promised him there and then that I would get him a day in the cutting room with Pakula and the film editor, as he had originally been promised, and urged him not to give up on it.

I knew I would have a tough time making good on that promise. The Hollywood culture thrives on people saying, and even writing, things they claim they are going to do, when in fact they have no intention of sticking to their word. It is just done so that they get their own way at a particular time. The legal contests over film contracts are legendary and a promise made by word of mouth is hardly worth the breath that carries it from the speaker's lips. In Hollywood, if someone says 'Trust me' the odds are you will be betrayed.

Fortunately, I was on very good terms with Frank Wells, a Rhodes Scholar who was then president of Warner Brothers, and called him to see what he thought of the film. 'I never did think it had great dramatic content or potential,' was his blunt assessment. This, however, gave me my opportunity. 'It's a total bore! It's a terrible waste and a great shame but something can be done with it,' I told him. 'Redford has spent a lot of time in the cutting room and I really think that Dustin should have time in there with the director as well.'

However reasonable that might have sounded, the bottom line was that Warner Brothers wanted to make more films with Redford and were very wary of upsetting him. So I pointed out to Frank that, big star though he was, Redford had his ranch in Utah which he needed to maintain and, financially, making films for Warner Brothers was as important to him as it was to the film company. A week later we had a result and Dustin was in the editing suite.

Once in there, Dustin played his hand very cleverly by suggesting that the first scene to be cut was one that featured him. That got rid of the idea that the whole exercise was going to be a battle of inflated egos and at the end of a very long day Dustin emerged from the room triumphant. Around half of the suggestions he had made were taken up, and although he would never, ever be totally satisfied with any film he made . . . he liked it. Not only was he more upbeat about it but so was everybody else, because all the essential ingredients were to the fore. It was intriguing, entertaining, tense and delivered at just the right pace. At the premiere, I told Redford: 'Congratulations. You've got a hit here, Bob.'

His response was cool. He was nothing like that humorous but sharp fellow I had met months before in his New York office and a number of times since on the film set. I mentioned as much to Frank Wells, who burst out laughing. The reason was simple. Frank had told Redford, word for word, what I had said about his needing Warner Brothers as much as they needed him. Redford had understandably taken offence.

The drama surrounding 'All the President's Men' was not yet over. Bernstein and Woodward, the reporters who broke the Watergate story and then wrote the book which became the basis for William Goldman's script, wanted more money, especially as the film had been a box office smash. Some months after it came out, Bernstein came to see me in Los Angeles. He wanted me to represent him and put his case to Warner Brothers. I couldn't do that because I had not been party to the original deal, but I did mention it to Frank Wells.

I pointed out to Frank that Woodward and Bernstein had very powerful pens and they had, in fact, brought down a President, so surely Warner Brothers should not appear to be treating them less than well. Frank nodded and said, 'I think you have a point – I will find a way to get them some more money even though they are not legally entitled to it.'

Later that year I met Bernstein at the home of a writer in New York. He was with Kathleen Tynan, the writer and wife of Kenneth Tynan, and as he came up to me he told her, 'This is the man who got me my money from Warner Brothers.'

The success of 'All the President's Men' made Dustin even more sought-after and despite his behaviour people put up with him. His insecurity was excused by many in the business as that of a dedicated, self-critical professional tortured by his work. People tolerated extraordinary abuse from him on the grounds that this was a perfectionist at work. I've met other perfectionists and they are nothing like as temperamental as Dustin could be. But in Hollywood, of course, when you are a star they will say you are a 'perfectionist'. If you are a lesser actor and give the same trouble you are a 'pain in the ass'.

When Dustin started out in New York as a poor actor desperate for parts, people would describe him as crazy. Success changed that to perfectionist. Strangely, the monster only emerged when he was working. When he didn't have a script in his hand or a camera pointing at him he could be charming and very generous, and off the set he was terrific company. Ever the showman, he had a passion to shock. He could be outrageous and you knew for sure he was doing it deliberately, relishing the fact that he was making you cringe.

So who could tame him? In my years with Dustin the only man that he seemed afraid of was his father Harry, to the point that if he wanted to get in touch with him he usually got me to do it for him. Harry was a first-generation American Jew who had survived tuberculosis twice and moved from Chicago to California because he wanted to be a film producer. He ended up as a furniture designer but the fight and the will to win never left him. I saw him, at the age of seventy-five, playing tennis and there was an astonishing aggression burning inside him. The paternal influence left its mark. When Dustin played Willy Loman in Arthur Miller's 'Death of a Salesman' on Broadway in 1984, it wasn't just Dustin up there on stage, it was his father too. The play had first been a huge hit back in 1949 when I saw Lee J Cobb playing the role of Willy Loman and Cobb used his physical stature as a metaphor for the big man going down. Dustin, because of his size, couldn't play it that way, so instead he squeezed every drop of emotional angst out of the part by becoming the little man overwhelmed by life, the man with hands too small to hold the American dream. I saw both versions and they worked superbly well for both actors.

Insecurity and a feeling he was a failure gnawed at Dustin. I remember going to see him on his fortieth birthday. It was August 1977 and he was laying in bed in a house he had rented in Los Angeles, looking very depressed. I asked, 'What's the matter? It's your birthday!'

He said: 'It is tragic. Did you know my chance did not come until I was thirty? Now I am forty perhaps I will go down as the greatest Jewish actor,' and he laughed bitterly.

I told him about the actor Paul Muni who was in his fifties before he became a star, and in order to get Dustin out of his depression I went to Brentano's bookshop in Beverly Hills and bought the book 'Actor', the biography of Muni which I had read previously. His real name was Muni Weisenfreud and he started in the Yiddish Theatre in New York and went to Hollywood after a successful career on the Broadway stage. What Dustin made of Muni's story I do not know, but his attitude that day illustrated how insecure he could be at times.

In 1972, two years before I started actively to work with Dustin, he had joined the film production company First Artists, which had been set up by Paul Newman, Steve McQueen, Barbra Streisand and Sidney Poitier with the express aim of giving the stars before the cameras complete artistic control of their projects. There were certain ground rules: films had to stay within budget, they could not run for more than two hours ten minutes, and the actors would only get a nominal fee for their work but would take a percentage of profits. In exchange for agreeing to all this, they were given final editing rights. To Dustin this was ideal – just how he liked it – and he signed up to do two films for the company.

The first of these was due to start shooting by late September 1974, just when I was becoming ensconced in the job of managing him, and was meant to be delivered a year later. By the summer of 1975 nothing had happened and Dustin wanted to push the project back until the spring of 1976. For First Artists, backed by Warner Brothers, this was bad news. I went to see the First Artists president, Philip Feldman, and their lawyer, Steve Cooper. They were in a prickly mood, not because Dustin wanted another delay but because of why he wanted that delay – to make another movie, 'Marathon Man', for a rival company, Paramount. At the meeting with me was Dustin's lawyer, Lee Steiner, and we were faced with the prospect of First Artists taking out an injunction to stop Dustin working on 'Marathon Man'.

This would have been a disaster for us because the producer Robert Evans had spelled it out quite clearly that shooting for 'Marathon Man' would start on time and if Hoffman was not available, he was out (which would have been no loss to the film's director – John Schlesinger). That was the last thing we wanted because 'Marathon Man' had the feel of being a superb commercial proposition. We had to do a deal.

Without saying as much I hinted to Feldman that I would be agreeable to renegotiating Dustin's contract with First Artists, conceding percentages due to him when he made a second film for them, and I also pointed out that if Dustin was allowed to make 'Marathon Man' it would actually be to First Artists' advantage, because he would become a bigger box office star by the time he started working for them. Furthermore, they would do better with a star who was happy working for them, rather than one disenchanted because he had been forced to drop a role he really wanted.

On top of this, I promised that as soon as 'Marathon Man' was completed Dustin would begin work on the First Artists project, the dramatization of a book by ex-convict Edward Bunker, 'No Beast So Fierce', which would eventually become the film 'Straight Time'. The deal offered to First Artists also involved the budget for 'Straight Time' being raised from $3 million to $4 million, again to their advantage because they would have a classier-looking project. Feldman agreed and Dustin was free to do 'Marathon Man', scripted by William Goldman from his own novel.

Work started in the autumn of 1975 and Dustin played a New York history student called Babe Levy, who was training to run a marathon. In the film, Babe's brother, played by Roy Scheider, becomes embroiled in a plot involving some diamonds hidden by a notorious Nazi concentration camp torturer, the role taken by Laurence Olivier. When Babe's brother is murdered, the Nazi comes looking for Babe, convinced the brother has left the secret of the diamonds with him.

Olivier was not well at the time and Paramount had a lot of trouble getting him insured. The rumours quickly made the rounds that Hoffman, in normal obsessive form, had driven the ailing Olivier into the ground, with constant tinkering with the scenes, requiring them to be done over and over again. That was just not true. Dustin had compassion and he had the utmost regard for his co-star. Besides, Olivier wouldn't have stood for it. Dustin's methods, however, did leave the great man somewhat bemused: 'My dear boy, when you are called upon to act, why do you not just act? Why do you agonize so? You are trying too hard,' Olivier told him.

Olivier was very charming and actually remembered in detail meeting my mother in the lift at Fortnum and Mason a few months earlier.

'Marathon Man', just as I had expected, turned out to be a huge hit, but the next project, the First Artists film 'Straight Time', was not to be one of Dustin's more auspicious contributions to the cinema. Again the start time was missed and, worse, Dustin was far from happy with the script, about the convict released from prison trying to go straight but finding society so rigid and inflexible that he reverts to his old gun-toting, bank-robbing ways. His tinkering with it caused more delays and by the time the film was completed, it was three months behind schedule.

For this movie, Dustin was not only the star but was also the director. However, he quickly realized he could not combine the two roles. An example of his failure to grasp the nettle was one scene which required Folsom Prison in California to be shrouded in fog as a backdrop. Instead of using a machine to manufacture the fog, Dustin kept the cast and crew standing by – on overtime – until the fog descended. But it did not. Everyone had heard of waiting for fog to clear, but no-one had heard of waiting for it to arrive!

He agreed to step down as director but had to find a replacement, and eventually he turned to his old friend Ulu Grosbard, who had made 'Who Is Harry Kellerman and Why Is He Saying These Terrible Things About Me?' Dustin had starred in that after 'The Graduate' but it had not been well received, nor was it a success at the box office. Although free, Grosbard was reluctant to take on 'Straight Time' for a number of reasons: the budget was running out, he had to slot into a framework that was already developing and worst of all the First Artists' contract gave final cut approval to Hoffman. Whichever way he turned, Grosbard could not come out of the film a winner, but to help out a friend he relented. Whether he would have done so if he had thought that eventually seven writers would be employed on the film I would think is most unlikely.

It was to end a twenty-year relationship, as Grosbard found Dustin harder to work with than he could possibly have remembered. He was not the only one. I began to feel that being Dustin's manager was an intrusion on my life, shackling me to his needs when I had other pressing business matters to deal with. Part of the attraction of our partnership was our independent status. I didn't need Dustin for my living and vice versa, yet here I was, stuck on the set for days on end, something I had vowed I would never let happen to me again when, all those years before, I was James Mason's very bored double.

For the first time, serious cracks appeared in our relationship. It did not help matters that this was a fraught period for Dustin personally. His marriage to Anne was beginning to crumble, although the actual divorce did not happen for another three years. When I went on holiday to Monte Carlo, Tim Zinneman (the son of director Fred who made 'A Man For All Seasons' and 'The Day of the Jackal'), who was employed as the day-to-day producer on 'Straight Time', bombarded me with phone calls about Dustin's behaviour. Even Anne Hoffman called, increasingly worried by her husband's erratic ways. These calls were nearly all to do with trivial matters that could have been sorted out then and there on the set. But they were not and I became even more embroiled.

In July 1977, Dustin, almost burned out, took a break from the film and just before that happened Feldman suggested that, against all First Artists' principles, perhaps the company should take over the production and editing of the film, if only to get a completed picture! But the fear was that if that happened – and Feldman was genuinely reluctant to follow this course of action – Dustin might just walk out and First Artists would have no film, let alone the two he had been signed to make.

Eventually 'Straight Time' was completed, but again at a cost. There were two endings, which revolved around a bank robbery. Dustin's character comes out to find the getaway driver, an old friend played by Gary Busey, has fled, but tracks him down. In version one, Dustin forgives the man and embraces him. In the other, he shoots him. There was no doubt in people's minds that the first ending had more impact and would have elicited sympathy from audiences for Dustin's character. Yet when pressed to make a decision, and in my view just to be perverse, Dustin exercised his artist's right by opting for the latter climax, which everyone else involved with the film felt merely served to alienate the audience.

Finally, Grosbard retreated to edit the film, only to find that Hoffman was gathering up his completed work and going back in the cutting room to re-edit it. He only got through about twenty minutes of the film before Feldman and First Artists did what they had been threatening to do all along and seized the movie from him. They felt Dustin was no longer in a position to damage their investment and his part in the project was done. Eventually, the film, all one hundred and fourteen minutes of it, came out to die a rapid and undignified death at the box office, despite some good critical reviews.

I met Dustin by chance in New York soon after the reviews came out and commented on them. He replied, 'You can see how much better it would have been if I had my way.'

THE saga of 'Straight Time' had been trying but it proved a prelude to the next First Artists project, 'Agatha'. A more apt title for it would have been 'Agony', for it was the film that brought about the end of my period as Dustin's manager. Yet when we started out on the project it was all so very promising, so much so that I backed it financially at a time when the dramas of 'Straight Time' were reaching a crescendo.

The beginning of my involvement in 'Agatha' came when I was hailed at Los Angeles airport by a young Englishman I knew who was beginning to make a name for himself as a film producer. It was David Puttnam, destined for greater glory and a short stint as the head of Columbia Pictures before his career went into a tailspin.

I had first met him in the late 1960s when he was running a photographic agency and I was involved with an agency providing photographers to take commercial photographs. In the long run the business was not successful because photographers were hardly a reliable breed. They tended to earn a stack of money and then disappear to Spain or Greece for several months until the cash ran out. Several times we had to turn work down because there were no photographers around to do it. So it was suggested we needed to retain the services of more photographers and I heard of a photographic agent who wanted to sell his business – David Puttnam. I met with him and agreed to buy him out for £34,000. A contract was signed and exchanged.

Puttnam arrived in my office on the day of completion looking pale and overwrought and at his wits' end. The deal, from his side, was falling apart because his photographers didn't want to be sold out and if they were, they wanted as their agent the brother of one of their colleagues, David Montgomery. I was not bothered but Puttnam was clearly agitated. He told me that he wanted to get into the film business and had committed £5,000 of the money I was going to give him for the photographic business as a payment that was due for a film script he wanted to buy. He was overdrawn at the bank and, with family bills on top of all that, he was in deep trouble, to the extent where, he said, he could not pay off his debts. He was so distressed, I had my secretary draw up a cheque for £5,000 made out to him and said, 'Pay me back when you can.'

He was overwhelmed, said this was the most generous gesture he had ever experienced and insisted that I must benefit from any future success he had in the film business. I didn't want this but he was adamant. He wanted to put it down in writing that I should take fifty per cent of his earnings from films in the future, but I persuaded him to cut back this offer to include just his career in films over the next seven years. Of course, he went on to produce some very successful pictures but I never made any attempt to get the money. As for the original debt of £5,000, it was repaid five years later without interest, after a few requests.

In those early days Puttnam invited me to all the private screenings of his films and would turn to me for advice on financial and other matters. So when he grabbed me at the airport in Los Angeles I was not that taken aback when he said he had a project he wanted to discuss with me. I told him to call me at my hotel and he left a couple of messages before we met up.

What he had was a script called 'Agatha' by Kathleen Tynan, about the eleven days in December 1926 when the crime writer Agatha Christie vanished. Puttnam already had Vanessa Redgrave contracted to play Agatha and a production office had been set up, but attempts to find backers, in both Britain and America, had been unsuccessful. The Rank Organisation had agreed to the project but then pulled out because Christie's husband, who was portrayed unfavourably in the script, had been a director of Rank. Puttnam proposed a budget of $1,750,000 to get the picture started but, looking at the figures and with some payments deferred, I reckoned that could be cut by $250,000. A publishing firm was willing to put up $1 million and I told David I would read the script and, providing I liked it, I would come up with the remaining $500,000.

I took the script down by the pool at the Beverly Hills Hotel and didn't leave until I had finished it. 'I loved it,' I later told Puttnam and said that I was definitely 'in' but wanted to offer Dustin Hoffman part of my share. I saw Dustin for dinner later that night and handed him the script. At about eight o'clock the following morning he called my room to say he had read about sixty pages and he, too, loved it. Furthermore, he liked the idea of doing something with the part of a journalist, Ian

Villiers, in it. I told him to forget that because playing Villiers would not fulfil the First Artists criterion that he took a leading role. I asked him to finish reading the whole script and we would then talk again.

When we did, Dustin's enthusiasm of the early hours was unabated and he was convinced the Villiers part could be developed and expanded enough to satisfy First Artists. I could see that Dustin saw this role as a quick fix, a chance to fulfil his obligations to them and move on to some of the meatier roles that were coming his way in bigger and better films. I told him again that he could put some money into it but added that he shouldn't get too excited about appearing in it. We agreed to meet with Kathleen Tynan, Puttnam and the film's director Michael Apted, all of whom happened to be in Los Angeles, later that day.

When the meeting took place, it was unbelievable, in that all egos seemed to have been left outside the door. Puttnam delivered a slick eulogy about the film while Hoffman was eager, complimentary and amiable, talking positively about the script and asking questions about Christie and her books, none of which he had read at that stage. For Puttnam, Apted and Tynan this was incredible – one of the world's top box office stars was eager to get in on the action. The only query was raised by Dustin after the meeting ended. He wanted to have a look at some of Apted's directing work. The message was passed on to Puttnam, a couple of films were delivered and Dustin was left happy with what he had seen. 'Let's go ahead,' he declared when the credits of Apted's second movie started to roll. He was less certain about Puttnam, but I reassured him that David would not do anything against my interests.

Location shooting – in York for the railway station, Harrogate and Bath – had to start in November 1977, just two months away. Vanessa Redgrave had other commitments once the film was over but the overriding problem was the considerable rewriting of the script that was needed to beef up the part of Dustin's character, the journalist now rechristened

Wally Stanton. Dustin's method of experimenting with his role, plus the presence of Murray Schisgal, the New York playwright friend of Dustin's brought in to work on his scenes, caused considerable unrest. There were often times when the cast had assembled on set and had no idea what lines they had or what scene was going to be shot. And Redgrave was not happy about a romantic development between her Agatha and Dustin's Stanton, which she said had been written in the wrong style for 1926.

There were just seven days before rehearsals were due to begin when Apted and the assistant producer Gavrik Losey, who had been tied up with the project long before I became involved, came to see me in my London office. They asked me if I knew that Puttnam was going to resign as producer of 'Agatha'. I was stunned. He couldn't do that so close to work starting. I phoned him in Malta, where he was completing another film, 'Midnight Express'. He claimed that his accountants had told him he could not spend more than another twenty days in Britain that year, for tax reasons.

It made me livid. Why had he kept this secret for so long? And when would he have told me, had I not challenged him because of what Apted and Losey said? Dustin and I had been sold on the project by him and we believed he was going to be steering it through. He had led us to believe the break in Malta was going to take up just three weeks. I was being taken for a ride and, because of the contract with First Artists and Warner Brothers, I was expected to step in and become the producer. This was all the more necessary because the film was attracting government subsidy under the scheme known as EADY, which provided substantial sums to producers of British films provided the vast majority of people involved in making the film were British. Very, very reluctantly I agreed to take on the job, on the proviso that I would only do it until another British producer could be found. But it was still a big mistake on my part. As I took on this onerous responsibility, I couldn't help but reflect on what I had told Dustin when he asked me whether Puttnam could be relied upon. I had said I was sure he would not do anything to harm me. How wrong I was. I had not expected to be spending seventy-five per cent of my time involved in the day-to-day business of making the film, particularly when Puttnam had made himself the executive producer – a title which meant nothing – without mentioning a word to me, and Losey was co-producer!

Five years later, in a deposition for a legal action involving claims and counter-claims running between Dustin, First Artists, Warner Brothers and myself following First Artists seizing control of both 'Straight Time' and 'Agatha', I was able to ask Apted about Puttnam's behaviour and on oath he called it 'reprehensible' that Puttnam had not been more straight-forward with me and First Artists about his commitments. Pressed to expand on that, Apted agreed that Puttnam had let me, Dustin and First Artists down. He said Puttnam had known that he would not be available, for tax reasons, when we first discussed the film. Puttnam had betrayed me and his actions bore out a favourite saying of Sammy Cahn's: 'No good deed goes unpunished.'

So there I was, propelled quite against my will into becoming the producer of 'Agatha' and the problems erupted from day one. Timothy Dalton, the man who was to become James Bond version 004, was to play Agatha's husband, Colonel Christie. This was a tough part to cast and Dalton was eighth choice, but nevertheless he was piqued that his name was not going to appear above the titles, since Puttnam had apparently promised him as much. Dustin called me from the rehearsal rooms to come along and sort it out, which I did. I just acted the stern uncle and, though it wasn't easy, we finally resolved the matter at my home the following morning after a two-hour session with Dalton. The only good thing about this episode was that Dalton appreciated my role and has always been extremely friendly whenever we have met.

If only all the problems with 'Agatha' could have been resolved like that. Down in Bath all hell broke loose over

Schisgal, who was being exceptionally aggressive and difficult. Along with Redgrave, I agreed that his rewriting was hopelessly inconsistent with the period. New York Jewish humour has its place, but not in upper-middle class England of the 1920s. Redgrave tore some of the scenes he handed her into shreds. Then there was his influence on Dustin, who seemed to be more glib than ever and was dwelling for longer and longer over his preparations before each scene. Dutsin's long-time creative adviser, Stanley Beck, challenged Schisgal about the way he was developing the Stanton character, but there was never any change and by December, Dustin had fired Stanley, leaving Schisgal as the sole spokesman for him on creative matters.

The final showdown between me and Dustin was looming and again at the heart of it all was Schisgal. He was determined to create some romantic interest between Agatha and Stanton. I agreed to talk to Redgrave about it and went to her hotel. She was not against the idea at all – what she objected to was the way Schisgal had developed it. There was, she argued, no plausible chance of Agatha responding to Stanton in the way Schisgal had constructed it. She was happy for a decent professional scriptwriter to come in and sort out the mess, but Schisgal had to go. I tried to get Tom Stoppard but he said he would not get involved unless Kathleen Tynan, the original writer, asked him to.

I thought this was a very sensible idea and approached Dustin, thinking the news that Redgrave had no objections about the romance being in the film might soften the blow that we had to get rid of Schisgal. For me the progress of the film was the one and only consideration. Professionalism could not bow to the whims of friendship. I went to see Dustin in the restaurant of the Priory Hotel but he was deaf to everything apart from the news that Schisgal was out.

'How can you agree for Murray to be dropped?' he yelled. He was raging so loudly that people at a nearby table asked me to control him, as in an hysterical tirade he accused me of being the originator of the plot to dump Schisgal. Rational conversation with him was out of the question.

Phil Feldman came over to have a look at some footage of 'Agatha' for First Artists and was far from happy with what he saw, describing Dustin's portrayal of Stanton as 'bizarre', 'overmannered' and 'inconsistent'. He laid down some ground rules that were to apply up to Christmas: Dustin and Redgrave were to do no more scenes other than those already scripted, nothing new was to be written for Dustin and only low-key bits involving him were to be filmed. The idea being that the Christmas break would give Dustin time to unwind and reappraise his contribution to 'Agatha' in a more constructive light.

When he met up with Dustin, Feldman expressed his horror at what he had already seen and talked about closing the film down until another writer could be found. Dustin listened, concerned rather than furious. Schisgal then asked Feldman what he thought about a scene that takes place in the Spa Hotel where Agatha has taken refuge. When Stanton approaches Christie, she asks him why he is in the hotel. Giving a false name – Curtis Schatz – he replies it is because he suffers from constipation and has not had a decent bowel movement for eighteen days, thirteen hours and forty-two minutes.

Apted and many of us had always hated that scene and when Schisgal asked Feldman for his thoughts, the president of First Artists said, 'Don't worry, we'll cut that line.' To Dustin that comment signalled that he had already lost control of the picture and he furiously attacked Feldman, arguing that a takeover by First Artists would be counter-productive. At one stage he had the nerve to turn round and ask me why I wasn't defending him! 'Because your position is indefensible, and if you were twenty per cent right, I *would* defend you,' I replied.

Feldman didn't take over the film until the beginning of February 1978 but during the Christmas break, when I was on holiday in Acapulco, I received a phone call from Dustin's lawyer Lee Steiner, with some news: I was no longer to represent Dustin. That made life difficult when I returned to 'Agatha' in the New Year. Dustin refused to talk to me and I eventually gave up my attempts to contact him. Not only that, I was barred from the set when Dustin was there. He had become paranoid and developed the view, quite wrongly, that if we were both on the set at the same time I would be undermining him. I continued, however, to handle business for the film, particularly dealing with Vanessa Redgrave – who was not, by that time, easily dealt with – and the important negotiations with the unions.

First Artists had taken control of both Dustin's films by the time I arranged to meet his accountant, Michael Hecht, to settle our outstanding financial matters on Sunday 20 February at the Beverly Hills Hotel. Surprisingly, Hecht was accompanied by a New York lawyer, Alan Schwartz, who had taken over from Steiner, and a Los Angeles lawyer, Bert Fields. They started to quiz me about Dustin and First Artists and, believing I still had a contractual tie with Dustin, I answered them openly and in some detail. It was a big mistake. Two days later Dustin filed a lawsuit against me, Feldman, First Artists and Warner Brothers, alleging interference in his creative control. I asked my lawyer to look into the conduct of Dustin's legal team in their interview with me. At no time had they advised me that the statement I was giving them might be used against me, and considering that was exactly what happened so shortly afterwards, it was obvious that this had been the sole purpose of the exercize. I counter-sued, claiming $3.5 million which was owing to me as, obviously on his lawyers' advice, Dustin was refusing to release my outstanding percentage of his income from several films including 'All the President's Men', 'Marathon Man', 'Straight Time', 'Agatha' and, by this time, 'Kramer vs Kramer'.

I had read 'Kramer vs Kramer' by Avery Corman while Dustin was making 'Straight Time', and had recognized it as the perfect vehicle for him, for some of the events of his own life at the time were mirrored in the book. He rejected it as 'soap opera' but was eventually won round and worked with Bob Benton, the director and scriptwriter, on tailoring the part of Tom Kramer for him.

I had actually tried to buy the film rights to the book but these had already been secured by Stanley Jaffe, then a producer, later president of Paramount Pictures. He called me about Dustin playing the part and Dustin was just intrigued enough to ask about other screenplays Benton had written. These included 'Bonnie and Clyde' and 'What's Up Doc?' and they whetted Dustin's appetite, but he was far from impressed with Benton's directing credits, which included 'The Late Show' and 'Bad Company'. He told me he would not work on the project if Benton was directing.

I kept that bit to myself and simply told Jaffe that Dustin was interested in Benton's script but was otherwise tied up at that point. I didn't want Jaffe to give up on him and believed Dustin could eventually be persuaded to come round to the project. The fact was that Jaffe was known for picking and sticking by directors. It would certainly be Benton and another actor if Dustin objected to Benton. That other actor was Richard Dreyfus, who was calling Jaffe every week to check on the progress of the film, which was set for a March 1978 start.

In my court case with Dustin, Jaffe gave evidence on deposition and was very impressive. He not only told the truth about the various discussions on the possibility of Dustin playing the Kramer part, he refused to go along with Dustin's lawyer, who suggested that I had deceived Jaffe by claiming Dustin had wanted the role all the time. Jaffe said: 'Jarvis may not have been doing any favours for me but he was doing the best for his client, Dustin Hoffman, because if he had told me about Dustin's reluctance to accept Benton as director, I would have signed Richard Dreyfus straight away.' I am certain what Jaffe said on oath in deposition helped in eventually producing a satisfactory out-of-court settlement.

A short time before Dustin and I parted ways, with 'Agatha'

now in the can, Dustin flew back to Los Angeles and was contacted by Jaffe. Dustin had some script reservations about 'Kramer vs Kramer' which Jaffe said had either been sorted out or could be in a meeting involving Dustin, himself and Benton. They did meet up and Benton made a good impression, tempting Dustin with creative control offers which made him ninety-five per cent certain he was on board. The rehearsals took place in August 1978 and shooting started a month later.

Dustin apparently was his usual self on set and was chastised by the Los Angeles *Herald Express* for the way he treated Gail Strickland, the actress picked by Jaffe to play the part of the Kramers' neighbour who is accused of breaking up the marriage. The woman, Margaret Phelps, befriends Tom Kramer and helps him adjust to his new life. Away from the cameras Strickland suffered from a stammer which magically went when she was working. But according to Larry Merchant, the *Herald Express* writer, Dustin's methods raised the temperature and tension so much that it struck her down in her 'on screen' persona, so badly that she was fired and replaced by Jane Alexander, who had worked with Dustin on 'All the President's Men'. Alexander picked up Oscar nominations for that film and for 'Kramer vs Kramer'. Ironically, on his third nomination and in 'a soap', Dustin collected his first Oscar. I felt it was a case of 'How to win an Oscar without really trying'. In fact, during a conversation at a deposition hearing, Dustin volunteered the view that 'Kramer' had not been his best work.

Our court case dragged on for five years, much to the delight of the lawyers, and nobody seemed to know how to bring a dignified end to the proceedings, which in California are played for very high stakes indeed. The law there exists only for the rich. Dustin and I, eventually weary of it all and prompted by a less than honest Californian official, sorted out our differences in thirty minutes, saving ourselves much money and time. I was glad to be completely free of the business of being his manager and in a way the break-up of our partnership helped me, because I was able to concentrate on more lucrative business concerns of my own.

Trying, tiring and exasperating sums up those years as Dustin's manager, but for all that, I have sometimes missed the wit and warmth of the off-screen Dustin and still take a great interest in his work on stage and screen. I saw Dustin and his wife Lisa in late 1994 and was pleased to be warmly greeted by him with an embrace as he brought Lisa over to say hello. I also met him recently with his son at a theatre in London and we had a nice friendly chat. These occasions reminded me that my days with Dustin were unique, enlightening and rewarding – but I would certainly not want ever to repeat them.

5

Business Genius

Clore, Wilson and Goldsmith were the names of the most influential political or business geniuses I have ever known: Charles Clore, Harold Wilson and Jimmy Goldsmith. I was fortunate enough to be associated with all three of them. They were all different but each, in his own way, quite special.

Charles Clore was Britain's version of Rockefeller. In America, if someone made an eyebrow-raising financial demand you would say, 'Hey, do you think I'm Rockefeller?' In Britain we substituted 'Charlie Clore' for Rockefeller.

I first came across Clore in a social environment, during a holiday weekend at Deauville, the fashionable resort in northern France, in the 1950s. He did not leave that much of a mark. He was already well known then as one of the country's leading entrepreneurs, but that weekend he did not seem anything special. If great men carry a certain aura about them, then it was completely absent with Clore. Far from being at the centre of the social group, he was at the edge, more a listener than a talker, an observer rather than a doer. As I was to discover, he liked the company of friends but never dominated proceedings. In the boardroom it was very different. There he moved with a swiftness of thought and purpose that was truly breathtaking.

I was to fully appreciate this other side of Clore, the one that made him a business genius, when in 1959 my partner Charles Burkeman and I sold the jewellers Mappin & Webb to him. To us, his involvement in the deal was manna from heaven. In effect Charles rescued us from a business that was proving a terrible burden.

We had acquired Mappin & Webb as the price to be paid for getting out of a messy business situation. I had moved from retailing – I had a chain of menswear shops – into property, having realized that property development would be a lot more profitable than running a retail business. Burkeman, who was also my brother-in-law, agreed and we decided to concentrate our efforts in that area. We started our partnership in a room loaned to us by our solicitor, David Freeman, who was in his early days of practice and had some spare space. David eventually enjoyed great success and became one of London's leading solicitors.

Our first property venture resulted from a conversation on a tennis court in Bournemouth when one of the players, an estate agent, mentioned a site in Edgware, a north-west London suburb. We built, on vacant land, six shops with offices above and those offices were let to a young man named Stanley Kalms, who used them as the headquarters of his retail and mail order photographic equipment business which has become one of the best known names in shopping centres and high streets: Dixons.

Urged on by our father-in-law Abraham Oppenheim, a brilliant property developer himself, I found myself in a three-way partnership with Charles Burkeman and my wife's brother, Henry Oppenheim. But the arrangement did not work and Charles and I wanted to break away from Henry, whom we found to be devious and not to our liking. The idea was that Henry would buy us out and we could go on our way. What happened in fact was that we ended up buying Henry out, and part of the deal was that we acquired – or were stuck with – some business luggage we were very reluctant to take on: Mappin & Webb shares.

It was a big, prestigious public company with a lot of kudos. It held royal warrants and had jewellery stores in Oxford Street, Regent Street, the City of London and Sheffield.

There were also factories in Sheffield and overseas shops in Buenos Aires, Rio de Janeiro, Johannesburg and Paris, as well as the Robinson & Cleaver department stores in London, Newcastle, Liverpool, Belfast and Bournemouth. All this sounded grand but in buying these shares, which gave us control of Mappin & Webb, we had overstretched our resources. Putting it bluntly, we fell into almost unmanageable debt. The whole saga was long, complicated and not particularly pleasant.

It was then that Charles Clore came along. He had just failed in his bid for the brewers, Watneys, in the face of hostility not only from the company but from the brewing community generally and even Parliament. It is hard to imagine now but in 1959 there were people, even MPs, who thought only those already in the industry could own breweries. Clore had to withdraw from the bid. It was the first time he had tasted failure and it left him wounded and sore. He was in need of a successful and high-profile move in another direction. Mappin & Webb certainly filled the role. If Clore came along at the right time for us, then it was also good business for him.

Most important for us was that, relieved of debt, we were able to concentrate on developing shopping parades and particularly supermarkets, of which we were among the pioneers in the UK. I was certainly fortunate to have a partner as intelligent and as conscientious as Charles Burkeman.

It was now that I began to appreciate Clore. As I showed him round the Mappin & Webb shops, I could see how quickly he grasped things. He might not have been university-educated – in fact his years at elementary school in London's East End and at an Anglican school in north London were fairly undistinguished – but he was 'switched on'. The son of a Russian Jew who fled Latvia because of anti-Semitism, Charles was brought up in a family that made a living from the textile trade and small property deals. However, throughout his business life he favoured controlling firms that the man in the street knew about. New technology and greenfield sites never really attracted him.

We had something in common. As I would in time be successful putting on Muhammad Ali's fights in the cinemas, so Charles had landed his first big deal with film of the Gene Tunney versus Jack Dempsey fight in 1924. He picked up the rights for South Africa and sold them on the boat going over to Cape Town. The money from that deal allowed him to buy a derelict roller-skating rink at Cricklewood in north London, where he had skated and worked as a boy collecting the admission money. From there he went on to acquire a stake in the Prince of Wales Theatre and invested in a South African gold mine, buying shares for six shillings before the war and selling them later for £7 each. He bought the Richards dress shops and by 1950 had expanded the chain from thirty shops to forty-five, before selling out for £1 million. Clore's great ability was approaching problems from an angle that no-one else had seen or thought about, and this was to lead to his huge success with his company Sears Holdings.

Charles would look at companies with a Stock Exchange price well below the value of their assets and then approach the shareholders with an offer they could not refuse. He did this with Sears, offering forty shillings a share against the quoted price of fourteen. Now, such a way of doing business is so commonplace that during takeover battles the bidder positively advertises the fact that the shares being bid for are much below their asset value. When Clore did it with Sears, it was a totally unheard of tactic and caused controversy. The City was outraged and dubbed him, with no affection what-soever, the 'Takeover King'. He was accused of asset stripping but his crime was simply to be ahead of his time. Indeed, far from stripping companies, he built them up. A typical example of this was Selfridges department store, which he acquired after a bitter battle. He certainly made great improvements there.

When Clore moved into Sears they had 2,000 employees.

By the time he died in 1979 there were 60,000. After he bought the company he sold off its freehold property for £6 million, giving him more capital to invest, and rented back the same property at market rate. If he had been the asset-stripper he was accused of being, he could have exploited the business for the value of its property and cut and run. But that was not the way Charlie Clore did business. 'Find your opportunity and work hard' was his creed, and he was true to that. Often in the office by first light, he would work late and then enjoy an evening socializing before snatching three or four hours' sleep, all that he ever needed. He brought a desperately needed dose of realism to the City and was hard-headed and pragmatic. Nor was his almost visionary development of property restricted to London. In America, with Jack Cotton, he built the famous Pan-Am building in New York. The partnership with Cotton ended in acrimony and upset both men, but the building is still a New York landmark.

Charles was not a man to suffer fools gladly and had a reputation for rudeness, particularly to women. Really he was more brusque than rude, although I would admit that his attitude to the fairer sex did leave a certain amount to be desired. The reason was his one experience of marriage, which had left him somewhat bruised. He had wed Francine Halphen, a French Resistance heroine, in 1943, but fourteen years and two children later the marriage ended in divorce. She had run off with someone else and it left him bitter. If someone irritated him he would not bother to talk to them, but that did not mean he was not a kind and good friend, or even an ungenerous man, and by that I am not just referring to his wealth.

His philanthropy was legendary and he was knighted for it in 1971. It was reported that he gave £500,000 away annually and among the beneficiaries was London Zoo, which received £400,000 for the Mammals Pavilion and the Lions' Terraces. London University was given £750,000 and benefited from a charitable foundation that Clore set up, while his other great passion as a Zionist was Israel. During the Six Day War of 1967 he provided the country with £1 million for war relief. His love for Israel and his loyalty to his religion meant that he refused to go to the wedding and reception of his daughter Vivien, when she married the stockbroker John Duffield, because he was not Jewish.

He was also keen on the horses, and we were often to meet at a race track. His colours of royal blue and pink were a common sight and he enjoyed his greatest success with Valoris, a filly trained by Vincent O'Brien in County Tipperary, which won the Irish 1,000 Guineas and The Oaks at Epsom in 1966.

Clore's personal kindness and thoughtfulness to me was considerable. After my wife Phyllis died he was very kind to me, calling me every weekend to see how I was and to find out whether I was doing anything. But for all his immense wealth and business triumphs, he could be envious of other people's success – even friends of his. I was left in no doubt about that after his reaction to the film 'Marathon Man'.

It was September 1975 and I, of course, was involved in the film through my association with Dustin Hoffman. I met Charles in New York on the way to the Philippines for the third Muhammad Ali v Joe Frazier fight, billed as 'The Thrilla in Manila'. (Charles' interest in boxing was for rather sentimental reasons – it reminded him of that Gene Tunney v Jack Dempsey deal which set him up). On the way to the airport, he asked me what my financial share from 'Marathon Man' was going to be. I had no reason not to tell him and he also asked me about the plot of the film. I briefly explained it and then at the airport I saw a copy of the book by William Goldman on the news stand, bought it and gave it to him. In spite of his legendary lack of need for sleep, he would catnap, especially on flights – but not this time. The book had him riveted and by the time we touched down, he had finished it.

Some months later I was in New York, sandwiching the premiere of 'Marathon Man' with the Ali v Ken Norton fight. Charles called me from the Waldorf Hotel, where he had a permanent suite, and I told him he was welcome to join me and some friends for dinner at '21'. He came along and during the course of the evening one of our friends mentioned the film premiere, which had been the previous night. Now it was being shown in an uptown cinema and Charles was keen to see it, so the next evening he and I went along to a Third Avenue cinema to see 'Marathon Man'.

Charles had a well-known habit of falling asleep when watching a film but half an hour into the screening he nudged me and said, 'This is a good film.'

After an hour he nudged me again.

'This is going to make you a lot of money.'

The hour and a half point arrived and another nudge.

'I don't think you realize how much money this is going to make.'

We came out of the cinema and there were people every-where, wall-to-wall people, and Charles looked up at the huge hoardings towering over the street, showing Dustin Hoffman and Laurence Olivier. 'This is going to make you a fortune,' he said again, and in a very bad-tempered way added: 'Nothing like this ever happens to me.'

'Do you realize what you have just said?' I asked, totally amazed by his reaction. But Charles stamped his feet and said, 'I know what I have just said!' and then we headed off to Pearls Chinese restaurant in mid-town Manhattan. We had a fifteen-minute ride in complete silence. When we arrived at Pearls, someone at the table asked him what he thought of the film and he pointed at me and said, 'Ask him, he's the one making all the money out of it.'

How could a man as rich, successful and powerful as Charles Clore be envious? It was just part of his character. This, after all, was the man who, when he could not find a hotel to buy in London, built one instead, the Park Lane Hilton. He was used to getting his own way. I suspect being envious of others, even those who were nowhere near as rich as he was, motivated him and drove him on to seek more riches.

Two years before his death, he stepped down as chairman of Sears and became a tax exile living in Monte Carlo. It meant that his money could be handed over to charities without being taxed, but it was not the life for him. He appeared to be very miserable because he missed the activity of business and every morning he would be on the phone to London to keep up with what was happening. No amount of luxury could ease the emptiness in his life. He bought a magnificent penthouse apartment in Monte Carlo with its own private swimming pool, but even so he only occupied it for two weekends. On one of them his daughter and two grandchildren went to stay with him and the following weekend I was his guest. He even said to me during that weekend, 'I don't know what I am doing here.' I told him, 'Well, Charles, you have to understand: Charlie Clore is a legendary figure in London, whereas here you are just another rich man.'

He then came back to London for the Ascot races and immediately afterwards went into hospital to have an operation. He seemed to be on the road to recovery when he died on 29 July 1979. A few months before his death he sold his 16,500-acre estate in Herefordshire to the Prudential for £20 million, which at that time was the biggest land deal in history. He had originally bought it for £1.25 million from Guy's Hospital in 1961. Yet none of the money from the sale was due to the tax man, because it was left to the Charles Clore Foundation.

His son Alan, however, contested the will on the grounds that the daughter, Vivien, was a beneficiary and he wasn't. The son claimed that because Sir Charles had become domiciled in Monte Carlo, Napoleonic Law should apply. There was a court case and the three principal witnesses for the estate were Leonard Sainer, Charles' lawyer, Janet, Marchioness of Milford Haven, another close friend, and me. My evidence was believed by the judge and the estate successfully defended the action.

THREE years before Charles' death, I met another man who

was to become a leading figure in the global business world. Through a mutual friend in Philadelphia, back in 1976, I was introduced to Ronald Perelman, who was thirty-three at the time, and found him a charming and ambitious young man. I had not appreciated just how ambitious he was until I met up with him again after he had acquired Technicolor, the largest international film-processing company in the world. Knowing of my involvement in the film industry, Perelman asked me to join the board. He had acquired the company, based at West Drayton near Heathrow Airport, for $125 million and would sell it later to Michael Green's Carlton Communications for £850 million.

In the meantime, he had fought and won a bitter takeover battle in 1985 for the world-famous cosmetics company Revlon, and after completing his deal with Michael Green he also asked me to join the board of Revlon International, which is based in London and operates in the eastern hemisphere. Following this Perelman acquired a number of television stations, which he sold two years ago to Rupert Murdoch's Fox Network for a very substantial profit. Among other businesses he owned was New World Entertainments, a major supplier of programmes to television in the United States and which he recently sold, again to Murdoch, for $2.6 billion.

Because of his heavily fought takeover of Revlon, Perelman was unfairly regarded as a predator of established businesses. I can say, without fear of contradiction, that he is a true business manager first and foremost and has surrounded himself with top-class lieutenants, including Howard Gittis, a leading Philadelphia lawyer, and Richard Halperin, an in-house lawyer, formerly with the New York District Attorney's Office. Perelman has also used for many years, in a roving capacity, one of the most amusing men I have ever met.

Dennis Stein had a successful career in the jeans business before he joined Perelman, and was such an outstanding jeans salesman that on one occasion the owners of a large manufacturer, Sergio Valenti, in the persons of Brian Leung, a Hong Kong Chinese, and Martin Haiflink, a Polish survivor of the concentration camps, asked me to persuade Dennis to join them, saying he could write his own salary cheque. But what makes Dennis captivating is not so much his business skill as his almost unmatched capacity for one-liners – you can recall them days later and burst out laughing. Indeed, Elizabeth Taylor found Dennis so amusing that she became engaged to him and it lasted six months.

Mel Brooks told me once that on a one-for-one basis Dennis was the funniest man in the world, and that, coming from a master of the comic art, is some compliment. One of my favourite stories involving Dennis occurred on a night flight, known as the red eye, from Los Angeles to New York. On board was the actor Jose Ferrer, who had been somewhat demanding of the stewards and when the plane landed, Dennis leaned over Ferrer to take his coat from the compartment above. Ferrer snapped, 'Why don't you sit down until the plane stops?'

Dennis, already fed up with Ferrer's behaviour during the flight, replied, 'Why don't you mind your own business?'

To which Ferrer promptly said, 'Do you know who I am?'

Dennis called out to a stewardess: 'Miss, you'd better get a doctor quickly, there's a man here who has amnesia.'

Through Dennis I met Frank Sinatra, as he had been a friend of Sinatra and his wife Barbara for many years. We were in Monte Carlo on holiday when the Sinatras were staying in the same hotel and we spent a great deal of time together. I had been a Sinatra fan for as long as I could remember but was not keen to meet him, mainly because of the bad stories I had read about him.

I was, however, surprised and delighted to find him a very knowledgeable and obviously well-read man who was very friendly. After a few days, when we were alone at the Beach Club I asked Sinatra about the stories concerning him and American mobsters. He explained that when he was starting his career in the Thirties, the men who gave him his chance in nightclubs were the same men who had run the illegal clubs known as 'Speakeasys' during prohibition. When they came to see him after shows in his dressing-room, he obviously couldn't refuse to see them even when they brought a photographer – hence the publication of all those photos in the newspapers. I must say that this seemed a reasonable explanation, even if it only dealt with part of the problem. To me, the simple truth was that having grown up with these people, he never felt uncomfortable being around them.

IF Charles Clore was a genius, so in his own way was Sir James Goldsmith, or Jimmy Goldsmith, as I knew him. My association with him came about in a curious way and almost despite myself.

Taking over Mappin & Webb meant we became involved with GN Vansittart. Known as Nick Vansittart, he had been one of the first sales directors for General Motors in Holland and Belgium and ultimately became the chairman of their subsidiary, Vauxhall Motors, and Frigidaire, the leading refrigerator company also owned by General Motors.

Nick joined us on the board of Mappin & Webb and his experience and contacts proved very useful when dealing with institutions and also when we were thinking of going into the second mortgage business, which was thriving at that time. I was advised against it by my guru for many years, Morris Finer QC, a friend since our days at Kilburn Grammar School. He later became a High Court Judge but tragically died very young. The main objection Morris had was the existence of the Moneylenders' Act, which he argued was likely to cause us endless problems.

When I happened to mention this to Nick Vansittart he said he was on the board of a company, Anglo Continental Investment and Finance, which had a secondary banking firm, Continental Bankers Agents, as its principal subsidiary. Nick thought we could buy a controlling interest in Anglo Continental. The deal went ahead and it led to a very interesting period in my life because having been a borrower for many years, to be sitting on the lending committee of this banking subsidiary was quite an education. Moreover, it was Anglo Continental that made me take a fresh look at Jimmy Goldsmith.

It was Harry Recanati, of the Discount Bank of Geneva (which had been founded in Israel), who proposed that Goldsmith should join us at Anglo Continental. I was not keen and told Harry my view of Goldsmith which, at that stage, was extremely negative and based on a deal I had done previously with him. Just before the Mappin & Webb deal there were movements on the property development front and Charles Burkeman and I had pulled off a few successful deals, among them acquiring a company called Lewis & Burrows, which had thirty-four chemist shops. It was a public company and we sold half of it to Mappin & Webb when we took control there, but still retained the other half. One day Charles Clore rang to say that the previous evening he had met Jimmy Goldsmith at a nightclub in Paris and that Goldsmith was interested in buying up our joint interest in Lewis and Burrows. We did a deal with Goldsmith that just about trebled our original investment.

But Jimmy made nothing of the business and I was struck by his failure with Lewis & Burrows. There was also the matter of his wild social behaviour, which had created the initial reserve I felt for him. He had eloped with Isabel Patino, the daughter of a famous Bolivian tin millionaire, in his early twenties, but she had died giving birth to their first child in 1954, a daughter who was named Isabel. Jimmy then married his French secretary Ginette Lery, but left her to live with, and ultimately marry, Lady Annabel Vane Tempest Stewart, the former wife of Mark Birley, (who named the famous London nightclub Annabel's after her). Not long after marrying Annabel, Jimmy took a French journalist as his mistress and until his death lived in homes supervised by both his mistress and Annabel, who occupies a magnificent home in Richmond, Surrey. He was also one of the biggest casino gamblers in Europe.

However, Harry Recanati had been extremely helpful when we went into the Mappin & Webb business and we felt we owed it to him to seriously consider Goldsmith's approach. Harry said that Jimmy was an entirely different person to the one who had been involved in Lewis & Burrows. Goldsmith, he said, had been running Generale Occidentale SA, a bank in Paris, and was now a very successful businessman. We naturally made inquiries and found out that he had indeed been very successful in France.

Jimmy made it clear that he wanted to use Anglo Continental as his financial vehicle for expanding into the UK, and in the end I expressed the view to my brother Edgar, a successful stockbroker, and Charles Burkeman that we should take a gamble with Goldsmith. Jimmy was not the only player in town. Two brothers called Davidson, who were running a secondary banking firm called Eagil Trust and were very closely associated with the Eagle Star Insurance Company, had also approached us. Compared to Jimmy, the Davidsons appeared very conservative. So to go with Goldsmith was a gamble, but it soon paid off. Jimmy took off like a rocket once he was on board.

The activities of the company were expanded tremendously and there was a large excursion into the insurance brokerage business which was particularly notable. Jimmy did one deal after another until Anglo Continental ended up owning twenty-seven percent of Cavenham Foods, which was a remarkably successful retail food business. The share price rocketed and I came to regard Jimmy Goldsmith as a genius, particularly in the way he would explain his strategy at board meetings.

Much as I admired Jimmy in the boardroom, I was not blind to the other, more controversial side of him which set him apart from me. If before Jimmy had come into Anglo his social behaviour had raised alarms, now it was his politics. He had come from Conservative stock. His father Frank Goldsmith was the Tory MP for Stowmarket in Suffolk and had owned hotels such as the Carlton in Cannes. However, Jimmy's political views were not what would be called respectable, mainstream Conservatism but of the extreme right, maverick and unpredictable. This was demonstrated many years later when, having become a Euro MP in France, he intervened in the 1997 British election by setting up the Referendum Party.

In the end his intervention had little or no effect on the overall election result, except in a couple of constituencies. Even without him the Conservatives were headed for defeat but Jimmy's style was shown on election night as the votes in Putney, where he was standing against the former Cabinet Minister David Mellor, were counted. Traditionally everyone behaves very decorously at such occasions as, despite all the bitterness that might have marked the election campaign, a certain kind of British manner and propriety prevails. However, Mellor launched into a diatribe against Jimmy, who tried to disrupt his speech by clapping and chanting during it. Mellor, riled, advised him to return to his hacienda in Mexico. What none of us knew then was that Jimmy was very ill and he died soon after of cancer.

Such behaviour was rarely seen in the boardroom, where I enjoyed an extremely friendly relationship with Jimmy during our time at Anglo Continental. However, even as we did business together, politics did cast a shadow, as in 1976 when Jimmy was trying to buy the *Daily Express*. I had been attending a party at a house in Belgravia and at about one o'clock in the morning, I came into conversation with Jocelyn Stevens, then managing director of Express Newspapers, and Lord Shawcross, who at the time was chairman of the Press Council. They were discussing Jimmy's attempt to buy the *Express* and I told Jocelyn that I wouldn't forgive him if they sold the newspaper to Jimmy, because I felt someone with such extreme views should not own such an important arm of the media. Lord Shawcross said he had already said as much to Stevens. I immediately qualified my remarks by saying that if anyone asked me whether they should go into business with

Jimmy Goldsmith, my unhesitating reply would be yes.

At 8.30 the next morning, my phone rang. It was Eric Levine, Jimmy's solicitor at that time. He told me Jimmy was very upset to learn from Stevens of my remarks. I thought Jocelyn's passing on my comments reprehensible, the more so as he did not add my rider that I would unhesitatingly recommend going into business with Jimmy. When I pointed this out to Jimmy, he said he understood and realized what I had said was not meant to be personal but reflected the fact that we held diametrically opposed political views. Jimmy never did get the *Express*, and tried and failed to start his own media empire in Britain through the ill-fated *Now!*, a weekly news magazine. *Private Eye*, his great enemy, dubbed the magazine the Talbot and all that remains of the venture is a cricket team composed of journalists, some of whom worked on *Now!*, called the Old Talbotians. For a time Jimmy's wife Annabel was a patron of the team and it still flourishes, although very few cricketers who turn up ever worked for *Now!*. It is, in a way, an appropriate commentary on Jimmy's desire to become a media magnate.

After our business dealings I had little to do with Jimmy but watched with some amusement when, in his battles with *Private Eye*, he formed the view that there were people in the City and the establishment out to do him down. He even began to regard criticism of himself as being anti-Semitic, and this from a man who was only partly Jewish and not in any way practising or affiliated with Jewish affairs.

But then that, in many ways, summed up Jimmy Goldsmith. As a businessman he could be a genius, as demonstrated when he withdrew from the Stock Market before the 1987 crash, almost anticipating that dramatic fall. Yet he could be ruthless and a bit of a bully, as when having just got into the boardroom of a company, he decided he did not like a particular director, Eric Sosnow, and from the very first board meeting so bullied the man that he forced the poor chap to resign. I prefer to believe, however, that his obsessional behaviour in forming the Referendum Party was caused to some degree by the effects of his fatal illness. Jimmy was a man of light and shade who often gave off a brilliant light, but also had his moments of great, almost forbidding darkness.

6

Wilson and the Honours List

Harold Wilson was no businessman, but he completes the trio of brilliant men I have worked with. In his own way he was no less a genius than Charlie Clore and Jimmy Goldsmith.

Wilson was a man completely lacking in what would now be called charisma yet he was a remarkably effective political operator. What he was above all was a survivor. He won four general elections as Labour leader and lost only one, making the most of his skill as a down to earth campaigner with a memorable turn of phrase.

I met Wilson years after I had begun my long and profitable business dealings with Clore and Goldsmith. My personal association with him did not begin until very late in his political career, a few days after the February 1974 election, but I had been a Labour supporter since my youth and worked with and for the party since the 1970 election.

I make no apologies for being a socialist or, in the modern idiom, a social democrat. The fact that I drive a luxury car does not make me a champagne socialist because it is what you believe in that matters, and I believe in social justice. I don't, however, hold with the idea of equality, because the able are always going to rise above the less able. There are many policies of the Labour movement with which I haven't agreed. I was strongly opposed to unilateral nuclear disarmament, for example. But then there are a lot of Conservatives who don't hold with everything under the banner of Toryism. Politicians like to say their parties are a broad church and I have always believed that.

My direct involvement with the Labour Party came after they lost the 1970 general election, a stunning result brought about by complacency. The Labour government of that time just did not think it could lose. Certainly it was a time when British politics was undergoing a radical change, the contest turning into a battle between talking heads on the television and having the look and feel of an American-led vote for the personality. That defeat for Labour left me quite disgusted.

Soon after that, an old friend, Stanley Clinton-Davis, who would later become an MP and is now Lord Clinton-Davis, until recently a Government Minister, was elected mayor of Hackney. I went along to the ceremony where he was sworn in as mayor and spoke to him about my anger and frustration at the way Labour had handled themselves through the 1970 election. He suggested I join the Finance and Industry Committee of the Labour Party, comprised of businessmen who backed Labour. Their brief was to advise and give an overview of business reaction to policy matters.

It proved interesting and invaluable. On the committee were Lord Gregson, Sigmund Sternberg, Michael Montague, Lord Wilfred Brown and quite a few powerful lawyers. Because of the calibre of the committee it also became a useful advisory unit to the Labour Party. I spent several months on a special sub-committee dealing with company law reform and I was pleased to see that even under a Tory government some of our recommendations were eventually accepted, particularly in the areas of insider dealing and share options for employees.

As a member of this Labour advisory group, I found myself involved in some fascinating and informative debates with some very lively minds. We had regular sessions every few months, meeting near Lord's at the Westmoreland Hotel, since renamed the Regent's Park Hilton. There were also general sessions when forty or fifty people would turn up. It was structured with an executive committee and then smaller committees with briefs to deal with specific areas.

At around the same time, I met Samuel Fisher, later ennobled, an old-time Labour man who was mayor of St Pancras and Camden and a close ally of Wilson's. Fisher invited me to dinner where he explained that Wilson, as leader of the opposition, was seriously underfunded but that a number of businessmen who supported Labour were making donations through a trust run by a partner in Lord Goodman's law office. He asked me if I would like to join in and donate £1,500 a year to that fund. I was happy to do so. However, despite offering continued financial support, I have never become a member of the Labour Party, tending to misquote in jest the old Groucho Marx saying that 'I didn't want to join any party that wanted to have me as a member.'

In 1974, Prime Minister Ted Heath had his confrontation with the miners and called an election. It was held at the end of February, just a short time after my first wife Phyllis had died. Needing a diversion, I threw myself into that campaign at full tilt. Believing as I did that Labour had lost in 1970 because of complacency, I was determined to make sure there would be none of that this time. I became involved in canvassing, although in a general sense rather than door-to-door.

Canvassing is one way of getting the vote out, and I was very keen to make sure Labour's supporters actually voted. A large turnout was essential to Labour's ambitions because I felt our supporters had somehow got out of the habit of voting. Something was needed to stir them up and I came up with a scheme to get them to the ballot box, by taking out full-page adverts in the sort of papers that Labour voters read, the tabloids. These simply urged our sleeping voters to make the most of the democratic process, using the headline 'DON'T VOTE – If you want to lose the right to complain about what the government does in the next 5 years.' It was eye-catching and it proved an effective move.

A friend, who preferred to remain anonymous, and I

between us covered the costs, somewhere in the region of
£15,000. We had the idea cleared by the Labour Party's press
adviser, Alf Sherman, who liked it, but I did not think anyone
else, apart from Sam Fisher, knew of our efforts. Later I
realized that Wilson, of course, was well aware of it.

Heath had challenged the country to say who ruled it, and
the country's reply was certainly not you. No party had an
overall majority but Heath hung on in No. 10, trying to strike
a coalition deal with the Liberals. When that fell apart he
resigned and Wilson, with the most seats in the House of
Commons, was invited to form the new government. A day or
so after he moved back into power, I received an invitation to
go to lunch on the following Sunday at Chequers, the official
country home of the Prime Minister.

I was met by Marcia Williams, Wilson's political secretary,
and we sat down to a crowded lunch table. Among those
present were Donald Gosling and Ronald Hobson, the men
behind the NCP car park business, Charles McCarthy, Sam
Fisher, Eric Miller, Rudy Sternberg, Sigmund Sternberg,
Wilfred Brown and Bernard Donoghue. One or two were
familiar faces, people I had met on the advisory committee, but
a number I had never seen before, although I assumed they
had contributed to the fund being run by Lord Goodman's
partner.

Wilson was very impressive and he stressed the importance
of Labour holding on to power because the revenues from
North Sea oil would soon start flowing. He was sure that whoever was in power when that happened would remain there for
years to come. How right he was. After Labour lost in 1979
they were in the wilderness for eighteen long years.

By this time, I had already met up with some of the party's
leading lights including Michael Meacher, Anthony Crosland,
Dennis Healey, Michael Foot and Tony Benn. Benn, of
course, I had met before when trying to arrange closed-circuit
coverage for Terry Downes. But what he said at one of our
House of Commons meetings rings in my ear and still appals

me. He said he would rather the Labour Party, then in opposition, lose the next election than win under the policies that had prevailed the last time Labour was in power. It seemed perverse. I told him such an attitude meant he was betraying all the people who had been voting for him. So following the Chequers lunch when I got to know Wilson, I asked him why he stood for Benn's nonsense. 'He's a cross I have to bear,' he said. He also admitted that his way of handling it was to have Benn in the government, along with Michael Foot, another left-winger. It was the English version of US President Lyndon Johnson's view that 'it was much better to have the sons of bitches inside the tent pissing out, rather than outside pissing in.' Wilson's suspicion of Benn, I later learned, was matched only by a similar mistrust of civil servants. He told me: 'You find me the man who can control the Civil Service and I'll show you a miracle worker.'

I remained an active member of the businessmen's advisory committee and was invited to Downing Street on several occasions, once for Trooping of the Colour. I also made other visits to Chequers and there was one amusing evening when after dinner we gathered around the piano, with Lady Wilfred Brown accompanying Harold Wilson and me singing together 'On Ilkley Moor Ba T'at', obviously a favourite of Yorkshire-man Harold, and 'Ole Man River'.

My involvement in and knowledge of the film business meant that this was an area where I could offer advice, and on one occasion I came back from the Cannes Film Festival to attend a dinner at No. 10. The Prime Minister wanted to form a committee to promote the film industry and I had already made suggestions as to who they should invite for the occasion.

However, that evening was to have annoying repercussions. Wilson and Marcia Williams were very interested in films, Marcia so much so that I offered to take her to a charity film premiere I was attending the following night. Our trip was innocent but we were photographed going in and finished up in the gossip columns, the subject of a supposed romantic link. It sparked off a lot of silly speculation. Marcia was always portrayed in the public's eye as a virago. In reality she was nothing of the sort but rather a shy person, quiet, soft and very emotional. She was less sophisticated than she was made to appear. The stories about her benefiting through land deals were rubbish and she has never been able to enjoy a luxurious lifestyle. I remember winning a car in a raffle at a charity dinner and giving it to my mother to replace her old Triumph. I loaned Marcia that old Triumph, which she eventually bought from me for £100.

An example of how the public perception of her was so unfair came when I put her name forward as a patron of the Royal Free Hospital, of which I was the chairman of the Appeals Fund. She seemed an ideal candidate, yet in spite of my being a major benefactor of the hospital, my nomination of Marcia was opposed by a number of doctors. In the end I was forced to withdraw her name. It was very embarrassing for me and unfair on Marcia because the doctors were acting on what they had read without bothering to get to know her. I know she would have worked hard on behalf of their hospital.

In 1974, Wilson's hold on power was tenuous and clearly another election was around the corner. It came in the October and after my experiences the first time round, I was eager to become more involved this time. At my own request, Marcia put me in touch with John Key, then Labour's chief organizer in London, and I was sent to work in the capital's constituencies, where I became involved in grass roots politics, organizing and devising local publicity campaigns. I found out pretty quickly that it was not the life for me. It was boring and I was interested in involvement at a higher plane, though I knew this could not be achieved without an apprenticeship at constituency level. You cannot win an election without a comprehensive and thorough grass-roots system. It is here that people are persuaded to go to the ballot box.

Wilson won that October election in more convincing style.

He had a small working majority and seemed well placed to remain in Downing Street for a very long time. However, over the next eighteen months, leading up to his resignation, he seemed to lose his stomach for battle and his grasp of what was going on appeared to fade. My early meetings with him had been filled with lively discussion about politics in general, the international scene, domestic problems – now he was more introspective, talking about himself and reminiscing about the past to the extent that it seemed like a preoccupation. Looking back, I was left with the distinct impression that he was no longer interested in the affairs of the country. I noticed, too, that he tended to repeat himself very frequently and I've since learned that this is a symptom of Alzheimer's disease, or what used to be called senile dementia. My father, who died at the age of 89 in 1988, showed the same symptoms and after Wilson died it was revealed he had indeed suffered from the disease for some time.

He never told me why he resigned and the only explanations I know are the various ones published at the time. My own feeling is that while his resignation appeared very sudden and took us all by such surprise, it was to a large extent planned. I believe its primary aim was to bed James Callaghan down in the role of Prime Minister and prepare him for his first election. There would be time enough for Callaghan to make his mark with the electorate and make sure, as Wilson said, that Labour was in power when the North Sea oil began to flow.

But Callaghan miscalculated by not going to the country in October 1978 and I know that Wilson and Marcia Williams were far from happy with the way he behaved once he was in power. They felt Wilson did not get the respect he deserved, that Callaghan did not defer to him as he should have done – and they remained bitter about it for some time after. In 1983 I arranged a charity lunch in aid of the Variety Club and committed the cardinal sin in Marcia's eyes of asking Callaghan, as a former Prime Minister, to be one of the guest speakers. Marcia was livid that I had not asked Wilson instead and called me in a fury when she saw the event on television.

THE Wilson resignation honours list was a shambles and one in which I found myself, quite unwittingly, embroiled. Wilson announced his resignation on 16 March 1976 but stayed on as Prime Minister until 5 April. His honours list had been expected on 15 April, but remained a subject of much speculation and talk for more than ten weeks, finally coming out on 27 May. The delay proved deadly.

I had never given any thought to getting an honour. In fact, I had no idea such a thing as a Prime Minister's resignation honours list existed. The first hint that anything was afoot came while I was away in Israel, visiting Jerusalem as a guest of Charles Clore, who was endowing an educational establishment out there.

It was the first weekend in May. I had booked into the Hilton Hotel in Jerusalem but then gone away. I returned there on the Friday to be given a message to urgently phone *The Sunday Times* in London. I got through to the reporter, who asked me how I felt about my impending peerage.

'What on earth are you talking about? You're talking nonsense, absolute nonsense,' I told him. Of course, that denial was not enough. I was asked if I had 'seen the official letter' and again I said, 'It's nonsense. I haven't seen the letter because there is not a letter for me to see.'

The reporter then said that the letter was waiting for me at home, so I hung up on him and phoned my daughter Susan, asking her to go through the post and weed out anything that looked vaguely official. She called me back in half an hour, and as I expected all along, she confirmed there was no letter. As far as I was concerned that was the end of it.

The next thing my name and sometimes my picture appeared in a number of newspaper articles, most notably on the front page of *The Sunday Times* in a display which was clearly intended to look like a rogues' gallery of people who were apparently being honoured by Wilson. I was featured with James Goldsmith, Lew Grade, Bernard Delfont and Joseph Kagan among others. All of us, of course, were regarded as Jewish and it appeared to me that the way we were referred to in the stories was done to denigrate Wilson. I was described as a bookmaker and boxing promoter, Kagan as a raincoat manufacturer and Grade and Delfont as impresarios. I actually got to see all this three days after it was published, when I got back from Israel. I made a point of not contacting Wilson or Marcia because it seemed wholly inappropriate while this storm was raging.

Eventually the honours list came out and I was not on it. Nor was David Frost, who had also been tipped to be on it, although Grade, Delfont and Kagan were all given peerages. It was only then that I contacted Wilson to discover if there was any truth in the story that I had been proposed for a knight-hood and then had the honour taken away at someone's request. What worried me was that if that was true, it meant someone with influence had it in for me in a very big way and I had no idea that such a person existed.

I went round to see Wilson, who was then staying in Lord North Street, for my first contact with him since his resigna-tion. I told him that I had not expected to be on the honours list but I wanted to know whether there was any truth in the press rumours. He said that I had never been on the official list he submitted, and went on to add that – and I remember it for his choice of words – neither had there been anyone who had said anything about me that was not 'qualitative'. In other words, not a soul had uttered a bad word about me. Wilson then went on to say that there were two other people proposed who had been questioned and that had led to an investigation which cleared them. Now for me, that was enough. I took Wilson at his word.

The really intriguing question was who had actually done the leaking of the names supposedly on the list – and it is worth emphasizing that there had never been such a leak before. It could have been one of many people. Marcia reckoned Bernard Donoghue was responsible because he had been passed over for a peerage. Many years later I travelled to Birmingham with Bernard, by that time a peer, for a Variety Club lunch in honour of Denis Howell, and he suggested that any leak was down to the bitter dislike between Marcia and Joe Haines, Wilson's press secretary. The pair were in a state of 'open warfare' and Donoghue's feeling was that Haines had caused the problems out of spite, while the civil servants, also at loggerheads with Marcia, had got wind of the length of the list and pre-empted its arrival by insisting that it be cut back.

I don't think we will ever know now what really happened, but the fact that Sir Philip Allen, former Permanent Secretary at the Home Office, fronted a Civil Service inquiry into possible leaks was a clear indication that a lot of the material appearing in the newspapers was a great deal more than educated guessing.

I was particularly annoyed, however, when *The Sunday Times*, which of course had kick-started all the speculation in the first place, described me on the Sunday following the eventual publication of the list as 'an embittered casualty' of the affair. I was so annoyed at the description that I telephoned the Editor, Harold Evans, to complain. I had met him on a few occasions and he was understanding and appeared to feel that I had a grievance, so he invited me to write a letter which he undertook to publish, unedited, the following Sunday. It read:

To The Editor
Sunday Times

How can the author of 'The Wilson Connection' take it upon himself to describe me as 'an embittered casualty'?

I have had three conversations with members of your staff in connection with the Retirement Honours List Affair. During all those conversations I expressed the firm belief that I had never been on any Honours List whether 'preliminary', unofficial or official, and I have maintained this view throughout the numerous conversations with journalists who have spoken to me about the matter as well as with friends, acquaintances and members of my family.

The only facet of my attitude in conversations with your staff, as in conversations with other journalists, which could in any shape or form be regarded as indicating bitterness has been my unhappiness about the fact that whenever I have been referred to in the Press, in connection with this matter, it has been as either a (mere) boxing promoter or, occasionally, with the added description of bookmaker. These descriptions have quite obviously, in an apparent desire to denigrate Sir Harold Wilson, been used in a derisory fashion, and a number of journalists employed by the newspapers concerned are well aware that these particular activities are only a minor part of my business interests which are, I think it is fair to say, substantial by any standard.

Furthermore, there has been a complete omission of any mention of my activities in public life which include membership of the Executive Committee of the National Association of Boys Clubs, being Treasurer of the London Federation of Boys Clubs, Chairman of the Royal Free Hospital Appeal Trust and a Vice President of both the British Olympic Appeal and the Commonwealth Games (England) Appeal, when a number of journalists know about me occupying these positions.

It is just not true to say I am bitter and I am certainly not a casualty.

Jarvis Astaire
London W1

If the whole thing was an unholy mess from start to finish, I had the consolation of receiving praise from a surprising quarter. A columnist called Philip Wrack, whom I had never heard of, met, nor talked to at any point, wrote in the *News of the World* on 30 May 1976 that I was the only person who came out of it with flying colours because I had remained dignified and silent. It is worth quoting in some detail:

'I simply cannot understand all the yapping and yelping over Sir Harold Wilson's Resignation Honours List. By tradition these Honours are the personal choice of the outgoing Prime Minister. Why, then, astonishment that they go to his pals? He wished to honour and thank his family doctor. And did so. Which doctor was supposed to get a Wilson peerage? Mrs Thatcher's? The honours system is rather fun. Quaint, maybe, but lovely. Amid all the sneering, the man I felt most sorry for was Jarvis Astaire. Through all the speculation that he was to be honoured, he quietly did his best to get the record straight. Quite simply, he told his friends, it just wasn't true. In the end plain Mr Jarvis Astaire, embarrassed as he must have been by the whole fiasco, emerged uncomplaining, with the greatest honour of all. The Most Noble Order of Dignity.'

I still saw Wilson several times after that and solicited his help with the Independent Broadcasting Authority when I was involved in a bid for Lew Grade's company ACC and we were being given the runaround (see Chapter 7). He was very helpful but as is the way of the world, it seemed that once out of office he was tolerated rather than respected. Not fair at all and I feel the country let him down by letting him plod on, with no support at all, in spite of his years of great public service.

This was graphically brought home to me in the mid 1980s when I attended a lunch for the Jewish Board of Deputies and the main guests of honour were Harold Wilson and his wife Mary. Wilson, at that time, had been the longest-serving Prime Minister of this century, yet at the end of the lunch, when I came out on to the street, there he was trying to hail a taxi. It was a sad and undignified way to treat a man who, in my opinion, had served his country with courage, fortitude and skill for many years. In his old age, and after his tremendous public service, his country was not prepared to support him. His car and driver had been taken away and there was no personal detective. I was so incensed that I wrote about it to Neil Kinnock, then Labour leader.

They seem to order these things better in America, where former Presidents get an office, car, driver, security and even help with organizing their archives. Johnson, Nixon, Carter, Reagan and Bush all have their libraries recording their years in office, as do other former Presidents. Americans seem to accept that their former leaders served the nation and deserve the nation's support. We, arising from the days when all our politicians had their own independent means, cast off our Prime Ministers as so much useless furniture and that day, seeing Wilson trying to hail a black cab, made me feel that it was indeed a black day.

I had been courted by the group starting the SDP but was not impressed by their initial composition. So Wilson's departure meant that my active involvement with Labour ceased until a couple of years before the 1992 election when I met Jack Cunningham, who impressed me greatly with his views and ideas. I worked closely with Jack, who led the Party's campaign and although Labour lost that election, great inroads into the Conservative majority in the House of Commons were made. They were not enough to take Neil Kinnock to Downing Street, but then I do not believe Kinnock was electable as Prime Minister. He had changed too rapidly from a policy of unilateral disarmament and, strangely enough, there appeared to be a certain amount of antipathy towards him because he was Welsh. The Tory press also succeeded in making his wife Glenys some sort of ogre. All this combined with the forecasts of doom, gloom and ruin should Kinnock get to Downing Street – I recall *The Sun's* front page on the day of the election showing Kinnock's face in a light bulb over the caption: 'If Kinnock wins today, will the last man leaving the country please turn out the lights' – created an intense climate of fear and loathing. It also, it seems, galvanised the Tory voters, who turned out in large numbers to make sure John Major won.

The pundits who had confidently predicted a Labour victory had a tricky task explaining their misjudgement and made much of the so-called triumphalism displayed at a rally in Sheffield ten days before the election. This, they claimed, made all the difference as the supposed air of exultation exuded by Kinnock and Labour turned the British public off. What nonsense! For a start, Sheffield was not quite the premature victory celebration it has since been made out to be, and certainly in the Labour circles I moved in nobody expected to win. I remember talking to Jack Cunningham on the Sunday night before the election and we both agreed that the best we could hope for was a hung Parliament. Curiously, I have since learned that John Major and his people had also given up any hopes of victory. As the election approached they consoled themselves with the thought that Kinnock would get a very small majority and would have to call another election pretty soon.

All this shows how amateurish political forecasting can be. The simple truth is that after three successive defeats at the hands of Mrs Thatcher, Labour had a mountain to climb and did well to come as close as they did in 1992. It provided the springboard for the great victory of 1 May 1997, as was generously acknowledged by Tony Blair. I was present at the Labour Party's celebration at the Festival Hall after the 1997 election and when Blair spoke to the ecstatic crowd, the first thing he said was how much was owed to Neil Kinnock, who was standing nearby at the time and who received an enormous ovation.

Some credit should be given to Ken Follett, the famous author, who at Jack Cunningham's instigation was the main fundraiser for the 1992 election. Ken procured a number of Labour sympathizers who contributed £10,000 a year for three years running up to the election, while Jack organized the 1000 Club which is still in being. Many people formed this group a short while before the 1997 election, for which the main fundraiser was Michael Levy, a successful record producer who had been an outstanding fundraiser in the Jewish community for many years. Michael was rewarded with a peerage and although I am sure that for Ken, his wife Barbara's election as MP for Stevenage in 1997 was reward enough, I do believe he was entitled to receive some personal recognition for his work in the 1992 election.

Just a few weeks after the 1992 election defeat I was given an inkling of 'things to come', although I didn't realize it at the time. Jack Cunningham called a debriefing meeting at Millbank for campaign organizers, where he was accompanied by his friend Tony Blair, and we were all invited to express our views. When my opportunity arose, I said, 'You fellows have to change your act because if you don't, you are just going to be, at best, a good Opposition and frankly, I am sick and tired of supporting an Opposition, however good it may be. You have to accept the fact that there is no longer a majority of people in this country who are prepared to accept old-time socialism.' With Jack Cunningham I knew I was preaching to the converted, but I felt from his body language that Tony Blair also agreed with my view.

So it has proved. In fact, about six months after he had assumed the leadership of the party following the death of John Smith, I met Blair at a lunch and during a short conversation I said, 'I don't suppose you recall what I said at Millbank in '92? He replied, 'I certainly do.' By that time, of course, he was already propagating the cause of New Labour and I said, jokingly, 'I didn't expect you to take me so seriously.'

7

Lew and I

I never got on with Lew Grade. You could say we were two Jewish boys but cut from very different cloth. He was of a very different generation and had some of the mentality of the market trader. The problem was he felt he could hustle me and when he found he couldn't, he did not like it.

Our battles centred around closed-circuit TV and began with the screening of the Ali fights. As we have seen, I had promoted them all except for the Brian London fight in August 1966, which was a mismatch from the off. I wanted nothing to do with it and passed up the option. Grade, who then ruled independent television through ATV, took it up and was about as successful as London was in the fight. The Englishman landed on the seat of his trunks in the third round from a mysterious punch while Grade burned a hole of £75,000 in his bank balance, a huge loss in 1966. I cannot say I shed any tears, the more so as Grade had joined forces with the promoter Jack Solomons, my old foe – of whom more later.

In February the following year there was another Grade attempt to hustle me. I had bought Ali's heavyweight title fight against Ernie Terrell in Houston. I had done the deal with the promoter, Bob Arum, and it was cut and dried. Then out of the blue I received a call from Mike Malitz, Arum's TV man, saying that Grade's company had not only paid more for the fight than me but the money was up front and, what is more, already sitting in their New York bank account.

Furious at Grade muscling in after the event, I got my lawyer to deliver a very strong letter to ATV. The crucial card was my contact with Robert Clark, then chairman of ABC which was then part of the commercial television network. I knew him through the pay-TV experiment in England, which he had backed. Now that Grade had apparently secured the rights to the Terrell fight, ABC were involved. Grade, in effect, was buying for the entire ITV network.

Clark was a workaholic and I went to see him in his office at around 9.30pm. He didn't approve of this double-dealing and promised that first thing the next day, ABC would pull out of the deal. True to his word, Clark and ABC did and Grade was forced to retreat as well. All this did little to endear me to Grade, but a while later we met head-on again.

This time he was trying to buy a fight from me and was pushing like mad to get the price down. He tried to trump me by saying: 'I don't need this fight, I can put on John Wayne in "Rio Bravo" instead.' As a result of his wrangling the delayed showing of the fight was sold to the BBC and ITV missed out. A while later he approached me about another fight but I told him he could show John Wayne's 'Rio Bravo' instead! Those clashes meant there was always some hostility in my dealings with him and it surfaced again in the early 1980s during the ACC business.

ACC (Associated Communications Corporation) had become the parent company of Grade's TV and film interests and by this time Grade, having once been the master of commercial television in this country, had begun to lose his power. His early influence was based, apart from his natural ability, on the success of ATV which became the dominant company in the ITV network, partly because it had the London franchise for all seven days of the week. Grade also had contacts with the top American artists and consequently was able to put on the big shows – programmes that he was then able to sell on profitably to the Americans.

The first dent in his power base came in the late 1960s when the Independent Broadcasting Authority took away ATV's weekend franchise for London and awarded it to London Weekend Television. But Grade still remained very important. Indeed, when it came to his enforced retirement – under the regulations of the IBA, which insisted on retirement at the age of 70 – he was given licence to stay on for another year, based on his past performance. That showed the pressure he was able to put on the IBA. Bit by bit his power was being eroded, yet he had far too much energy and was too vigorous to retire. His counter was to move into films. As the IBA chipped away at ATV, Grade broadened the scope of the company, going into films in a major way and acquiring a number of theatres in the Stoll Moss Group and various other businesses.

The problem was that he did not understand the modern movie business. Here we were in the late 1970s and early 1980s and we had Lew Grade, then in his seventies, launching a new business producing films. He had a disastrous time of it. As an old-fashioned impresario, more at home with the ways of the music hall, he brought old-fashioned style and ideas to an era in cinema history where the trend was very modern. Some of the films he made were quite good, but they were just completely out of touch with the cinema-going public of the time.

His first venture saw a link-up between ATV and the American exhibitors Associated General Films, which resulted in 'Voyage of the Damned' and 'March and Die'. The failure of those films at the box office ended the deal, but then in 1979 Grade, now finally removed from ATV after his stay of execution, linked up with EMI to form Associated Film Distribution – and came up with more box office flops, notably 'Raise the Titanic' and 'Can't Stop the Music'.

'Raise the Titanic' was a classic example of how to make a great, loss-making film. It was an epic with an all-star cast that included Jason Robards, Anne Archer and Alec Guinness, it cost £19 million to make, and it proved a complete box office disaster. Worse still, the critics savaged it. The magazine *Variety* said of it: 'Hits new depths hitherto unexplored by the worst of Lew Grade's overloaded ark melodramas.' The *Guardian* commented: 'The longer it all goes on, the more one hopes that if they ever do raise the Titanic, they'll leave the film overboard to replace it.' While *Halliwell's* – the film industry's bible – summed it up with a terse 'heavy-going exploiter with little action and even less plot.' Even Lew himself always admitted, 'It would have been cheaper to lower the Atlantic than to raise the Titanic.'

His only real success had been 'The Muppet Movie' of 1979. He did have one other hit with 'On Golden Pond' but it came too late to save him. Grade's movie disasters led to a power struggle in ACC, leaving him weakened and ill-equipped to cope with the predator who had now got the company in his sights.

Grade's closest associates at ATV had been Jack Gill, who had stood by him through thick and thin; Louis Benjamin, who managed the theatres; and Lord Windlesham, at one point managing director of ATV and later a non-executive director of ACC. And it was Windlesham who, following a trip to Australia, introduced Grade to the entrepreneur Robert Holmes a'Court.

Holmes a'Court was becoming a big noise in Western Australia and Windlesham returned to Britain raving about him, so much so that he insisted that Gill and Grade should meet him. At the same time, and probably at Windlesham's instigation, Holmes a'Court started buying up shares in ACC. He eventually came to London and a meeting duly took place. Windlesham was enthusiastic about Holmes a'Court becoming involved with ACC, while Gill was more sceptical. But Grade was won over, the overriding factor being that he wanted to keep ACC afloat so that he could continue with his film-making.

Gill, a financial man rather than a daring entrepreneur, could see problems looming on the horizon, with Grade over-speculating in pursuit of his film ambitions. Fearing this was going to bring the company down, Gill even tried to mount a boardroom coup. But the tables were turned on him. Grade mounted a counter-revolution and it was Gill who was ousted. But that battle weakened Grade's position still further and left him totally vulnerable to Holmes a'Court.

Grade had been warned about Holmes a'Court. Gill had told him to be careful and so too had Grade's brother, Lord Bernard Delfont. I remember Bernie telling me that he had been in California with Grade and Holmes a'Court and the three of them had gone to dinner. It was obvious to Bernie what Holmes a'Court was trying to do and he had a word in his brother's ear about the 'charm job' the Australian was putting on. But he refused to listen and now with Gill gone and Grade weak, Holmes a'Court made his move, a bid of 36p a share for ACC. The first I knew of it was when I read about it in the *Daily Mail*. It seemed a cosy deal.

At the same time as this drama was unfolding, I was involved in film production with Gerald Ronson, who had become extremely wealthy and powerful mainly through property deals in his Heron Corporation. We knew each other through various charity functions and had met socially. One day at a cocktail party he had said to me that he felt there was a great future in the communications business and he was keen to get involved. He thought my knowledge and experience could be of some use to him and wanted me to help him move in this direction. That resulted in my doing the deals and him becoming a backer for, among others, a picture called 'Buddy, Buddy' with Jack Lemmon and Walter Matthau, directed by Billy Wilder for MGM. We also did 'A Stranger is Watching' with Rip Torn and 'Loophole' starring Albert Finney, Martin Sheen, Susannah York and Robert Morley.

Now, with ACC ripe for takeover, it was something to go for and we went for it. Ronson, who had been in America, arrived back in London on the day after the *Daily Mail* article unaware of what was going on. I spoke to him on the phone and he asked if I could pick up copies of the ACC accounts, which were freely available. The company headquarters, ACC House, were at Marble Arch and I passed them on the way to my office. I collected two sets from the girl on reception and immediately sent a copy over to Gerald – this was ten o'clock in the morning. An hour and a half later he was back in touch with me to say he liked what he had read and we should stage our own bid for ACC, offering substantially more per share than Holmes a'Court.

Immediately contacts were made with bankers, in our case Barclays Merchant Bank and their director Michael Peterson, and we tried to make an approach to ACC. A day passed and we heard nothing. The next day, a Wednesday, we were told that the ACC board were meeting and were considering our approach. When it takes a company which is up for sale two days to get that far, it can only mean they are stalling. The messages from ACC seemed to reinforce this view when they said that while they would be prepared to meet our lawyers and bankers, they would not meet us.

All this was soon confirmed. Ronson and I were having dinner at the Grosvenor House when Peterson and Giles Ridley, our solicitor at Slaughter & May, came in and said they were getting nowhere in their talks with the ACC company secretary, a man called Lucas. We agreed that we had been given the runaround for long enough and it was time to do something about it. We decided that we would barge in on the ACC meeting at eleven o'clock that evening – it was the only way we were ever going to get any reaction. In we marched and made our position crystal clear to the representatives of the ACC bankers. They tried to stall us but eventually Grade agreed to allow Ronson through and he met the board.

Grade wouldn't have *me* in the room, though – partly, I think, because of our less than fraternal past. But the fact that only Ronson was allowed in was also a neat move on Grade's part because he knew that Ronson was not completely au fait with the business. His Heron Corporation was providing the main finance while I was a junior partner and investor in our bid, which was a multi-million pound deal. Ronson made his pitch, pleading with Grade and the ACC board to listen to our offer, and eventually left.

But despite this, at two o'clock in the morning, the board completed their deal with Holmes a'Court. He had manoeuvred them into accepting his proposals because he had already bought 40 per cent of the company in the form of 'A' (non-voting) shares. This was his enormous advantage over us. Although these 'A' shares did not carry voting rights, he was able to outbid us because it was cheaper for him, having bought the 'A' shares much earlier at a time when nobody thought the 'A' shares would ever play a part in the control of the company. I believe this was always part of Holmes a'Court's strategy.

Our immediate reaction was to seek an injunction to stop the deal going through, but a hearing before Appeal Court judges led to them deciding to hear the whole case, and that lasted for two weeks. The findings overturned the ACC directors' deal with Holmes a'Court and he ended up having to pay 60p a share instead of 36p. The Appeal Court findings were quite damning of him and he was ordered to pay half the costs of the case.

Soon after the end of the hearing, Grade realized that he had made a terrible mistake and said as much to me when we were both in Los Angeles for the 1981 Academy Awards, when 'Chariots of Fire' won best picture and Colin Welland took the Oscar for best script and made his famous 'The British are Coming' remark. One of the other films nominated for best picture was Grade's 'On Golden Pond'. Although it didn't win that, it did collect the best actor award for Henry Fonda, in his last film, and best actress for Katharine Hepburn, for a record fourth time.

I was staying at the Beverly Hills Hotel, as was Grade, and he made several attempts to speak to me. At his third attempt, at 7.30 am, he finally got through and I agreed to go up to his suite. There he was in the plushest and biggest suite in the whole hotel – it was as if nothing had changed, that he was still ruling the world. He could not change his style in spite of what had happened to him. He handed me a pink slip of paper from Holmes a'Court, a memo. It said that Lew Grade, the man who had constructed the mighty ATV Independent TV Company, was permitted to attend the Academy Awards ceremony in Los Angeles but his expenses were limited to £500.

'Look what's happened to me,' he wailed. 'Please, please phone your friend Ronson and get him to increase the bid.'

I told him that I was sorry but I couldn't do that. Grade had made his own bed and he now had to lie in it.

Later we met outside the hotel. Grade was being picked up and I was climbing into my car. I stopped and told him that his biggest mistake had been letting Jack Gill go. He still couldn't see it; he believed that Gill had been out to remove him. 'He was after my job,' protested Grade. The truth was that Gill would have been his best defence against Holmes a'Court. He had seen through him and was totally loyal to Grade, yet Grade had allowed this brash Australian to split them up, to sow discontent and then pick up the pieces on the cheap.

The fight for ACC also provided an insight into the bitter rivalry between the Australian moguls. As we went for ACC, Rupert Murdoch was inundating Ronson with faxes about Holmes a'Court and then following that up with phone calls. There were also all sorts of spies and counter-spies in on the act. Louis Benjamin, a director of ACC and ostensibly a stooge for Grade, was playing every which way, covering himself for every eventuality and often ringing me at home.

If we had won, Grade would, of course, have been eased out. We would have softened the blow by making him life president, but that would have been it. As it was, Ronson and I lost money in the unsuccessful battle, my part of that being about £20,000. But the whole thing made Ronson a public figure and while it cost him a lot of money, he got publicity that would otherwise have cost millions. As a result of that, people started coming to him with deals because he was now seen as an international player and in the long run it opened doors for him that would otherwise not have been easily accessible.

Holmes a'Court did not come out of the saga smelling of roses. As I said, the legal reaction to what he had done was quite damning. Yet he was still allowed to carry on wheeling and dealing on the London Stock Exchange, bidding for Dalgety among other companies. It made me wonder what on earth was going on. Holmes a'Court died suddenly some years ago and as a result of a deal he did with Alan Bond, another Australian, now in jail, his widow Janet is today the owner of Stoll Moss Theatres in England.

Lew Grade mellowed with age and died only recently at 91, and we had many pleasant meetings and conversations after the end of the ACC affair.

HOLMES a'Court was not the only one to get away with it. Robert Maxwell did it with even more disastrous consequences. A Department of Trade and Industry inquiry had ruled him unfit to run a public company, yet he did and the fallout from that was terrible. I had met Maxwell a number of times. On some occasions it was to do with the Labour Party – he had been an MP – and at other times it was at charity functions. It hadn't taken me long to form the opinion that he was a bully. I also met his sons, Kevin and Ian, and found them to be completely different. Both of them were very charming men and it was clear that they were being dominated by their despotic father.

The person I most worried about was my entertainment lawyer Oscar Beuselinck, to whom I had been originally introduced by Robert Patterson. He was an expert in libel law and show business and a nice man, although prone to occasional bouts of aggressiveness. That said, we always got on famously. He was my friend and his involvement and expertise in the entertainment business was considerable – at one stage he had been heading MGM's UK operations. Suddenly, around 1990, Oscar called me to announce that he was leaving his firm,

Wright, Webb and Syrett, to go and work for Maxwell's Mirror Group.

'You're crazy,' I said.

He told me that he'd won a few cases against the Mirror Group and in the process had obviously impressed Maxwell. The charm had been turned on, Oscar had received a proposition that seemed too good to turn down and he was off. I warned him against it and said that Maxwell was only being charming because he wanted him. Once Oscar had made the jump, Maxwell, I was certain, would treat him, as he treated other employees, like a dog. I told Oscar that I had read Tom Bower's book about Maxwell, 'The Outsider', and that 'if even fifty per cent of what was said about him in the book was true, then he gives crooks a bad name'.

As it turned out, a lot more than fifty per cent of the stories about him were spot on. I was on my way to the airport in New York when the story broke that Maxwell had drowned, and as soon as I reached London I gave Oscar a call to see how he was. It appeared that Maxwell had been acting oddly, even by his standards, and from the various accounts I heard, I had the impression that he had committed suicide. A few months later the full implications of what he had done were revealed in the Mirror Group pensions fund scandal. Fearful that Maxwell might somehow have got my friend involved in all this, I again rang Oscar.

He reassured me, saying the only work he had done for Maxwell had been newspaper legal work and on the one occasion that a business matter had landed in his lap, it had been taken out of his hands after he had raised a few questions. He went on to add that in the previous few weeks my words to him about Maxwell had been playing on his mind – he had been frequently reminded of my warning and he now knew I had been right all along. The fall of Maxwell's *Mirror* saw Oscar move back into mainstream legal work and he joined Davenport Lyons. He still did legal work for me until his sad death from a sudden heart attack in August 1997.

As for Gerald Ronson, his meteoric rise led to his eventual involvement in the notorious Guinness case and the company's takeover of Distillers. Ernest Saunders, the Guinness chairman and chief executive, had so turned round an ailing business that Guinness was in a position to acquire other companies. The whisky firm Arthur Bell & Co. became the first target, then Saunders set his sights on Distillers. However, that company was also being hunted by the Argyll Food Group. The takeover battle for Distillers was one of the bitterest seen in the City. Guinness won but soon faced a backlash when, following a series of allegations and revelations, some of them in America, there was a Department of Trade Inquiry which in turn led to a Serious Fraud Office investigation and criminal prosecutions.

Saunders was initially charged with intending to pervert the course of justice and destroying and falsifying documents. Then more arrests followed: Anthony Parnes, the City stockbroker known as 'The Animal' for his aggressive dealing methods; Sir Jack Lyons, the UK adviser to Bain & Co. management consultants in London; Roger Seelig, the corporate finance director of Morgan Grenfell; Lord Spens, a corporate finance director at Henry Ansbacher & Co., merchant bankers to Bells; and of course Ronson. Between them the group faced 104 charges. Only Saunders, Parnes, Ronson and Lyons were convicted.

I am quite sure, having spent so much time discussing business with Ronson, that he would not have become involved if he had realized what he was doing was illegal. At the very most I would imagine he thought it was unethical and sharp – but not an act that could have led to criminal charges being brought against him. He seems to have weathered the storm and a subsequent six-month jail term with extreme fortitude and it would not surprise me to see him rise up the business ladder again in the coming years. He certainly seems to continue to command the respect of bankers and financial institutions in the City, which is quite remarkable in the circumstances and a tribute to the way he conducted his business with people prior to Guinness.

I must say I never saw any sense in sending Ronson to prison, but there was a strange sense of injustice about the whole Guinness saga. As a result of the acquisition of Distillers, the people who came into Guinness after the Saunders regime was removed benefited enormously, while the people responsible for it were jailed. It seemed to bear out the saying, 'There ain't no justice.'

8

That's Entertainment

We all have Ifs in our lives. 'What if . . .' is a phrase often used as we wonder how our lives might have turned out had we taken an opportunity that came our way or chosen a different path to the one we did. In my case, the 'what if' is . . . What if I had decided to manage The Beatles? For I was offered the chance to buy up their management contract from Brian Epstein early in 1964.

One night I walked into the Hilton Hotel on Park Lane and by chance met Michael Black, an agent and brother of the songwriter Don Black. Michael was talking to a group of men but immediately broke away when he saw me and said he had a deal he wanted to talk about. I told him that if he wanted to put the proposition to me then he had better come up to Wembley Arena, where there was a boxing show on. As we drove to Wembley in my car, he explained the situation to me.

Epstein, a notorious gambler, was badly in debt, so much so that he could not pay off his creditors. He was desperate for some quick cash and was prepared to sell ninety per cent of his Beatles management contract for £250,000. At that time the group were in Paris for a three-week stint at the Olympia Theatre, their record 'I Want to Hold Your Hand', the Christmas No. 1, having been replaced by 'Glad All Over' by the Dave Clark Five. Epstein had done a deal with a French promoter called Bruno Coquatrix, who was paying them less than it was costing them to stay in Paris for the run (which, incidentally, was treated with magnificent indifference by the

French, compared to the fever The Beatles stirred in Britain and were about to stir in America).

On the face of it what Michael told me sounded like a good deal, especially as I knew through my great friend Walter Hyman that The Beatles had been booked for a night at Carnegie Hall in New York on the strength of the mania breaking out in Britain. The booking of the venue had to be done months in advance and Sid Bernstein, the show's promoter, had got 12 February, Lincoln's birthday – perhaps not the most sensitive of dates to launch an invasion by a British pop group. When Bernstein called to make his reservation for the Carnegie Hall and explained he wanted to put on The Beatles, the Polish woman at the other end of the line had no idea who or what he was talking about.

'What are they?' she asked.

'They're a phenomenon,' Bernstein replied, wary of admitting that they were a pop act for fear of not getting the booking. That seemed to satisfy her and he put down the phone convinced the woman thought phenomenon was something to do with the Philharmonic and the hall was being booked for a string quartet!

Talking to Walter reassured me about the potential of The Beatles in America. Michael Black and I returned from Wembley in the early hours and by then I was quite committed to the deal. The plan of action was to meet later that same day with Epstein. I got home at around two in the morning and my wife's sleepy voice asked, 'How was the show?' I said it was fine and then added, 'I have bought The Beatles.' She said, 'Do be quiet and go to sleep.'

Later that morning Michael called to arrange the meeting with Epstein and I chatted away to him, not really noticing my wife taking an interest in the conversation. When I put the phone down, she became very agitated and it led to the worst scene in the whole of our marriage. She was adamant that I was not going to sign them up. Her list of objections summed up what many thought of The Beatles then – they were regarded as rebellious and a disruptive influence on their youthful fans.

To my wife, who was chairman of every charity committee she sat on, The Beatles stood for everything she despised. She had a certain style that came from having spent a number of her formative years in the United States. She had the English-ness and yet, having spent something like eight years from the age of twelve to twenty in America, she had a trans-Atlantic style. She liked music – light music – her favourite song was 'Raindrops Keep Falling on My Head' and she'd go anywhere to see Steve Lawrence and Edye Gormé, the husband and wife singing and comedy duo in the United States.

Marriage to me meant that while she wasn't particularly interested in sport herself, she put up with it. She liked boxing to a degree – she enjoyed world championship contests and was interested in Muhammad Ali's fights, not because she found him fascinating but because it was a major event. I think that was the American in her. She liked going to watch Wimbledon, too, for the same reason.

But when it came to managing The Beatles, she drew a line. She was a strong traditionalist and she didn't like the long hair, the drugs and that sort of thing. She thought it would ruin my life and that of the family if I got involved with people like them. To be fair, it was a rather popular view at the time.

Contrary to the impression this episode might create, Phyllis was not a dominating person. She was very intelligent and you could reason with her. But on this issue she knew what she wanted and couldn't be pushed around, not at all. That morning she made her views known so relentlessly that it was clear there was no room for negotiation. She was unimpressed by my assertion that Epstein was going to carry on with the day-to-day management. She felt it would not be long before I became actively involved, and she was probably right.

I ultimately saw the logic in what she was saying, decided it was not worth the family conflict to go on with this and called Black to withdraw from the deal. But I don't regret not signing The Beatles, not for a minute. What happened at home really reinforced my own opinion of that time. I didn't like their music then, although I have since had great pleasure from it. As for Epstein, he sorted himself out somehow on that occasion but committed suicide in August 1967 and was really something of a pitiful figure.

I did work with The Beatles, videotaping their shows at the Intertel Studios and we also videotaped the Rolling Stones, who were very professional.

They were not the only pop groups we worked with. Intertel provided extracts for an American show called 'Hullabaloo' which featured the main British rock acts, and in the mid-1960s we worked with Billy J Kramer and Gerry and the Pacemakers. They were as good as gold to work with and so, too, were their managements, who realized that being on TV was good for the group because it helped sell records and brought fatter royalties. The situation changed later in the decade when every Johnny-come-lately was a pop manager, promising the best for his charges and turning up with out-rageous demands, absurd schedules and ludicrous obligations to be satisfied on our part before they would perform.

Two cases spring to mind. I was running shows at Earls Court and I remember booking David Bowie. The only prob-lem was that nobody told him! He had taken himself off to the Bahamas, claiming his management had said nothing about the date. On another occasion we booked the rock group, Slade. The stage was set up, the equipment all set and every-thing in place for the show. Then I received a call from the manager of Earls Court, who had noticed that there were cameras set up, obviously to film the show. There had been no mention of this in our initial contract and as far as I was concerned, they had no right to be there. If the band wanted to film the concert, they had to pay a rate for that facility at the venue. I raised this with their manager, Chas Chandler, who bluntly told me they were not going to pay and if anyone tried to make them, he would make sure the group didn't appear and he would sue, sue, sue. He might have thought he had presented me with a fait accompli, but he was in for a surprise.

The show went ahead, cameras and all, but the band's percentage of the box office takings could not be paid until the following week, when all the accounts were drawn up. Now it was my turn. I adjusted their percentage accordingly to allow for the extra filming facility and sent them the remainder of the money they were due. If they wanted to sue, I was quite happy for them to go ahead and do that. I had an irate call from Chandler, but I brushed him off and I never heard another word. He had been outwitted and he knew it. It took a bit of time for rock music to catch up with the real world and get away from their earlier, cavalier management style. Today, they realize that time and money are part of the equation and they are far more professional and businesslike in their dealings.

It was my business partnership with Robert Patterson that brought me into contact with these rock stars. Patterson, a promoter and impresario, was a lovely and very talented man who was destroyed by a natural weakness in that he always needed someone to prop him up, notably his German wife Sybil. When she left him, he turned to drink in a heavy way, became rather reclusive and died.

Patterson had been Stravinsky's private secretary and then worked with the concert impresario Victor Hochauser before striking out on his own and concentrating on the pop business. Our partnership did various things, one of which was obtaining the exclusive rights to Earls Court for live events, hence the Bowie and Slade involvements.

It was while I was involved with Robert that I did a property deal in which the singer Andy Williams played a crucial role. By this time I was involved in developing office buildings with my partner Charles Burkeman and in 1974 we had this building for which we wanted to charge around £300,000 a year in rent. Although it was in a good location in the centre of London, Soho Square, there was a mini recession at the time and we could find no takers. The only one on the horizon was CBS Records, who were looking for a UK headquarters and were very keen, but their company secretary was proving so awkward that the deal was going nowhere fast – a worrying situation, considering our investment. Then Andy Williams intervened.

Through Robert and our joint entertainment interests, I had got to know Andy quite well and he called to say he was in town. We had breakfast together and I happened to mention to him that we were hoping to let a new office building to his record company, CBS. That evening he had dinner with Dick Asher, head of CBS Records in Britain, and Andy mentioned that he had met me, described me as an 'old friend' and said he understood CBS were renting a building from me. Asher mentioned that the deal had stalled and said something about sorting out problems and how he had gathered I was a difficult person. 'No,' said Andy, intervening decisively, 'Jarvis is anything but. In fact, he is a very nice guy.' He persuaded Asher to give me a call the following day, promising that the deal could be resolved if he talked directly to me.

Andy tipped me off that I might receive this call and when it came, I was ready. Just as Andy had promised Asher, the problems were resolved and CBS Records had their new headquarters in Soho Square. It was proof that it is often not what you know, but who you know that counts – a classic case of contacts and coincidence coming together to make something happen. We ended up with a very good deal that could so easily have gone bad, and whenever I run into Dick Asher, who remains an important man in the music business, even today he still calls me his landlord.

For all the highs working with Robert Patterson brought, there were also frequent crises and they grew more regular as the years rolled on. On one occasion he was presenting Andy Williams at the Palladium for a week, but after the first show Robert was 'out of it'. He had drunk himself to the point of no return. When it came to the after-show party, he was in no fit state to go and I remember driving him back to his flat in New

Cavendish Street, putting him to bed and then making excuses for him, telling everyone that he had food poisoning.

On another occasion he was badly unnerved when someone tried to muscle in on him. Robert had discovered a young black singer who had a hit record and I had used this chap in a charity show, although in the long run his career never amounted to that much. Robert operated from an office in Wigmore Street and one lunchtime a man arrived there claiming he had the rights to the black singer. Robert was at lunch but the visitor overturned the receptionist's desk and said that was the message he was leaving for Mr Patterson. Of course, when Robert returned he was in a terrible state, very upset by what had gone on and he called me immediately. He started going on about getting some bodyguards. I told him that the best bodyguards he could possibly have were the ones dressed in blue.

I called Savile Row police station and told the Superintendent, Arthur Phillips, an old friend of mine, what had happened, and Arthur made sure that this hoodlum knew 'his card was marked' – if there were ever any more threats to Robert, then he knew where to start the investigation.

That incident, however, is really a microcosm of my eventual parting with Robert on a business front. He was becoming increasingly more unreliable. The work he was supposed to be doing was not happening and the air around him was one of constant crisis. The separation from his wife left him vulnerable and he then lived with a girl who came from a family where the father had been an alcoholic.

If the parting with Robert saddened me, I had fewer regrets about the break-up, not long after, of the association I had with Trevor Wallace of Wallace and Style's Intertel. As I have already described, my closed-circuit television activities meant using Intertel's facilities several times and as we had worked together with some success, Wallace and Style asked me to become more involved in their operation. Neither was a great businessman but they were sharp enough to realize that I had

My mother's family, with Esther, the youngest, at 2 years old.

The wedding of Esther and Max, December 20 1922.

My grandmothers, Leah and Rebecca, show their happiness on my wedding to Phyllis in March 1948.

A page at my aunt's wedding and my earliest Frankie Vaughan impression, 'Give me the moonlight, give me the girl.'

(Above left) Me at 20 about to make my 'acting' debut.

(Above right) Esther and me.

(Left) Me with Phyllis and our son Steven, aged 1.

Muhammad Ali at a press conference before his return fight with
Leon Spinks at New Orleans.

Lester Piggott, 'the Master', rode a winner for me.

With Dustin Hoffman at the premiere of *Lenny* at Cannes.

Laurence Olivier the dentist and Dustin Hoffman in *Marathon Man*:
'Is it safe?'

Trying to persuade Gregory Peck to play the lead opposite Dustin Hoffman in *Nightwork*, a film of Irwin Shaw's bestselling novel.

Amusing Jack Lemmon by reminding him of the Neil Simon film 'Out of Towners' in which he starred. The picture became a cult film for my family and we used to recite the dialogue over dinner.

Singing on 'Ilkla' Moor Baht 'at' with Harold Wilson after dinner at Chequers 1975.

With Marcia Williams at a film premiere. The publication of this picture led to unfounded rumours of a romance.

With Elizabeth Taylor at the party following the first night of her play *Little Foxes* in London.

Joan Collins helps the Variety Club and the Royal Free Hospital with the presentation of a Sunshine Coach.

With fellow judges Alan Wicker and Ivana Trump at Miss World, Sun City, South Africa, 1992.

A judge with Miss Venezuela (voted 'Miss World'), at Atlanta in 1991.

With Charles Clore and Nat Cohen, my guru in the film business at Cannes. My pals would rather have been in the picture above.

At the Variety Club Guildhall lunch in 1983 with the guests of honour, left to right, the Archbishop of Canterbury, the Chief Rabbi and the Cardinal Archbishop of Westminster.

(Below left) With President Reagan at the White House.
(Below right) With Bob Hope at the dinner in his honour at Palm Springs, California 1993.

With Mike Tyson and Frank Bruno on formal occasions.

Variety Club dinner at the Waldorf Astoria, New York, 1992, with
Margaret Thatcher, Henry Kissinger and Anthony Quinn.

With Nadine and Sammy Cahn at our wedding reception for friends in
New York City.

Princess Diana at a charity greyhound race meeting at Wembley. I said 'Ma'am, you look wonderful,' and she replied, 'Well, you did say black tie.' Brian Wolfson looks on.

Variety Club lunch with Princess Anne and Dean Martin.

A youthful Prince Charles at a Commonwealth Games dinner with, left to right, Arthur Wint, Olympic athlete; Ray Illingworth, England cricket captain; Lord Westmorland and Sir Alec Douglas Home.

At the Pro-Am revue at the Fortune Theatre, Prince Edward wondered how I managed to get Samy Cahn to write special lyrics to 'Strangers in the Night'.

excellent contacts and could find work for them. The actual deal I did, along with Charles Burkeman, was to invest in a debenture in their company, but the major contribution was those contacts. Before I joined them, Intertel had made £18,000 in the previous year. Two years later the company was making £130,000 – and that was after Wallace and Style had taken their handsome salaries out of the business.

Intertel were responsible for all the pay-TV shows and I was able to find them additional work from the United States. This was a crucial development for one simple reason: the Americans had moved into colour television and Wallace and Style managed to get some colour cameras and therefore could satisfy the American demand. This was, of course, the time when The Beatles were taking off and Carnaby Street culture was very much the vogue, and we started video-recording programmes, stage shows and sports events for the Americans, who could not get enough. You name it, we would do it and business boomed, as no request was beyond our resources and, in effect, we were the one and only provider. Nothing was beyond us, nothing surprised us – except maybe one request that momentarily threw me.

It came one evening as I was sitting at home. The phone rang and the voice at the other end said, 'Hello. This is Bing Crosby and I need your help to produce a show in Ireland.' I could hardly believe my ears and my first thought was that this must be some friend playing a prank. The caller fortunately did not seem to hear when I said, 'Just a moment, I'll call Frank Sinatra.' After a few minutes' conversation, I realized it was not a joke, it really was Bing Crosby. He was making a film about fishing in the Lake District and he wanted my, or rather Intertel's, services for another project in Ireland, a television programme which was to be called 'A Little Bit of Irish'.

I was more than happy to do business with Bing Crosby, although it made me realize how stingy and mean he was. He was supposedly doing this as a favour for a friend, but it turned out that the favour eventually cost the friend a whopping

£10,000, even though the Irish characters and artists in the show gave their services free. Crosby had run up the extra costs himself but refused to reimburse his friend. I later learnt he was notoriously tight-fisted when it came to money.

We also made 'A Winter's Tale' for Warner Brothers with Jane Asher and Laurence Harvey in it, after I was approached by a young Canadian, Peter Snell, wanting £60,000 to make the project possible. It struck me that Shakespeare is, as he probably always will be, a good bet and Harvey's name carried enough clout to make it work, so we did it. The American distributors proved that when they returned a £250,000 profit. Another project was the 'Xerox Hour' on American TV and we were commissioned to film the John Osborne play 'Luther'. A week before shooting was to start, Richard Harris pulled out to make a film in Spain titled 'A Man Called Horse'. Stuart Burge, who was directing this teleplay, was left in the lurch with what looked like a hopeless situation.

As it happened, I was in the White Elephant Club in London having dinner when across the room I saw Robert Shaw and William Conrad, the burly actor who enjoyed big success in a long-running detective series called 'Cannon'. It struck me that Shaw could fill the gap left by Harris and I went across and introduced myself. I told Shaw about the problem with 'Luther' and though he was sympathetic, he told me that he had a pact with his wife, Mary Ure, that if one of them was working, the other didn't, because they had a number of small children – and that at the moment it was her turn.

It was, however, a plum part and Conrad was very helpful in promoting my cause. I left my phone number with Shaw and he said he would call me. Shaw was a hard drinker, a larger than life man and he and his wife in fact shared ten children, but he was as good as his word and did call me to say that, having sorted it out with his wife, he would do it. The only unwelcome part of this deal was that once Shaw agreed to take part, he expected me to be around the set and I ended up as a reluctant producer of the show. It was, however, a big hit and was nominated for an Emmy, television's version of an Oscar.

By now our work for the American companies with the colour television cameras had put us so far ahead of the game that we really had a licence to print money. All this should have made working with Trevor Wallace a joy. It was not.

Wallace's behaviour became more and more erratic as time went on. The fundamental problem was that he despised the producers and directors with whom he was working and always felt he knew better than them. He was a frustrated Cecil B de Mille, or a Steven Spielberg. He was constantly wanting Intertel to go into production, something that I and the other directors made sure to block. That was the route to destroying the business, because there was no need to risk our capital when so many other people wanted to invest, using our equipment. It got to the stage where Wallace said he had a company called Commonwealth United interested in backing a spy thriller he was going to make, starring Joan Collins and Gene Barry. They were, he promised us, going to provide 100 per cent of the finance. Wallace was instructed by the Intertel board that he could only make the film once the money was in place.

A few days after this, I was in New York, where I ran into my old friend, the agent Jack Green. He told me that Gene Barry was off to London the next day to make this film with my company, news which caught me by surprise because it seemed to me that the money had come through very quickly, in fact within two days.

When I returned to England I discovered that no money had been forthcoming from Commonwealth United. But that had not stopped Wallace, who was shooting the film just off the Edgware Road. I went down to see him and he tried to bluff his way through when I questioned him as to how the project was being funded. Realizing he could not justify himself, he turned on me and was very unpleasant. As a result of his folly, Intertel was left to pick up costs of $350,000 for the film. The Commonwealth United deal, of course, went belly-up and Wallace, with everybody now aware that he was deceiving them, fled to Australia and then America. The salvage operation involved my selling the film in Cannes for $250,000 plus a percentage of the profits, but it was never seen other than on airlines. Ironically, it was not a bad film at all, although today I can remember little of it apart from the fact that it had a theme song entitled 'No Escape', sung by Malcolm Roberts. The title of the song was a fair reflection of the predicament Wallace had got us into.

The problem now was what should we do with Intertel? Here fate intervened, in the shape of the IBA. As we have seen, they had decided to take away the weekend television franchise for London from Lew Grade's ATV. Among the groups bidding for the franchise were London Weekend Television, with David Frost and Humphrey Burton to the fore. Like all bidders, they had made great projections about what they would do and made optimistic noises, but I don't think they were expecting to win. When to their surprise they did, they had nothing to run the channel with! No studio, no equipment; nothing but the paper spelling out their bid terms. Their lack of resources was Intertel's salvation. We managed to sell our studios and equipment to LWT and the company was liquidated.

The sale of the Intertel studios to LWT had one other happy consequence, in that it brought me in to contact with David Frost and a friendship began which I value and which has endured. I already knew David from the time he had come, with the beautiful actress Ursula Andress, to one of the first Ali satellite shows I staged. I remember seeing them together in the foyer of the Leicester Square Odeon and asking if they would do a pre-fight interview, which they did. From that point on, David and I became good friends and were later to become involved in a business venture with Charles Clore, a production company called Paradine Productions, the title coming from David's second name. Paradine produced the famous interviews in 1977 with the disgraced US President Richard

Nixon, and a major film for television called 'Centennial'. Although the partnership with Charles didn't last more than a couple of years, largely because his right-hand man Leonard Sainer, who was always difficult about money, could not come to terms with the sort of expenses people in television like David incurred, it did not harm my relationship with David.

Over the years David has proved to me what a very fine human being he is. Both my first wife Phyllis and my second wife Nadine died, and on each occasion it was David who was the first to call me up and ask me out. I don't believe that it was just a coincidence, not with those two unhappy moments in my life happening twelve years apart. On the second occasion he was with his wife Carina, the daughter of the Duke of Norfolk, and despite my sadness it made me glad to see David, who, as the newspapers have painfully, and sometimes glee-fully chronicled, has not always been lucky in love, so happily settled as a family man with three lovely children.

Most famously, David had a traumatic experience with the *Vogue* cover girl, the American model Karen Graham. She had moved to Europe to work after the break-up of her romance with Del Coleman, a man known for his jukebox business. Karen and David hit it off, all was progressing well and a wedding date was set for a Saturday in New York. David and Robert Patterson were, at the time, involved in a partnership that was doing live shows in Australia featuring artists like Neil Diamond. On the Monday before the wedding, Coleman arrived in London and booked in at Claridges. According to Robert, Coleman called David and asked him to come and visit. David, and I think it was remarkably gracious of him to go, arrived and was virtually threatened by Coleman, who told him, 'If you know what is good for you, you will call off your wedding to Karen.' David's cool response was to tell Coleman that he was in London and not Las Vegas or Chicago. Even so, he left somewhat perturbed by this encounter and in fact took the precaution of booking Karen on a flight to New York on an airline which she would not normally have travelled on, at least not to New York. She flew there with Pakistan International Airways.

The following day, the Wednesday, after some business loose ends had been tidied up, Robert and David set off for New York. Some hours later, I received a desperate call from Robert, who recalled that I had a contact in the District Attorney's office in New York. Robert said that Coleman had not only been stirring things up with Karen's mother but had Karen as his prisoner in his New York flat. The address was traced through my DA contact but it was learned from him that Miss Graham was not there against her will and, in fact, she was going to Chicago with Coleman the following day, where they were to marry.

You can imagine what a shattering experience it was for David. The next I heard from him was a few days after what should have been his wedding day, when he called me from Paris. He was on his way to Australia but had chosen to change planes in France, because he could not face the prospect of the British press at Heathrow. I reminded him that newspapers are here today and gone tomorrow, when they are only useful for 'wrapping fish and chips'.

Indeed, hindsight has proved that in the long run, those events led David to a happier private life. As for Karen and Del Coleman, their marriage, predictably, didn't last more than a few years.

ALAN Crawford is not as well known as David Frost, but he proved to me that contrary to what the pessimists say, human nature is not quite as bad as it is often made out. Crawford, a young Australian, came to my office in 1963 and told me he had been working on Radio Veronica, a commercial radio ship anchored off the Dutch coast, claiming an audience of around five million listeners. He wanted to start a similar operation off the east coast of England and I immediately sat up and took notice. The Pilkington Report had recently come out and it had concluded, wrongly, as I felt at the time, that there was no demand for commercial radio in this country.

I had spent a lot of time in the United States and my experiences there had proved to me how tremendous the commercial radio industry could be. It seemed clear to me that a similar operation would work in Britain. I was convinced there was a demand here and Crawford impressed on me that he had the necessary experience, not only with Radio Veronica but from his time back in Australia. He told me of his plans involving a ship, the *Atlanta*, which was being refitted at the southern Irish port of Greenore. What he did not tell me, because he did not know it at the time, was that Captain O'Rahilly, who was refitting the *Atlanta*, had a very bright and enterprising son named Ronan who, having heard of Crawford's plans through his father, was having another vessel, a ferry, refitted and it would be ready before the *Atlanta*. That boat was the *Caroline*.

After talking to my lawyers, who confirmed that there was no legal reason why ships should not broadcast from off shore, I agreed to make an investment in the project and persuaded some of my friends to follow suit. One of them was Leslie Grade, brother of the famous Lew, but he withdrew some time later because the interests of the Grade family in commercial television might have been prejudiced had the legality of the pirate radio stations been challenged.

Of course, with two ships on the high seas there was obviously going to be a clash between Radio Atlanta and Radio Caroline, but it was only a matter of weeks before the two operations merged under the Radio Caroline banner and became a huge success. Caroline had been launched on Easter Day 1964, with Simon Dee the first DJ. Within three weeks the audience was one million and a few months later some seven million were tuning in. The Parliamentary lobby against it grew stronger and stronger and eventually brought about a change in the law. Radio Caroline was finally killed off when the Marine Offences Act became effective in August 1967.

We had quite a cast of people involved with Caroline. It

included Oliver Smedley, a very active businessman; Jocelyn Stevens, at the time managing director of Express Newspapers, now chairman of English Heritage; Air Commodore Freddie West, VC, chairman of the Hurst Park Syndicate, and Philip Solomon, originally from Ireland and manager of The Bachelors singing group. Also on board were, of course, Ronan O'Rahilly and Alan Crawford, who could claim to have changed the sound of radio in this country.

The irony is that only a few years after Radio Caroline was closed down, commercial radio started and the likes of Capital Radio in London and Radio Piccadilly in Manchester were huge successes. Many of the disc jockeys who cut their teeth with Radio Caroline were now working in either commercial radio or for BBC Radio 1.

One or two of the business people involved with Radio Caroline tried similar projects, hoping that they would be within the law, but ran into problems. Oliver Smedley came into conflict with a man who was operating a radio station from a tower in the Thames Estuary, off Whitstable. The result was a violent confrontation, ending in a shooting and a death. Smedley faced a murder charge but was cleared, thankfully, for though he was not an easy man to get on with, he was certainly no murderer.

As for Alan Crawford, as I said, he restored my faith in human nature. A short while after Radio Caroline ceased broadcasting, he came to see me and asked for a £750 loan so that he could buy a ticket to fly back to Australia. I was more than happy to oblige, as I felt he had been very unlucky and deserved success. I was not surprised that I didn't hear from him and was taken aback when, seven years on, he appeared in my office, ready to pay back the £750 plus interest. In the time since I had last seen him, he had enjoyed some financial success with a business venture in Pakistan and, like the man of the calibre that I always thought he was, there he stood, insisting on repaying the loan with interest added on. I had a lot of difficulty in persuading him to pay back just the original £750.

9

Sport on the Screen

The sale of Intertel to LWT did not mean my involvement in the TV and film business was at an end, particularly when it came to sport. I still had my closed-circuit TV company Viewsport and I had been able to arrange for the former Intertel facilities which now belonged to LWT to be available to me.

Viewsport was a winning concept, a real forerunner of the satellite TV stations that now dominate the sporting scene. I feel it would have been even more successful had the bodies that controlled sport, notably the Football League, been more far-sighted. Yes, again it was a battle to make them see the sense of it, and the commercial opportunities that were there for them.

The most glaring example was the Tottenham v Arsenal match towards the end of the 1970-71 season when Arsenal were on course for the Double and needed to win at White Hart Lane to lift the League title. Now if ever there was a game people wanted to see, that was it. On the night of the game, 50,000 were locked out. Viewsport could have put it on in a number of cinemas and everyone would have been happy, even the football authorities and the clubs, because they would have got revenue from it. But a joint committee of the Football Association and the Football League had drawn up a list of conditions, absurdly impractical, that had to be met.

Conditions! They were more of a stumbling block. For example, they insisted that closed-circuit screening could only be into a football ground and that there should be no other matches being played within a certain radius at the same time. That was clearly daft. Imagine the situation. Chelsea are involved in a sell-out match away at, say, Newcastle; on the same night, Fulham, Chelsea's neighbours, are at home. Therefore no show can go on at Stamford Bridge. The point is that Chelsea fans would not go to Fulham anyhow, and vice versa. Football fans just don't work that way.

The main opposition came from Alan Hardaker, secretary of the Football League, a man who thought no idea was any good unless he had come up with it. To be fair to him, he did have some good ideas. He instituted the League Cup, took the Final to Wembley and gave it stature. But I could never persuade Hardaker to agree to closed-circuit television taking big matches live to cinemas. We had more luck with the pay-TV experiment in the 1960s. Earl Mountbatten's son-in-law Lord Brabourne was involved in it and he was able to speak directly to Lord Harewood, then president of the Football Association. An agreement of sorts was reached for a handful of Cup games to be shown on pay TV.

I kept persistently lobbying Hardaker about closed-circuit screenings and eventually I was invited to meet the Football League management at the Great Western Hotel in Paddington. I told them that there was no risk capital involved on their part, but it was clear that Hardaker was very much against the plan and they argued that people should be encouraged to go to football grounds to watch. Their attitude was hardly surprising. They had been anti-floodlights, slow to make innovations with substitutes and had hardly pushed out the boat when it came to English club sides competing in the early days of European competition. The chairmen and directors of clubs, the men with the power to vote, were in a large part motivated by the privileges and prestige that came with being a director of a football club. They were not prepared to agree to scheduled League matches going on closed-circuit TV.

Hardaker was, of course, a bit of an actor. In 1967, the year of the first League Cup Final at Wembley, Queens Park Rangers beat West Bromwich Albion 3-2. Hardaker was in his pomp at the match. The FA Cup Final later that year was between Tottenham and Chelsea. It was not the greatest of finals – Tottenham won 2-1 and were well in command, Chelsea only getting a late consolation – but Hardaker made out it was so boring that he pretended to be asleep throughout the match. I could see him doing it, and pointed it out to the people I was with. It was clear Hardaker was making a point. The League Cup was his baby. The FA Cup Final, probably the most prestigious event in English football, was not, so he was determined in a bloody-minded way to appear dis-interested and bored. And he did not care who knew about it.

Eventually the Lord Brabourne pay-TV experiment col-lapsed with losses of around £1 million when John Stonehouse, who had become Postmaster General in succession to Wedgwood-Benn, refused to sanction an expansion of the service to 250,000 homes, limiting it instead to 150,000. The collapse, however, did not mean the concept was wrong. Cup ties had been run successfully both for the cable television network, as it then was, and for Viewsport. The popularity of satellite and cable today has also more than proved that even back then the idea was right. Its worth would have been proved earlier if some football chairmen had been more receptive than others.

In 1976, QPR were pushing hard for the First Division Championship and football had a deal with LWT, who showed the games in a Sunday highlights package, 'The Big Match'. The home clubs at the time received £300, QPR's final match was at home to Leeds United, interest was huge and clearly there were going to be people in Yorkshire who wanted to see the game as it happened but would not be able to get there. I told the QPR chairman Jim Gregory that his club could make £10,000 from a live closed-circuit screening and he challenged LWT to match that offer. It didn't mean that we were shutting LWT out of the picture, just that they could not show any of the action until the following day as usual. But they wouldn't budge and we were not able to show the game.

In 1981, I put the American Football Super Bowl on live in England for the first time, at cinemas, and the same year I had another big shot at football. I wanted a minimum of twenty-four matches a season, with the fixture list arranged to show midweek games, not unlike the satellite position now. On top of that I wanted various foreign matches involving England and English teams, a cure, I would have thought, for a number of ills that beset the games at the time. The hooligan problem could have been controlled, the grounds would have been utilized more and therefore become more economic, and parking problems would be eased. In fact, the whole package was aimed at making football a modern sport and a modern entertainment.

This bid came on the back of a very successful and lucrative broadcast of a League Cup quarter-final clash between West Ham and Tottenham Hotspur in December the previous year, a sell-out that we managed to beam to four London cinemas. That made it all the more frustrating when I was unable to get the Football Association or the Football League to back my proposal to set up a programme of matches for the season to be shown on the big screen.

In many ways, I look back now to the 1970s and 1980s and I see that Viewsport was way ahead of its time. These days, in conjunction with Jeff Petts and his Satellite Express company, I show games regularly at the grounds of the away team, a situation brought about to a large extent by the change in ground capacities because of the Taylor Report, meaning fewer tickets for the travelling fans. We have shown games at Manchester United, Blackburn, Chelsea, Newcastle, Liverpool, Arsenal, Preston, Fulham, Sunderland, and Birmingham – the list goes on and on.

The pity is, had the football authorities shown a bit of

vision, the game and the fans could have benefited and English football could have been transformed, even avoided some of the problems of hooliganism and crowd control that has so plagued it over the years.

FOOTBALL provided the most horrifying event that I have ever witnessed on 15 April 1989 when Liverpool were playing Nottingham Forest in the FA Cup semi-final at Hillsborough, the home of Sheffield Wednesday. I had a clearer view of the tragic event than anyone present at the stadium because I had been invited by Brian Barwick, an old friend who was Head of Production for BBC Television Sport, to sit in his control room so that I could watch both semi-finals being played on that day.

The first sign of trouble came through the BBC cameras outside the ground, where it became obvious about ten minutes before the 3pm kick-off that too many spectators were late in arriving at the entrance to the Liverpool end, causing a great crush in their anxiety to get into the ground. There was no question of orderly queues being formed up to the turn-stiles. The intensity of the pressure built up and when the people still outside the stadium realised from the noise inside that the game had started, the crowd outside became virtually uncontrollable. I am convinced that if the police had not decided to open the gates there would have been many people crushed, seriously injured, and possibly killed, in those circumstance.

We had been trying to tell the BBC commentators to warn people of the problem outside the ground for some minutes, but the answer we got back was they they were unable to contact anyone who could help.

I was particularly aware of the problem I was witnessing because on 15 February 1986, the day the new stand at Lansdowne Road in Dublin was opened, I had attended the rugby game between Wales and Ireland and on that occasion many of the spectators, including myself and some friends, arrived late. Most had stayed in the bars of the nearby hotels until almost the last moment, while my host had trouble finding a parking space. There was a tremendous crush leading up to the ground, which was compounded by the fact that the level-crossing gates at the end of the road had been closed. The crush was frightening and if I, and a man next to me had not held up my host's mother, a lady in her seventies, she would have been trampled on by the crowd. Only the opening of the exit gates allowing people access to the stadium prevented a disaster at Lansdowne Road that day.

At Hillsborough, of course, the respite was only temporary. As the crowds from outside poured into the stadium, there was no control over the number of people entering the central terrace 'pen' through the short tunnel under the seated areas above. This inevitably resulted in serious overcrowding in that particular pen, behind the goal at the Liverpool end of the ground.

Apparently there were no Sheffield Wednesday stewards supervising the entrance to the tunnel. They might have been able to divert people into the less crowded areas of the terrace, but I can only assume that any stewards who may have been there in the first place had now moved inside, the game having started some minutes earlier. It has always surprised me that in the various reports of the disaster, Sheffield Wednesday, as owners of the stadium, seem to have escaped serious criticism.

We naturally watched with horror as the police were pushing people who were trying to climb the fence, and come on to the pitch, back into the crowd, mistaking their attempts to get out of the crush for some sort of pitch invasion. The police could not have realised that those climbing the fence were trying to escape serious injury, or even death as it turned out for 96 tragically unfortunate souls.

The only benefit which was gained from this dreadful event was the Taylor Report, brilliantly prepared by the late and lamented Lord Chief Justice, Peter Taylor. His report resulted in every ground in the Premier League being required to become all-seater. Incidentally, we at Wembley had already gone all seater well before the Taylor Report was issued. I feel that this requirement should be extended to all Football League grounds because a disaster can just as well happen with ten thousand present as it can with fifty thousand.

The success I had with the live cinema screening of the West Ham v Tottenham Cup tie in December 1980 led almost by chance to a long involvement with American football and the NFL. And it all started as a result of a casual conversation which took place a few days later at the San Lorenzo restaurant in London.

I was lunching with a Canadian lady friend and as we went to sit down, an American at the next table, who apparently lived in London and had seen the match at the Odeon Marble Arch, told me how exciting he thought it had been. He asked why I did not also show the Super Bowl (NFL version of our Cup Final), which takes place in January and is a huge event in North America. I replied facetiously that I didn't show it because he and I would be the only ones who would want to see it. My lady friend contradicted me and insisted that the sizeable Canadian community in London would certainly be interested, as they were great fans of American football. She told me that she knew all about it because her brother had played for her home town professional team, Calgary Stampede, in the Gray Cup, the Canadian counterpart of the NFL.

I recalled this conversation when in New York two weeks later and arranged, through a friend, to meet Pete Rozelle, then the Commissioner of the NFL. He was very enthusiastic about the idea and I was able to buy the rights through the NFL TV agents, Mark McCormack's International Management Group, for the princely sum of $5,000. I was further helped financially by the fact that the game was already being shown by satellite to the American Forces in Germany. I took the pictures off the satellite to London.

When I held a press conference to announce the event, at

least one of the journalists present thought I was talking about the Soccer Bowl (Cup Final) of the North American Soccer League. I was asked whether I thought that the public would want to see the Super Bowl, but I jokingly commented that I wanted to see it anyway, so that was why I was putting it on.

It was, however, a great success and I discovered that the number of American Air Force personnel based in this country was far greater than I imagined. Therefore the Odeon Leicester Square was full to capacity in January 1981 for the game, between the Oakland Raiders and the Philadelphia Eagles. The match took place in the New Orleans Superdome and was very exciting. The satellite screening itself created a great deal of interest in the United States, where it was given much publicity on the television news.

For Super Bowl 1982 I repeated the experience at both the Odeon Leicester Square and the Odeon Hammersmith, with 5,000 seats, and this event was also a great success. As it happened, Channel 4 Television was starting up later that year and I invited Jeremy Isaacs, the first head of the channel, to come to the Odeon Leicester Square on that occasion. He fell in love with the game and as a result Channel 4 started its weekly programme on Sunday evenings at six o'clock, showing highlights of the previous week's games. It created tremendous interest in American football in this country, and resulted in my arranging with Pete Rozelle an exhibition game at Wembley in August 1986 between the Chicago Bears and the Dallas Cowboys. Rozelle, who had not fully appreciated the amount of interest there was over here in his sport, wondered whether we would attract a large crowd. Over lunch at Wimbledon, I told him I guaranteed 60,000 but in the event the attendance was 83,000.

This was the forerunner for a number of such American Bowl matches every year at Wembley, but the attendance gradually reduced for several reasons. Wembley became all-seater, reducing the capacity. Then the British press knocked the fact that these were exhibition games and to some extent this did discourage fans, who were used to seeing competitive games on Channel 4. Finally, and most seriously, the NFL succumbed to Channel 4's request that they be allowed to show the weekly games from the United States live, at eight o'clock on Sunday evenings.

This was the biggest mistake of all and I pleaded with Art Modell, owner of the Cleveland Browns team and chairman of the NFL Television Committee, to stick to the 6pm slot on Sunday, when the other major channels had religious programmes. I tried to explain to him that eight o'clock on Sundays is when most channels show their peak-time programmes and the competition would kill the Channel 4 audience. I added that for the majority of the British public American football works best in a highlights package, since they are not brought up in the traditions of the game and are therefore unable to sustain their interest, through all the stops and starts, for the three hours which a live game requires.

Modell did not seem to understand this and I finished the discussion by saying to him, 'Art, I promise that when *I* come to Cleveland, I will take *your* advice.' My advice on that occasion was correct, as the NFL learned to their cost. The audience on Channel 4 dwindled and eventually lost interest. Now American football is shown on Sky TV, to a minority audience, and there are no longer American Bowl games at Wembley. There was a tremendous start to the newly-formed World League some years ago by the London team, the Monarchs, but although they had two successful seasons at Wembley, we were unable to continue to stage their games because of our contract with the Football Association. The Monarchs moved first to White Hart Lane, home of Tottenham Hotspur, and then for one season to Stamford Bridge, home of Chelsea, but have now come to the small stadium at Crystal Palace which in previous years was only used for training. Mr Modell has a lot to answer for, although he continues to be a successful NFL team owner, having controversially moved his team from Cleveland to Baltimore.

American Bowls are still held in other parts of the world, including Barcelona, Mexico, Frankfurt and Berlin. In fact, when the first game was staged at the Berlin Olympic Stadium, coinciding with the unification of the city, Paul Tagliabue, who replaced Pete Rozelle as NFL Commissioner, introduced me to guests at the commemorative dinner as 'the Godfather of international American football'. Since becoming involved with the NFL I have attended various Super Bowls and they are always great events. I have also been to many games at Meadowlands, home of the New York Giants, where my late, great friend Neil Walsh had a private box. Neil was an Irish-American who had been on the New York City administration under Mayor Beame and was well-known because he arranged for the green line to be painted down the centre of Fifth Avenue every year for the St Patrick's Day parade.

Neil died of lung cancer in 1992 and I miss him greatly on my frequent visits to New York. The closeness of our long-distance relationship was reflected in Neil's will, where he asked for me to be a pall bearer at his funeral. It was a request I could not refuse.

I have never been involved in televising cricket but am very proud that on one occasion, when the game faced a sticky patch, I helped get things going. I was responsible for arranging sponsorship of the alternative series when the 1970 South African tour to England was cancelled. Various protests against apartheid – which I, too, detested – brought this about and when the cancellation was finally announced I obtained sponsorship from my cousin John Ashton, one of the owners of the Victoria Sporting Club. He was a keen cricketer himself and a useful wicket-keeper in his younger days.

I put the idea to Ted Dexter, who lost no time in conveying it to the cricket authorities and thus the five-match series between England and the Rest of the World took place, with cricket of a very high standard from both sides.

I have been a member of the MCC for thirty years and cricket is really my favourite game. I have travelled the world to watch it, including a trip to Sydney for six days in 1979 to see an Ashes Test, and the players I most admire today include two Australians, Steve Waugh and Shane Warne; the others being the West Indian Brian Lara, Sachin Tendulkar of India and the Pakistani all-rounder Wasim Akram.

10

The Fight Game

Although very often in public I am presented as a boxing promoter, boxing has never amounted to more than ten per cent of my business activity. Indeed, I must confess that I have always resented it when people, and particularly the media, refer to me as 'the boxing promoter, Jarvis Astaire'. I suppose my resentment is partly because of the way the description is couched, as if to imply something underhand, even undesirable.

Not that I have anything but fond memories of my boxing experiences, and in particular the fighters I have had the privilege and pleasure to meet. Foremost among them was Sugar Ray Robinson, who, as I have said, was quite the best pound for pound boxer I saw, and lived up to his name by being a very nice person.

I encountered Sugar Ray on my first trip to America in 1948. I had just got married to my first wife Phyllis. Her family had escaped the war by going to America in 1938. After the war they returned to London and I met my wife at a charity function when I offered to take her home. Some days after this, I saw her with some mutual friends and that encounter started our friendship and eventual marriage.

My father-in-law, who still lived on the west coast of America, was keen that I should try to live in the United States and so it was that in 1948 we crossed the Atlantic, taking the Queen Mary from Southampton to New York. The sight of the Statue of Liberty looming into view as we approached New York formed an indelible impression, as did the long train journeys we took to cross America from east to west.

Many European Jews had made their home in the States, particularly in New York, and both my wife and I had relatives in America. Fascinated as I was by America and much tempted to live there – and for a few months I did live in Los Angeles – I never wanted to leave England, and particularly London. I like visiting America and go there as often as I can, but London is home.

However, America has played a big part in my life in the boxing and entertainment business, and that visit in 1948 was memorable for my first sight in the ring of Sugar Ray Robinson.

Boxing was very much on my mind as I stepped off the boat on to the New York dockside. My first priority, on that same evening, was to go to Jersey City where the Frenchman Marcel Cerdan was fighting Tony Zale for Zale's world middleweight championship. To me Jersey City was just a name and I had no real idea where it was or how to get there. But like all boxing fans visiting New York, I had heard of Jack Dempsey's restaurant in Manhattan and that is where I headed, only to find that most of the people there who were going to the fight had already gone. I asked a cab driver to take me but he refused, saying he would have to go through the Holland Tunnel. I had never heard of the Holland Tunnel and did not know where it was, but quickly worked out it was on the way to Jersey City.

So I waited for him to pick up a fare then went up to the next cab driver in the rank and, putting on an American accent, told him I wanted to go through the Holland Tunnel to Jersey City and the Roosevelt Stadium. This seemed to do the trick – he probably took me for a New Yorker who could not be trifled with and not only did he take me and Phyllis, who was going to her first ever boxing match, he also agreed to wait for us and take us back to Manhattan after the fight.

The fight itself was sensational. Cerdan, the son of a butcher, was famous in France not only for his great boxing prowess but also because of his love affair with France's queen of song, Edith Piaf. That night in Jersey City he showed he was not only a great lover but a very good boxer as he knocked out Zale. Phyllis and I went back to our waiting cab and could even offer a lift to two rather perplexed Americans. One of them said, 'How is it that this Limey comes here for the first time today and he's got a cab waiting, and we have got to struggle back to Manhattan?' That little episode convinced me that in America you must grab your opportunities, whenever they are available.

As was only to be expected, the Americans were not pleased with Cerdan's victory and when on our return to Manhattan we went to a little Italian restaurant, the Italian-Americans were claiming that if 'The Rock' – Rocky Graziano – had been at the Roosevelt Stadium he would have beaten the Frenchman. That was nonsense. 'The Rock' would have been put away quicker than Zale was. True, Cerdan never got to fight Graziano and he did lose to an American when Jake LaMotta beat him, but I remain convinced that had he fought Rocky Graziano, he would have won easily. As it was, soon after his defeat by Jake LaMotta he was killed in a plane crash in the Azores, just as he was returning to America for a rematch.

It was the night following Cerdan's victory over Zale that I first saw Sugar Ray Robinson. It is rare, if not unheard of, for two big fights to be on consecutive nights. But at that time in New York there was a battle going on between two promoters, and Mike Jacobs slipped in the Robinson fight so as to adversely affect the box office for the Cerdan-Zale contest. On the Sugar Ray bill he also had Ike Williams, the lightweight champion, against Jesse Flores.

Robinson was up against Kid Gavilan, a very fine fighter himself, but the measure of Robinson's outstanding ability was in the way he so comfortably beat Gavilan. What should have been a tough fight was made to look remarkably easy. Robinson's best days were as a welterweight but he still came within a whisker of winning the light-heavyweight championship against a good champion, Joey Maxim. If Sugar Ray had not collapsed from heat exhaustion he would have done it, because he was that far ahead, despite giving away too much weight.

That first sight of Robinson made me fall in love with his boxing and convinced me that he was the best fighter in the history of the game. You won't find many in boxing who would disagree. That night I worshipped his skills from afar, like any other fan. It was another decade, 1955, before I met him. I was in Los Angeles and he was training locally for a fight with Carl 'Bobo' Olson, in which Sugar Ray was out to regain his world middleweight title. With the helpful introduction of my friend George Parnassus, I went to visit the Robinson training camp just outside Los Angeles and talked to him a lot. I mentioned to him that he should think about coming to England again. I knew he felt it was an unlucky place for him – he had lost in London to Randolph Turpin. But I tried to convince him we would make him welcome.

Robinson in England was an even more attractive proposition after the ease with which he beat Olson, finishing it with an uppercut followed by a left hook that put his opponent on the deck. I was sitting at the fight with the famous TV personality Eamonn Andrews, who was reporting for the *Sunday Telegraph*. As Olson went down, Eamonn said: 'The referee can count to a hundred and it won't make a difference.' He was right about that, although on that trip Eamonn had no luck playing the Las Vegas gambling tables. That was until, with his money virtually gone, we were waiting in the lobby for his taxi to the airport and he found one last silver dollar in his pocket. He put it in the fruit machine, and hit the jackpot – almost $1,000 came gushing out. We were picking up the money as the cab waited.

As for Sugar Ray, we did eventually bring him to London in September 1962 to fight Terry Downes. Robinson was forty-one but still a very big draw and Londoners loved him. He had become known for driving around in a pink Cadillac, and had a charming style. I didn't know Sugar Ray as well as I was to get to know Muhammad Ali, but I would meet him and his wife Millie in Los Angeles and I found them a delightful couple. His time came before television was the power it is today, or even in Ali's time, but I have to say that Sugar Ray was in his own way as big a draw as Ali, although his appeal was very different. While Sugar Ray was a very outgoing man, he was nothing like as big a talker and in public nowhere near as articulate. He was much more humble and allowed his ability to do the talking for him.

As had happened on his previous trip to London, his ability did not quite prove to be a winner and he lost to Downes. However, even Terry accepted that he had not beaten the real Sugar Ray. The fight, in fact, almost did not come off. Downes faced claims from Lou Leavey and Walter Cartier, the two men who had first signed him up in Baltimore. They were now suing him for $18,000 for breach of contract. I guaranteed to pay Downes' court costs and put him in touch with an uncle of mine, a New York lawyer called Herman Levine. We won the case but I still ended up with a legal bill of around £2,000.

Sugar Ray remained a favourite of mine and some years after the Downes fight, I brought him back to England for a personal appearance tour and then got him on stage for the 'Sunday Night at the London Palladium' show, co-starring Shirley Bassey. The audience loved him. In many ways his drawing power as a boxer never dimmed and I had vivid proof of this when his visit to London, for the Downes fight, coincided with an amateur contest I had organized at Wembley between Great Britain and the Soviet Union in aid of the Variety Club. I mentioned to the Russians that Sugar Ray was in town and asked if they would like to meet him. I didn't think the Russians would know who he was – but, boy, they knew all about him. They drove me crazy, it was as if they were lining up to see a saint; and of course, Sugar Ray was marvellous with them.

BOXING is like roulette. You watch the ball spin in the wheel and you never know where it is going to end up. I am so glad that in my involvement with boxing, the roulette wheel spun and pointed in the direction of Mickey Duff.

Mickey has succeeded in boxing because he is dedicated to it. He lives, eats and breathes the sport. He has no other major interest. Mickey is still associated with people he was doing business with thirty or forty years ago, including promoters and managers in the United States, people like me and Terry Lawless. You can't find anyone else in boxing who has lasted as long with their associates as Mickey Duff.

Just one example of his honesty will suffice. Mickey went to Japan on our joint behalf to promote a fight between Johnny Famechon and Fighting Harada. At the last minute, a Japanese businessman came and gave him $20,000 in cash to allow him to advertise round the ring. There was no possible way that I could have known about it. Yet Mickey came back with the $20,000 and split the money with me.

A very knowledgeable man, who reads a lot, there are not many subjects on which Mickey can't hold a conversation and he would have been successful in almost any field. If his politics, being Conservative, are opposite to mine – and we have argued long and hard about it – this has not affected our friendship or relationship.

The son of a Rabbi who came to this country from Cracow in Poland when Mickey was nine, he and I first came across each other at the gym in Fitzroy Square just after the war. I remember going to his father's synagogue in Bournemouth in the morning, then watching him that same evening boxing under the nom de pugilist, Mickey Duff (he took the idea from the name James Cagney had in the film 'Cash And Carry'). His father had no idea what he was up to, that this Mickey Duff was Morris Prager, his son. As a young amateur who used to box in the professional gyms, Mickey sparred a lot with a fighter called Dave Crowley, a former British champion, and was a very brash boy for his age.

Our friendship should never have got started, for on the first two occasions we met, Mickey stitched me up. The first piece of business I did with him was when he took £5 off me for a ten-shilling ticket to see a Canadian sensation called Danny Webb, who was fighting at the Queensbury Club, now the Prince Edward Theatre. Mickey was equally smart when we had our first encounter in the boxing game. As I have mentioned, the first professional boxer I managed was Billy Thompson, who introduced me to another promising fighter, a lightweight called Al Wilburn. He hadn't fought as a professional but looked a good prospect, so I brought him down to London to train.

The time came for him to be tested and the opportunity arrived out of the blue. Mickey, now fighting professionally, was on a show at the Mile End Arena. His opponent pulled out and when I heard this, I offered Wilburn as a substitute. The promoter jumped at it and Mickey's manager agreed. We arrived at the Arena and as I walked in, I saw Mickey standing at the door. I said, 'What are you doing? Why aren't you in the dressing room?'

'I haven't got an opponent,' he replied.

'What are you talking about? Al Wilburn's here.'

'I'm not fighting Al Wilburn.'

'What do you mean, you're not fighting Al Wilburn? Your manager has agreed to it.'

'In that case, my manager can fight him.'

Mickey, who was eighteen, didn't want the fight because he knew all about Al Wilburn, knew what a tremendous puncher he was and knew his amateur record. Even then Mickey, who was five years my junior, knew more about boxing and managing than his manager. I tried everything in the book to get him in the ring – the anger, the soft-sell – but he would not budge. From somewhere they conjured up an easy opponent for him, and Wilburn was left high and dry.

Needless to say, Mickey was right: Wilburn was a very dangerous man in the ring. Mickey is a tremendous judge of boxing and boxers and has won a fortune betting on fights, putting money on in Las Vegas and boasting a record that is probably around the eighty per cent mark, a phenomenal return.

However, despite this, I got to know and like him. Self interest played a part. I realized that if I was to be involved with boxing, I needed help. Mickey, who had had sixty-five professional fights, knew he was never going to be anything special inside the ring, but he knew the business inside out. I was well aware that while the number of boxers I was managing was rising, I did not know enough about the game to go into the corner during the fight. This amazed the old-timers who were managing in the Fifties. They would say to me: 'If you're not good enough to go in the corner, how can you manage them?'

I took comfort from the old story about a sexton who is sacked by the pompous chairman of the church committee because when the chairman asks the sexton to witness his signature on a document, the sexton says he can't do it because he can't write. Some friends take pity on the sexton and help him start a shop; the business expands and as the years roll by, he eventually ends up as chairman of the church committee. One day the current sexton comes to him and asks him to sign the parish minutes, and the chairman says he can't because he is unable to write.

'My God, sir, you've been so successful and you can't write. Imagine how successful you would have been if you could!'

'If I could write, I'd still be doing your job,' says the chairman.

That is how I felt with the boxers I managed. From the beginning I implicitly trusted Mickey and besides, as I said, boxing was a sideline rather than my main business. Mickey came on board not to manage but to travel with the boxers, who came to rely on him. These relationships were not always easy. I remember the problems Mickey had with Lloyd Honeyghan, whom he managed and who in 1986 was undisputed world welterweight champion. Honeyghan, a very difficult and arrogant man, had been sounding off abut Mickey and picking up a good few column inches in the press. When asked about this obvious friction that existed between Honeyghan and himself, Mickey replied that there was nothing in their contract that said they had to like each other! That said it all and really drew the sting from Honeyghan's attacks. He went quiet after that.

Mickey, in a classic case of poacher turned gamekeeper, would think nothing of driving fifty miles in the middle of the night to find a substitute fighter for a show. His other ruse in those early days, when there were a lot of homes without phones, was to call the local police station and persuade the beat officer to go and knock on the boxer's door to get him to call urgently. He did that more than once. My relationship with Mickey evolved and because he knew the business so well, he started promoting fights. He became a matchmaker for various promoters and in the process, a thorn in the side of Jack Solomons, the number one promoter of the time.

Solomons, an East Ender, had been a fishmonger. He got into boxing because he had tried to be a fighter, wasn't very successful in the ring but was so fascinated by the sport that he decided to become a promoter. He was something of a rough diamond but he knew what people wanted and he gave it to them, which explained his success. He had a great advantage in that soon after the war, he very quickly made a tie-up with Mike Jacobs and the International Boxing Club in America, so that all the American fighters who came over here could only come under his promotion. It was many years later that I broke the Solomons stranglehold when I brought over Jimmy Carter, a former world lightweight champion, and that opened the floodgates.

By the time Mickey and I started promoting, Solomons was well established, being much older than us. I suppose you could say we unseated him, although that wasn't our plan at the beginning. It came about because Solomons would not give us space to operate. In 1959, Mickey became the matchmaker for Ronnie Ezra and Dave Braitman, rival promoters to

Solomons who ran shows at the old Empress Hall. Through the British Boxing Board's Southern Area Council, which was controlled by Solomons, Mickey's licence was suspended and he was told that only if he stopped making matches for Ezra and Braitman could he have it back. The ironic aspect of it was that Solomons' opposition created the powerful alliance between Mickey and Harry Levene. I persuaded Mickey to go and make matches for him and the whole business just boomed, especially for Mickey. He never liked Levene, but the chance to rival Solomons was irresistible.

Levene was a very contentious character, honest but quick-tempered. His family had been killed in a bombing raid during the war and that made him very unsentimental and precise. As a young man, he travelled a lot, and managed his first boxer when he was still a teenager. These experiences made him a very dapper man about town and he managed Larry Gains and Kid Berg for a time. He was also closely tied up with a northern newspaper reporter called Norman Hurst, who was a very influential boxing writer. In a way Harry became the front man for Hurst, who obviously, because of his position, was not allowed to handle fighters himself.

Compared to the spiky Levene, doing business with Solomons was never unpleasant. He was very affable, generous and to the point. There was never any long, protracted haggling with him and in his day he did a marvellous job and was a great promoter. But like a lot of powerful people, when they have been unchallenged and ruled the roost for a long period, they can end up as dictators. Solomons was like that. You could do everything he wanted for 364 days of the year and then decide to go it alone on the 365th – and that was it, you were his sworn enemy and there was no way back. He would brook no argument.

Mickey's association with Levene only increased Solomons' anger and he blew his top. When the news reached him, he called me on the phone and was ranting and raving. When I was able to get a word in, I told him that he had brought this on his own head. After Mickey and I lobbied to remove his supporters from the Southern Area Council, he never forgave me, in particular, and kept trying to get at me by putting it around that I was manipulating the whole of the boxing scene. He was smart enough not to defame me, but nevertheless he created a storm and it resulted in a legal case that has become part of textbook law.

On Sunday 3 November 1963, *The People* newspaper ran a story on the front page: 'BIG BOXING PROBE IS ON – OFFICIAL'. It read: 'A full scale official enquiry is to be held this week into the operations of boxing managers and promoters – in particular a man known in the fight game as "Mr X". His identity is, however, no secret. He is Mr Jarvis Astaire, a wealthy 40-year-old company director. He is only called Mr X because other boxing personalities fear his growing power.' In this piece by Peter Campling, Solomons, described as once the biggest promoter in Britain, was quoted as saying he was fed up with a syndicate which, he claimed, was squeezing him out of business. He went on to say that other boxing managers would not place their fighters on his shows for fear of upsetting the syndicate. The day before this was published, Campling contacted me, saying he had just spoken to Solomons, who said I was Mr X. I told Campling that it was all rubbish and I was happy to meet him on the following Tuesday to explain everything to him, but publication meant the opportunity never arrived.

The papers had been speculating for some time about the power of Mr X and in my lawyer's opinion, had Mr X existed, what was being written about him was defamatory. Now, without repeating the allegations, *The People* had made me Mr X and as far as I was concerned, anyone who had read that *People* article, and the ones before it referring to all the misdeeds of this Mr X, would have linked the two. I stood defamed. I sued *The People* for libel, Campling and Odhams Press Ltd being named on the writ.

The case found its way to the House of Lords, where my

QC, Desmond Ackner, argued that a reasonable reader would have taken on board all the information about Mr X and then, having read *The People*, associated it with me. For the defence, Mr Colin Duncan, QC, argued that *The People* could not be responsible for what others had printed and that the words used would only have relevance to *The People* article. I lost the case on the grounds that it was not reasonable to argue that the readers of *The People* were thinking of me in a poor light because of what they read elsewhere. I was not allowed to use this as evidence of libel by *The People*. The claim ended up sitting on the books, unresolved.

The decision astounded me and my lawyers. Indeed, it became a major topic in the text books of law students because many in the profession regarded it as a wrong decision – and still do. Consider that then and today, you have media moguls who own many different newspapers and through a cross-fertilization they can allege what they like of someone, name him and get away with it. For example, *The Sun* could run stories about a Mr X as the keeper of brothels in London. That could be followed up by a different publication in the same group, say the *News of the World*, who reveal that 'Mr X' is Joe whoever, without mentioning the original allegations. If my case set the precedent then there is nothing Joe can do about it. It seems absurd.

I came out of the case facing costs of around £5,000. In the meantime, *The People* had a new editor, Robert Edwards, who had joined them from the *Daily Express* and was later to become the editor of the *Sunday Mirror*. I knew him well and at his invitation went with him to the Savoy for lunch, where we agreed to a truce and the paper picked up all the costs.

The allegations of *The People* prompted by Solomons' spite and envy were ridiculous, just as were the claims some twenty-one years later by the *Sunday Times*, in December 1984, that I was involved in a 'cartel' – their word – with Mickey Duff, Mike Barrett and Terry Lawless. According to the paper, we were operating a closed shop, where we cleaned up at the expense of everyone else – including the boxers managed by Lawless.

It was true that we had had an agreement since 1978 with Terry, guaranteeing him a share of the profits (or losses) from our promotions, but the idea that as a result he was a soft touch when negotiating on behalf on his boxers was ridiculous. I had a number of direct dealings with Terry and found out that when he is in there battling for his fighters, he wants the lot – the right matches, the easiest opponents and the most money. He was, and still is, a good manager. If I were a boxer, I would be more than happy to have him on my side.

After the *Sunday Times* story was published, the British Boxing Board of Control announced they were going to hold an enquiry. When it came, in February 1985, not only were we cleared after the six-hour hearing, we were given a commendation by the Board, who said had it not been for our very active participation, 'boxing would not be in as healthy a state as it is now'.

They had gone through the figures of the purses paid to boxers under our management and found that they compared more than favourably to those of boxers managed by others. The Board said there was overwhelming evidence that the boxers had not suffered financially. For our part, we agreed that we would make sure that all the boxers under us would be made aware of the agreement.

The *Sunday Times* reported that the Boxing Board had cleared us but said that it would be a different story when the Office of Fair Trading investigated. However, shortly afterwards, the OFT decided that the matter did not justify their involvement. The fact that they decided there were no grounds for an investigation passed by apparently unnoticed by the *Sunday Times*.

I've already talked about the affair of Harold Smith and the Wells Fargo Bank. On the back of that, *The Sunday Times*, in their 'Inside Track' column, claimed Mickey Duff had used stolen money for promoting boxing. He sued and won that libel case, receiving damages of £10,000 while the newspaper picked up costs of around £300,000. If Mickey had lost it would have cost him around £250,000 but at that time he felt the paper had gone too far and he 'had to stand up and be counted'.

There are a lot of myths about the boxing business, and a general belief that the people involved in the game are smarter than they really are. I recall Joe Bugner, a big draw in his way and a man of great talent who could swing wildly between the extremes of good and bad. On occasions he put on the most timid performances. When he fought Joe Frazier in 1973 at Earls Court – Frazier was an ex-world champion with a real chance of getting back into the frame – he put up a magnificent performance. He did the same with Ali in Las Vegas that year. But he could also blow it all. He had a fight with Jack Bodell and, amazingly, lost. That left Bodell free to fight Joe Solomons' man, Dan McAlinden, and Bugner was out of the picture.

The Bodell-McAlinden fight was in Birmingham in June 1972 but being shown on BBC Television, while in London, on closed-circuit TV, I had the Ali versus Jerry Quarry fight. On the day the fight was due to take place, I received a call from Fritz Wiener, a Hamburg furrier who was manager of the European heavyweight champion Jurgen Blin. He wanted to know whether I was going to Birmingham for the fight and if I was, could he come with me? I told him about the TV show at the Hilton Hotel in London and said he would be better off coming to that, even though he was meant to be meeting Solomons. I told him he could catch up with Solomons later.

Wiener did not speak English but, as I have said, I speak enough German, so he arrived in London with his agent Max Stadtlander and came to the Hilton, where I always had a suite when we were doing a satellite show. We had a control room there and we watched the Bodell-McAlinden fight in my suite. Bodell lasted just one round. McAlinden was flattered by his performance and he looked a 'killer'. This fight coincided with

London Fashion Week and among my party were two friends of mine who were in the dress business. They had with them two stunning looking models, both German, who wanted to come to the hotel to watch the Ali fight. Wiener developed a big interest in one of the girls and although I kept saying there was something I wanted to talk to him about, he kept making excuses. In the meantime he had seen McAlinden murder Bodell so I said to him, 'Why do you want Blin to fight him? He's a destroyer. Box Bugner instead.'

I had some standard boxing promoter contracts with me and eventually managed to detach Wiener from the girl and told him I wasn't leaving him until we had talked about a Bugner-Blin fight. In his eagerness to get back to the girl, he signed a blank contract, so I had got Bugner a fight with Blin and now it was McAlinden left out in the cold. By sheer chance, Bugner and his manager Andy Smith were downstairs in the Hilton, as guests of the Anglo-American Sporting Club. They couldn't believe what had happened – it was an opportunity not to be missed and Bugner went on to take the European title, which led to his second fight against Ali, for the world title, in Kuala Lumpur, Malaysia.

As for Wiener and the girl, she made a discreet exit and left, saying she had a sore throat. I suppose you could say the girl was being original at least. After all, she could have claimed a headache.

11

Frank and Mike

The story of Frank Bruno can be told in various ways. Frank, himself, has told it more than once. In my version Frank fulfils a very special purpose. As his promoter for many years, many of my various interests were brought together: boxing, the entertainment business and Wembley Stadium.

In some ways the fact that Bruno ever became a professional boxer was a major surprise. Poor eyesight meant he could not pass the medical demanded by the British Boxing Board of Control. David MacLeod, an eye surgeon at the Moorfield Hospital in London, recommended that Bruno see a surgeon in Bogota, Colombia. Bruno travelled there, the operation was carried out successfully and he was free to box, starting his professional career on 17 March 1982 against Lupe Guerra at the Albert Hall. He won in the first round, knocking out Guerra. I was involved in that promotion along with Mickey Duff and Mike Barrett. Terry Lawless was Bruno's manager and he is the man who made Frank Bruno – irrespective of what Bruno and others may have since said or claimed.

Our partnership with Bruno worked marvellously for many years. True, we got a lot of flak from the press that Bruno was a manufactured boxer and we were carefully selecting opponents for him. But in boxing that sort of sniping goes with the territory. The fact is that in that first year Bruno had ten fights and won the lot, stopping all of his opponents and boxing just seventeen rounds. They were all at home apart from the victory over Ali Lukasa in the October, which took place in Berlin. The furthest Bruno ever went in a fight in that first year was four rounds, against Ron Gibbs at Wembley in May. Over the years it grew tougher. James 'Bonecrusher' Smith knocked him out at Wembley Arena in 1984 and Bruno's career developed a pattern of easy wins followed by a check. Two years later he had his first crack at the World Boxing Association world title held by Tim Witherspoon, who stopped him in the eleventh round, at Wembley Stadium, although Bruno was ahead until the ninth.

However, by 1988 Bruno was ready to challenge for the title again, this time against Mike Tyson. By that stage Tyson had dismantled every other challenger apart from Witherspoon and held all three versions of the world title. Witherspoon had fallen out with Tyson's promoter Don King, so that meant he was out of favour with the King-influenced World Boxing Council and was pushed down the rankings. He also wasn't in training and so Bruno became the number one challenger.

Until then, arranging fights for Bruno had been routine. But with Tyson we found ourselves in shark-infested waters and it was an experience that neither I nor Duff will forget. We had begun by negotiating with Tyson's managers, Jim Jacobs and Bill Cayton. We felt the fight should be in London because Bruno was no draw in America – all they had seen of him was on television and then only to see him beaten. We managed to arrange a provisional date for the fight at Wembley Stadium sometime in May or June 1988.

Then the first spanner appeared in the works. The previous year, Michael Spinks, the International Boxing Federation heavyweight champion, had been stripped of his title after withdrawing from Don King's so-called championship tournament, a series of bouts promoted with the American pay-TV station Home Box Office to unify the heavyweight division. Now suddenly Spinks, managed by Ronald 'Butch' Lewis, a Philadelphia car dealer, took King, the Las Vegas Hilton and HBO to court for the right to fight Tyson for the undisputed heavyweight crown. The case was heard in

Nevada, where the Hilton Hotels Corporation were particularly strong. In America that sort of home advantage can count for a lot, but despite this Spinks and Lewis emerged winners. So Tyson had to fight Spinks and we had to take a step backwards. Tyson won that fight in Atlantic City in June 1988, knocking out Spinks in the first round, and Bruno moved once again to the top of the queue.

Now came a more troublesome spanner. In February that year, Tyson had married the black actress Robin Givens. She had become quite well known thanks to a television series called 'Top of the Class'. Their courtship and then marriage made her a lot more famous, but part of the baggage in this relationship was Givens' mother, a bright and fiercely ambitious woman. She started moving in on Tyson's professional life and he was so smitten with Givens and so impressed by the mother, an educated and sophisticated woman – the only people he'd met like that before were white – that he was happy for this to happen. Tyson felt that socially he had arrived. He was obsessed with Givens and for a while was totally dominated by her and her mother.

In the meantime, there were problems with Tyson's management. Jacobs had been ill for some time but now he was deteriorating rapidly. People who saw him every day probably did not notice it, but I met with him occasionally, often months apart, and it was very apparent to me that there had been a sharp and rapid decline. Cayton, too, had health problems and was in hospital with suspected heart trouble when Jacobs died in March from leukaemia. This was the opportunity for Mrs Tyson to move in. She rang Cayton, who was actually in hospital at the time having tests, and announced that he was out and she was now running her husband's affairs.

All through this we were keeping in close touch with Cayton and eventually were able to enter into a contract with him. A number of letters had passed between us and though there were some slight differences, there was nothing serious enough to put the deal in jeopardy. Cayton was keen on it because he viewed Bruno as an easy opponent and he and Tyson would be getting an awful lot of money for taking the fight. The complication was the involvement of Mrs Tyson and her mother. Cayton seemed to be walking something of a tightrope with them. Such was their influence that they had barred Tyson from seeing Cayton, his own manager. I saw for myself how hard Cayton had to work to even persuade his boxer to come and see him in his office in New York. Tyson came, but he did not stay long. Robin and mother-in-law proved too big a lure and he was quickly off back to them in Las Vegas.

Inevitably, lawyers were everywhere at this point. Tyson had his own, Michael Winston – who had acted for his mother-in-law – and we met in my New York hotel. Winston came along with a long list of creative demands which only served to demonstrate his lack of knowledge of boxing. By this stage we did at least have a new date for the fight, 3 September 1988, but Winston was clearly intent on cutting Cayton out of the deal as much as possible. I was not prepared to betray Cayton, even though his position was weak – he was threatening to take out an injunction against Tyson if he fought without his authority, but the bald truth is that in those sort of circumstances you don't get injunctions like that. A manager cannot stop his client from performing and earning a living; the only remedy he has is a claim for damages.

Cayton also had another interest in the fight going ahead that I did not know about at the time. He had an agreement between HBO and his own company Big Fights that he and Jacobs received a commission on the foreign sales of television rights. So not only did he want to win the battle of wills between himself and Tyson's new support team, the mother-in-law and her lawyer, he wanted to protect his commission on the foreign TV rights as well.

The final complication was provided by Don King, who was trying to play a more significant role in Tyson's career. Until then he had just been the promoter behind Jacobs and Cayton, but he had what are called 'promotional contracts' – a curse in the sport because it means in effect that the promoter is a manager, something which is not allowed in America. The effect of such contracts is that you are dealing with two managers, the men running the fighter and then the promoter. King had the heavyweight division champions and challengers tied to these promotional contracts and as a result Jacobs and Cayton had been compelled to use King as a promoter for the up-and-coming Tyson, because King was supplying the opponents.

Now King began to feel, with good reason, that Cayton was going to dispense with his services. Tyson, as the greatest heavyweight boxer, did not need King to produce opponents and his manager had every reason to fear King's role in the sport – he is a very expensive luxury and money just pours through him like water through a sieve. As luck would have it, King fell out with Tyson's mother-in-law and so his influence was suddenly brought down more than a peg or two.

Eventually negotiations reached a point where I met with the various parties involved. I laid it on the line. I told Cayton that he would never get an injunction, that I had a duty to Bruno to make the fight happen and that I had cleared everything to make sure Wembley Stadium was the venue. 'Bill, I think wisdom should prevail, discretion should get the better part of valour and you should reach some sort of settlement with Tyson,' I said. So the ground for the great reconciliatory meeting was laid. It took place in Donald Trump's office at his newly-built Trump Tower, the hotel and property tycoon having injected himself into the situation. He, Tyson, Cayton and the lawyers disappeared into a room and after a long wait they re-emerged to announce that they had finally reached an agreement – Tyson would go ahead with the Bruno fight on 3 September at Wembley Stadium.

So after many months of hard work, we at last had a result and a fight. A press conference was called for the next day to tell the world. But with Tyson things are never what they seem and when it was his turn to speak, he simply said, 'I'm not boxing on 3 September.' He went on to say that he wouldn't be ready for Bruno on that date and I left America for London with it all up in the air again. The lawyers met again to discuss this and agreed that once Tyson saw some sense they would get the show back on the calendar, a date eventually being chosen for early October. I was back in the States to see Tyson sign up for that 8 October date, which was about as late in the year as we could manage in England for an outdoor show.

But signatures on contracts meant little with Tyson and more trouble was brewing with him. First he had injured himself during a brawl in the street with another fighter called Mitch Green, who was eventually awarded $2,000 damages. Then he had a row with his wife, roared off into the night in his car and smacked into a tree, breaking his hand. The domestic unrest was becoming quite serious and Don King seized on it to force his way back in with Tyson. As King would modestly put it, he 'came to Tyson's rescue', seeing off his wife and mother-in-law and making sure that Tyson kept hold of his possessions, the cars and the money.

So here we were with a fighter with a broken hand and an erupting marriage but holding a contract for him to get in the ring with Bruno. The only problem is that contracts don't fight and it was the old 'you can lead a horse to water, but you can't make him drink' syndrome. We needed all the boxing organizations on board but now King, who had a great deal of influence with the WBC and particularly its president, Jose Sulaiman, was in a position to make waves and the WBC started making noises about removing Bruno from his position as number one challenger, on the grounds that he had been inactive for so long. On top of that, they started to question the validity of the Bruno-Tyson fight contract.

We were getting close to mid winter when an outdoor show in England would be impossible, but I bluffed by saying Wembley could be turned into an indoor stadium, something that had been investigated in some detail in the past but had turned out to be totally impractical. I also leaked the story to the *Daily Mail* and the paper published a drawing showing everyone how it could be done. I immediately faxed this to everybody I could think of in America – it implied we were ready for Tyson whenever he wanted.

By now there was yet another problem, posed by Cayton. He had negotiated a deal for Tyson to fight Jose Ribalta, who had gone ten rounds with Tyson two years earlier. This rematch, under a WBC banner, could have been a big threat to our promotion and through the British Boxing Board of Control – a very valued constituent member of the WBC – I managed to build up some support for our case that Tyson should not fight anyone before Bruno.

Meanwhile, King was still coming at us and he played a new card. Tyson, he advised, should not come to England to fight. His place was in America and besides, he had not been a happy traveller. Tyson had accompanied Robin Givens to a film location in Russia and fought Tony Tubbs in Japan, and on both occasions he had an unhappy time. But from what I'd seen of his visits to London, he had no problems with England. In the build-up to the long-delayed Bruno fight, we had brought him over for a dinner where he was the guest of honour, and he did TV comment pieces on the Bruno-James Tillis fight which took place at Wembley in March 1987. Tyson seemed fine with London, yet King convinced him that it was not a good idea to go there.

The positive side of all this was that the fight was becoming very big news indeed. Tyson's notoriety following the bust-up with Robin Givens, the fight with Green and the car accident had given it an edge. And we had not failed to make the most of it for Bruno, taking him to New York for a big press conference and getting him to issue a challenge to Tyson to 'come and sort it out'. From being a dull walkover for Tyson, his forthcoming battle with Bruno had become a big box-office draw and the interest in where it was eventually going to be staged also started to build up.

The whole thing started getting resolved when Donald Trump approached me and so did the people running the Hilton Hotel in Las Vegas, via a long-standing friend of mine named Ben Lambert, who was also a director of the Hilton Hotels Corporation. He asked me in late October, early November of 1988 if I would talk to John Giovenco, president of Hilton Hotels Nevada, which owned the Hilton in Las Vegas. I said I couldn't approach Giovenco direct – that would look as if I was going behind Cayton's back – but if he called me I would be willing to talk. I was still holding Bruno and Tyson to a Wembley date which, as I have explained, had now become a bluff but was maintaining interest in the fight and boosting the TV rights potential.

Giovenco did call and it became clear that he was very interested in putting the fight on in Las Vegas. Since I had everybody under contract, I felt at liberty to deal with him. There were, of course, certain conditions which I spelled out clearly. There had to be compensation for Wembley Stadium, and I would only sell the rights to the fight if Bruno was prepared to go to America for it and he was compensated for travelling. That brought Bruno and his manager Lawless in on the discussions. In truth, however, I was holding on to this whole package by the skin of my teeth. For all my public protestations about the fight still taking place at Wembley, I knew it could not and it was Giovenco's call that was making Bruno-Tyson possible.

I was well aware that time was not on our side. If the delays had gone on much longer, it would have been hard to refute the WBC claims that Bruno should be removed as number one challenger because he was inactive. Our objective had to be simply to get Tyson in the ring – only then were we in business and if Bruno had to go to America to achieve that, then so be it. We finally struck a deal which meant Bruno virtually doubled his money, getting a million pounds more, and I negotiated £125,000 compensation for Wembley. The finishing touches to the deal were done on my behalf by the World

Boxing Association lawyer James Binns, because my father had died in the first weeks of December 1988. These were tough, business-like negotiations and eventually I flew out to Los Angeles with Bruno and Lawless to officially announce the fight.

Again, if I thought the war was won, I was mistaken. Now there was a dispute with ITV, with whom we had not dealt for years; in our promotions we always worked with the BBC. ITV had dropped boxing for a number of years. Then when they became interested again, they dealt exclusively with Frank Warren, who had become a competitor - although as I saw it, the TV company were the competition. Warren had promoted all his shows with ITV for years and I had no wish to do business with them; my loyalties were to the BBC. However, when the Bruno-Tyson fight was scheduled for Wembley, ITV started proceedings against me to stop me selling the rights to the BBC. The basis for this was a contract they had with Don King and an agreement with Cayton which they claimed gave them the rights to a number of Tyson fights, including this one. It was a situation that I had foreseen and when dealing with Cayton, I had said that I could not possibly enter into a deal for the Bruno-Tyson fight which allowed ITV access to it. The BBC were confident they would have it, but all the delays meant that the case went on the back-burner.

Once the fight was switched to Las Vegas, I had the TV rights transferred to Bruno himself, believing that ITV would never sue him – but they did and lost. In the end, I sold the live rights to Sky TV, which was their first major event, and the BBC had a delayed showing of the fight. We also screened the fight live in many closed-circuit venues, as at the time only a few people had Sky.

As for Bruno, his quest to be world champion failed in Las Vegas on 25 February 1989 when Tyson stopped him in round five. However, he gave a good account of himself and, true to the British tradition of loving a loser, he returned home hailed as a hero. His chase of the world title, in between winters spent appearing in pantomime, continued. His third shot at it came in October 1993 when Lennox Lewis beat him in Cardiff, stopping him in the seventh round. Lewis, the Canadian Olympic medal-winning boxer who had rediscovered his British roots, could lay claim to be the first Briton to take the heavyweight title since Bob Fitzsimmons in the days of Queen Victoria.

Subsequently Bruno split from Terry Lawless and managed himself, with his lawyer Henri Brandman. At their request we initially continued to promote Bruno's fights, and we put him on against Jose Ribalta, Carl 'The Truth' Williams and Jesse Ferguson. After that, however, the BBC dropped Bruno from their schedules and Mickey Duff and I decided to follow suit. We made no attempt to renew Bruno's contract with us and he was promoted by Frank Warren in what turned out to be Warren's ill-fated partnership with Don King. Bruno finally achieved his dream at the fourth attempt in September 1995 at Wembley Stadium when he outpointed Oliver McCall, the man who had relieved Lewis of his title. Bruno, the perpetual challenger, had become champion. All that is not part of my story, but it is sad to note that somewhere along the way Bruno seemed to forget the people who had made it happen for him – particularly Terry Lawless – in those tough days when he was starting out and when nobody outside the small circle of Mickey, Terry and myself held out much hope for him.

BOXING has changed a great deal since the 1970s. Fighters have suddenly become rebellious and the likes of Barry McGuigan, Nigel Benn and Chris Eubank have all had their run-ins with managers. While you would never expect boxers to agree to all the wishes of their managers, I do feel there are offers floating around that make them suddenly dissatisfied. The British Board of Control is these days short of funds and is therefore to a large degree impotent in attempting to enforce its regulations. Its problem is always the fear that its decisions will be challenged in court, where it does not have the same kind of money to fight a case as the major players it is trying to keep in line. The current chairman is Leonard 'Nipper' Read, who at one time was head of the national crime squad and was a 'lion' tough policeman. Today he seems more of a 'lamb' as he allows the transgressors to go unpunished, a state of affairs he must find frustrating. I must confess that I don't often meet boxers nowadays. I can't remember the last time I was in a gymnasium and it is many years since I last managed a fighter – that was Evan Armstrong, who had been a particularly conscientious champion boxer and a good friend.

When Evan retired in 1974, I became involved only in promotion and then largely with television. I would say that ninety per cent of my promotional activity in boxing since then has been to do with TV, doing deals for live telecasts and for video, selling film rights of our fights, that sort of thing. The day-to-day management of boxers doesn't interest me, but I did enjoy the business side of it and the sense of achievement. It is exciting to steer a young boxer and watch him become a champion. However, I am very aware that the sort of boxing business I had could never be repeated. When I think of the deals I did with George Parnassus and how we didn't even have contracts, I realize what a pleasure it was. You couldn't dream of doing that today.

I have never taken a starry-eyed view of the fight game, so I have no truck with people who try to defend boxing on medical grounds. They are crazy. There's not a single boxer goes into the ring these days who is not fully conversant with the risks he is taking, just as every single motor racing driver always knows them. What I would say is that from my practical experience, dating from my earliest involvement in the Boys' Club movement, where boxing is probably the major sport, there is no question that it is beneficial for boys in certain socio-economic groups. It teaches them discipline which they might otherwise not have. It's the sort of discipline that a lot of boys previously picked up in National Service, which they now don't have the opportunity to do. It is a big chance for a boy from the ghetto who wants recognition and to be better than the next man.

Of course, I feel upset when I see someone like Michael Watson, who suffered a terrible brain injury in a fight with Chris Eubank, but then I feel upset when I see the burns scars of the racing driver Niki Lauda. My view is that if you banned boxing, you wouldn't necessarily drive it underground, because there wouldn't be enough money in it, but there would be a lot of bootleg fights. Certain countries wouldn't follow the ban. For example, Sweden has a ban on boxing but Finland and Denmark don't, so the Swedes go and box in Finland or Denmark. The same would happen here. Fights would move to France. What good would that do?

12

Bookies and Horses

Terry Downes has already figured in this story. It was in showing his fight in 1964 that I made the breakthrough in closed-circuit television, but he has played a more prominent part in my life. My association with him was fruitful, both in the ring and because of the avenues it opened up for me, and his is a story, now little remembered, that is fascinating.

The brief outline of his life is easily told. Terry Downes, the middleweight boxer, the Paddington boy who ended up in America, joined and boxed for the US Marines and then came back home to win the world title. Terry's sister Sylvia was a trapeze artiste with the Ringling Brothers circus in America and she had gone out there as a teenager to perform. While the troupe was in Baltimore, however, she had lost her arm in a freak bus accident. All the immediate family moved out to support her, Terry went to school there and then on to the Marines, for whom he boxed fifty-one times. He was actually selected for the US Olympic team before it was discovered he was British, and it was following a trip back to England that he turned professional. Fighting for the Fisher Amateur Club in the Seymour Hall near Paddington, Terry was ruled out of a bout after a clash of heads gave him a tiny nick under one eye. He was livid with the decision and said he would never box in another amateur contest – and he didn't.

I had been recommended to Terry as a manager by Harry Alley, a young boxer from Paddington, and Terry contacted me through Jack Solomons and I later co-managed him with

Sam Burns, a shrewd and experienced boxing manager who by coincidence was subsequently involved with me at the bookmakers William Hill. Sam had great success as a manager with Tony Sibson, who fought Marvin Hagler for the world title, and before that Kevin Finnegan and his brother Chris, who was the last Briton to win a boxing gold medal at the Olympic Games and came close to taking the world light-heavyweight title from Bob Foster in a great fight at Wembley Arena.

What helped Terry was his chirpy Londoner nature – he was a man who knew the value of publicity and was always ready with a quip. When he lost to Dick Tiger, a very surprising result, he held court in the dressing room afterwards and told the press, 'I suddenly thought to myself, this fellow is big for a middleweight . . . Then I realized I was lying down and he was standing up!'

But underneath this bonhomie was a tough man who did not stand for any nonsense. He made a lot of money and that allowed him to buy a luxurious home out at Mill Hill in north London. Shortly after moving there, he received a death threat. Someone said they were going to bomb his house unless he handed over £5,000. Terry called me and I told him he had to get in touch with the police.

It was agreed that Terry would deliver the ransom money and the police would be close behind. Somehow the police lost Terry and he was standing on the pavement when a man approached him dressed in motorbike leathers and with a crash helmet on. Terry at first thought this guy was a policeman, but the penny dropped when the man said, 'Have you got it?'

'I've got it for you, all right,' replied Terry and thumped the man. At that point the police and one of Terry's sparring partners, a man called Lenny Cain, came around the corner. The motorcyclist was arrested and carted off to the police station. Terry was allowed to sit in on the questioning and when the investigating officer asked the blackmailer why he had done it, the man said, 'I needed the money and he's got plenty.' Terry went potty and said, 'I've got something else for you,' and knocked the man out. The police started calling for a doctor and Terry told them not to bother with the doctor and instead send for a coroner. Terry wasn't charged with anything because the police realized that his wife and children had been threatened and the blackmailer had been trying to get his hands on some easy money, earnings that Terry had picked up through hard work.

Throughout his career, Terry was looking to invest his boxing money and then his father, Dick Downes, came up with the idea of opening betting shops in the high street. It was something I had seen in Scotland, where they were technically illegal, but run openly. Mr Downes' idea seemed good to me and I said so to Sam Burns, who had for many years run the trade betting department of William Hill, the business that bets with other bookmakers rather than the public. I suggested he should go into the betting business with Terry. Sam agreed, left William Hill and I backed them, basically by finding freehold properties for the shops.

William Hill could have done the same thing right at the start. I already knew William well enough to have been invited to his daughter's engagement party. He was a big man; physically large and the sort of fellow to dominate proceedings. Whenever I went to a racecourse around that time, he was always there and you knew about it straight away, he had that sort of presence. We used to talk and got on well. Just when Terry and Sam were launching the betting shops, I was in Deauville having dinner with William and another bookmaker, Willie Preston. The subject of betting shops came up and William said they would be a disaster. I dared to disagree with him and being the dominant sort of man he was, he didn't like it. He became very hostile and unpleasant. I felt some of this was directed at Sam Burns, whom he had not forgiven for leaving his William Hill firm. We didn't meet again socially for seven years. When we did, he was ready to admit he had been mistaken.

In those early days, in 1961, it was not easy to get landlords to let their properties be used for betting shops. The law to allow off-course betting was just coming in, but even then it required some doing to find a property owner prepared to accept this business. I always remember a man in Harlesden, north-west London, who piously refused to let out his property if it was going to be used as a betting shop, because he was a lay preacher. That didn't stop him *selling* me the same building, at an inflated price.

Downes, having just won the world title by beating Paul Pender, opened the first shop in his old car showroom and was behind the counter for business on the opening day. I phoned through a £5 win-treble bet as a 'good luck' gesture, but ended up taking £70 off him when my horses came home. In fact that first day was a bit of an eye-opener for Terry, who believed all bookies were rich. The favourites romped in, leaving him down on the day. At the end of the first year, however, the business had made £40,000, a figure that was to be doubled in the next trading year.

I became a shareholder in the business and it expanded until there were thirty-eight shops. It reached the stage where the best move was to become a public company. To sell out would have been difficult because the concept of betting shops was still not well-established and it was an industry that lacked respectability. Then, however, I was introduced to the Hurst Park Syndicate, the company which owned the famous Hurst Park racecourse in Surrey, and a deal was done. They would sell the racecourse land to Wates for home-building and the £800,000 raised would be used to acquire the Burns and Downes betting business, through a mixture of shares and cash to expand the business. Terry and Sam were paid £180,000, with the same amount in ordinary shares. Sam became a director of the company and Terry was bound to serve as a director for three years. They also got £750,000 deferred shares which could be converted into ordinary shares once the Hurst Park Syndicate's profits climbed to £127,000 before tax.

We expanded the business, the company was going along nicely and it was then that William Hill made their approach. William realized he had missed the boat. Ladbrokes and Corals were in the betting shop business now and Jack Swift, one of the William Hill directors and a man I had known for years, approached me with an offer for the Hurst Park Syndicate. The bid was going through when Jack had a major falling out with Bill Balshaw, the William Hill chairman, and quit. The deal would see me join the William Hill board but I wasn't happy that Jack had gone, because he was the link in the takeover. I talked to him about it and he advised me to go ahead without him because it was a good business. I've always respected him for that and although I was not in business with him, I valued his fairness and honesty and when his son Brian, who was a jockey, became a trainer, I was his first patron.

William Hill announced their acquisition of Hurst Park at a lunch at the Cafe Royal and I remember William himself made one of his rare public appearances. He said to me – and we had not spoken since his tirade in Deauville – 'I'm glad you've joined the company because I'm looking to you to turn it into a real business. These fellows don't know what they are doing.' Jack Swift's departure created another space on the board and I was able to bring in Sam Burns with me. We did some good work for them, made some excellent acquisitions in Manchester and picked up several businesses in London.

We made great strides in catching up with Ladbrokes but even so we were still striving for some sort of public respectability. The opportunity to achieve that arrived through a familiar figure – Charles Clore.

If Charles was the catalyst for a chain of events that shaped my life, then I was able to repay him with the William Hill bookmaking connection. Soon after becoming a director of William Hill in 1972, I met Charles at a party, where he told me he thought I had a good deal and that he wouldn't mind becoming involved himself. At that point I was unaware that there was bad blood between Charles and William Hill, so I told Charles I could probably have some shares placed with him because the firm needed cash for a number of acquisitions we wanted to make. Virtually the next day, Charles' lawyer Leonard Sainer came on the phone and told me that I had got Charles very excited about the William Hill business. He had got the bit between his teeth and was not going to let go.

I put it to the William Hill board that Charles Clore was interested in investing in the company, but I received a pretty sharp negative response. Through Roy Sutterlin, another director, I discovered the reason. It seemed that Charles and William Hill had fallen out because William, who advised Charles on the building of his Stype stud farm, felt he had not received enough credit. However, still figuring that Clore's money – which he wanted at that point to be his personal investment, rather than that of his company Sears Holdings – would be more than welcome, I decided not to relay this snub back to Charles. Instead I arranged for him and William Hill to meet at the races in Deauville and the two men talked very amicably, so I was hopeful that something could be salvaged. Then in October, William, who had been in semi-retirement, suddenly died. I went to the funeral and, by absolute chance, gave William's nephew Chris Harper a lift back from the private chapel on William's Whitsbury Estate.

Harper ran the stud farm and he told me that his uncle's will stipulated that it was not to be sold while his wife Ivy was still alive. This was clearly going to put a lot of pressure on the business, because through another trustee of the will I had heard that the death duties on the estate were going to be considerable.

Four weeks later Leonard Sainer was in touch with me again to find out what was going on with the William Hill empire, so I told him about the will and the likelihood of the estate having to sell shares to cover the death duties. Sainer then said there had been a slight change of heart from Charles. Instead of a personal investment, he was now talking of Sears making a bid for the company. Was this a serious offer? I asked Sainer. 'Yes,' he replied.

I called Bill Balshaw, who was staying at the company flat in Grosvenor House. I arrived there at 4.30pm to see Allan Wyborn leaving. He was one of the William Hill trustees, a member of the board and an accountant. Still in the flat with Balshaw was one of his closest allies, Harry Hodgson, the company secretary. It transpired that Wyborn had just left after spelling out loud and clear that shares had to be sold, and worse, he had brought news of an approach from Grand Metropolitan, owners of Mecca Bookmakers. So when I turned up to say I had been contacted by Sears on the same subject and with the first move in a bid, the William Hill men were delighted. I was the white knight in shining armour because it meant their jobs could be saved. Grand Met, with Mecca Bookmakers, already had staff who were experts in the betting business and would stick with their own management. Sears were making a first foray into it and would have to rely on the existing team. That night I was the toast of the William Hill chairman.

But then things changed. I was working on the price and putting together drafts for the deal when I had a hand-delivered letter brought to me from Balshaw, in which he said that he and the rest of the William Hill board now wanted to remain independent. This stunned me as well as Wyborn, who knew there was no alternative but to sell out, to raise the money for Estate duty. But Balshaw, who had risen from employee to chairman and during Hill's lifetime had been not much more than a yes man, now saw his chance of glory. He flooded the board with his own people and used Hambros Bank, where he won over one of their directors, to act as his adviser in this mistaken bid for independence. The director, Cecil Berens, said that Sears shares were nothing but Chinese paper, a ridiculous notion considering the standing of Sears and Clore at that time.

Balshaw was fighting a losing battle and all he did was delay the eventual success of the Sears offer, as Charles Clore typically remained on top of every twist and turn. Part of the package meant that Balshaw stayed on, but he continued to display his resentment and only lasted three or four months after the deal was completed. In the end Sears had control of the William Hill business, with Charles becoming chairman of the company.

His contribution to the industry is almost too great to gauge, for the simple reason that bookmaking then had a rather seedy image. Grand Met might have been a big company, but they had (equally 'disreputable') casinos. When William Hill became part of Sears they moved into a different league. Sears was part of the business establishment, part of the fabric of British life, and brought a gravitas to the bookmaking business that had not been there before. My William Hill shares were now transferred into Sears and I became, in effect, a Sears representative on the board, remaining there for several years after Charles' death in 1979.

As for Sears, in recent years that company has gone from bad to worse. An empire built on the flair of a genius crumbled without him in the hands of lawyers and accountants. In show business terms, the board of Sears 'managed to take a star and turn it into an unknown'.

I WAS first introduced to owning racehorses by Irving Allen, a neighbour of mine, who was a highly successful film producer of great experience. Amongst his credits were 'Genghis Khan', 'Cromwell', 'The Trials of Oscar Wilde' and 'Green Beret'. He was a man of sardonic wit and when he learned I was becoming involved with the film business, he said, 'Always remember there is nothing wrong with the movie business that killing all the actors wouldn't cure.'

Irving owned the Derisley Wood Stud at Newmarket and, in the mid 1960s he invited me to be a partner in a horse which he had bred. It ran in my colours, emerald green and royal blue stripes, and I called it Folie Supreme, which demonstrates my faith in the animal. It was trained by Lester Piggott's father-in-law, Sam Armstrong.

From that point on my interest grew, at first sharing ownership with Irving, then branching out on my own and enjoying some fine moments. Down the years I have had quite a number of horses which initially I bought from sales and then later on bred with. The high point came in 1975 when I had the fastest two-year-old filly in the country, which I bred myself out a mare of mine called Firenza Mia. At the same time I had a twenty-five per cent stake in an American stallion called Virginia Boy with Ben Schmidt-Bodner, a very close friend and an enthusiastic and successful racehorse owner. Another partner was David Fisher – the same David Fisher from the Tamarisk greyhound incident in my youth. Virginia Boy had won the Wokingham Stakes, a handicap race over six furlongs traditionally run on the Friday at Royal Ascot.

Firenza Mia was successfully covered by Virginia Boy and she bred a filly foal in 1973. It was a breeding line that I was told stood a very good chance of being successful. A few days later I happened to be having dinner with my brother Edgar and Virginia Wade. It suddenly occurred to me during the meal that it might be an idea to name my filly by Virginia Boy after Britain's favourite tennis star. I put it to her there and then and she agreed, which was fortunate because a few weeks later John Banks, a well-known bookmaker and racehorse owner, had exactly the same idea but, when he asked for her permission, was told that she was already committed to me.

As a two-year-old, the filly was very successful and recorded five wins and because of that and the name, the two-legged Virginia Wade became a source of much interest. Everyone thought Virginia herself must be involved in the ownership of my animal. She wasn't, but I kept her in touch with the progress of her namesake. TimeForm rated the equine Virginia Wade as the fastest two-year-old filly in Britain that year and as a three-year-old she won the Ladbroke Cup at Epsom, where Jimmy Hill presented me with the trophy. That was the end of her success on the track, but I bred with her and had a couple of winners before selling her on to Charles St George. He had her covered by Ardross, who was a proven stayer, and with that sort of chemistry he should have had a world beater. However, as can often happen, it did not work out.

I also owned a horse called Gusty's Gift, which I bought rather than bred myself, and this, too, was very successful. It broke the track record for six furlongs under my ownership at Kempton Park. Then there was a partnership with a man called Sidney Winton in a horse that carried his colours and the name of his business, Winton Hotel.

My interest in horses was, of course, fuelled by my director-ship of William Hill. I used to go racing regularly because the company had boxes at various racecourses up and down the country. Winton Hotel had not done badly, winning two or three races, when one day, completely out of the blue, I had a phone call at my home from Lester Piggott, whom I already knew through Sam Armstrong. He said to me, 'You've got your horse Winton Hotel declared for a two-mile race at Ascot and I think it stands a chance, a good chance.'

I told him that Peter Ashworth, the trainer, was not so sure because he doubted it could last the distance. Lester replied, 'With me on it, it will.' That made me sit up and take notice and I said to him, 'Will you definitely ride it?'

'Yes,' he said, 'because I think I can win on it.'

I told Lester I would ring Peter and try to persuade him to run the horse. Peter again voiced his fears about it making the two miles but then I planted the seed in his mind about Lester Piggott. He doubted we could get Lester, so I told him to give him a call and see what happened. If Lester accepted the ride, we would go with Winton Hotel and if not, then we would not run him. So Peter phoned Lester, who I knew all along would accept the ride.

Lester was right about Winton Hotel, although it was a close-run thing. It was a tactical race and Piggott was at his real best. He brought Winton Hotel to the front about fifty yards from the post and then, twenty yards out, Jimmy Lindley on Royal Echo came chasing through. It looked as if Jimmy would get it until, right at the death, Piggott seemed almost to lift Winton Hotel over the line. At the time, it looked to me like a dead heat. Afterwards, I walked over to the winner's enclosure and as Lester came in on the horse, I called to him, 'Do you think you've won?'

He turned around and in a very assured voice said, 'We've won alright.' Just then the announcement came: 'The winner is No. 10 – Winton Hotel.'

The timing, and Lester's certainty that he had won, made sure that I never forgot the number. As he dismounted, I thanked him for his efforts but he said, 'Thank you for letting me have the ride.' Lester rode my horses now and again and we always got on very well. In fact, when he started training and everybody was after him, hoping his magic in the saddle would rub off on the animals in his charge, he phoned me and invited me to have a horse with him, which I did. It was called Spoiled Brat and it did win for me.

I bred other horses and also had a very successful partnership with my brother Edgar in Harvard Boy, which Lester rode a couple of times. The amazing thing about that animal was that he came second five times but never won, a real case of seconditis. Then surprisingly, an American trainer called me and said he wanted to buy it, maybe because of the name, and we made a good profit. The Americans were so keen on him they sent over a jockey to collect the horse. Another animal of mine was called Ocean Diamond, which won a few races for me until I sold it to Ted Dexter, the England cricketer, who was always very interested in horses and greyhounds. It proved to be a good buy because Ted also had a few wins out of Ocean Diamond.

When I left the board of William Hill, my interest in racing started to wane and there were other diversions. I was involved with Wembley, where there was greyhound racing, so I started to wind down my involvement with horses. My son Steven, however, took over and kept the flag flying for the family's equine interests.

Another good horse and strong stayer which I bred was Just Because, and the biggest kick I had from racing came from breeding a horse and then seeing it win. It is really exciting, something special, because you have to make a decision about who the mare is covered by and then hope mother nature makes the best out of your calculations. You do all you can to eliminate risks, study breeding, look at the strengths of the two horses you are mating and hope that the foal will inherit the best attributes of its parents. Virginia Wade was obviously fast because the mare Firenza Mia was extremely quick over four and a half furlongs but did not have the stamina beyond that distance. Bill O'Gorman was Firenza Mia's trainer at the time and he said, 'Don't sell this filly, breed with her. I've got some very good two-year-olds in my yard at the moment, but over four furlongs she beats all of them.' Stamina I could get from the genes of Virginia Boy, who was also rapid but, as his record showed, could keep the pace up over a longer distance. So having him cover Firenza Mia to produce Virginia Wade was a good match.

Virginia Wade's jockey was Richard Fox, a great humorist and striking fellow with his distinctive red hair, but it was Lester Piggott who persuaded me she also wasn't going to train on after she ran on Oaks Day at Epsom in 1980. He suggested that I think about using her for breeding.

During those years when I owned, bought and bred horses, I made a profit and it was only towards the end when I was not really concentrating that I did not do so well. Overall, however, I don't think it cost me any money to have horses during that period of my life. Today, owning horses at any level is a vastly expensive luxury and the scene has changed, with the Arabs owning the best animals. They have strings of horses and have bought up the top trainers, so it is not easy for the man with a horse or two to have them placed in the right hands.

13

Wembley, Venue of Legends

Wembley Stadium has been as much a part of my life as boxing or show business. I have used the facilities for many years, going back to the 1960s, but it was in 1983 that I began to get involved in the management of the place. That year I was approached by an estate agent, Harvey Soning, and Elliott Bernerd, chief executive of Michael Laurie Estate Agents, a firm that acted as property advisers to British Electrical Traction (BET).

They had acquired Wembley Stadium some years earlier and the plan had been for BET, which owned Rediffusion, the holders of the first independent TV franchise for London, to expand the site as a television centre in the same way that the BBC has now done at White City. But Rediffusion lost their franchise in the first independent TV shake-up and so the plans for Wembley came to nothing.

I had known Bernerd for a number of years and done a considerable amount of business with him. He came to me and said a consortium was being put together to acquire fifty-one per cent of Wembley Stadium Limited. Bernerd said he thought I was 'perfectly cast' as a prospective member of the consortium. This was because BET wanted someone in the consortium who knew something about the Wembley business.

A strange choice of words, but that is why I remember them so clearly. And indeed once the shape of the deal was explained by Bernerd, all became clear. BET, who were retaining forty-nine per cent of the shares, had the right to veto the members of the consortium as they saw fit. I came to the conclusion that it was a long-term proposition and recommended that my family trust should become involved. I went to meet other members of the consortium and I also brought in Harry Goodman, who at the time was running Air Europe. He was making a personal investment.

The leading member of the consortium was the former Labour Cabinet Minister John Silkin, a man who in the long run did not impress me at all. I don't think he set out to be crooked but, having spent his whole life in politics, lying had become second nature to him. A lot of politicians lie – it is the only way they can get themselves elected.

Silkin was a lawyer and at first I think he was probably very honourable. His family had a strong political history and his brother, Sam Silkin, had been Attorney General. They had been fed Labour politics from the cradle by their father, Lewis Silkin, a lawyer and also an MP. But as the years rolled by, Silkin became more of an opportunist and was not unprepared to bend rules to achieve what he wanted.

Over Wembley, his behaviour was bad and he was a boor. Silkin lied because he pretended to have money and he didn't. I had approached the collaboration with Silkin in a positive frame of mind. Here was a man – a lawyer – who had been a Labour Minister. I thought it would be great and it was what influenced BET to enter into discussions with him. Both BET and I were to be proved very wrong, particularly in the hopes we had invested in Silkin.

The consortium he was heading at various times intended to include companies such as Bovis, who didn't come in, and a number of other building firms. The size of the investment was £28 million for fifty-one per cent of Wembley Stadium Limited with various options. My family trust, together with Harry Goodman, was putting in around £3 million. Silkin was saying that he didn't want any one member of the consortium putting up too much, because that would destablise the whole purpose of having the consortium.

One member of this group was a film producer called Ben Fisz, among whose credits were 'The Battle of Britain' and 'Heroes of the Telemark', and for a while he had been promoting the concept of building a new super arena for London. The idea of a new super arena for London or anywhere else (prior to Lottery Funds being available) seemed to me a non-starter. I wasn't close to Fisz but I knew him socially. Because of his past plans for a new London stadium I was somewhat surprised to find him involved and also surprised, given my interests, that he had not talked to me about that project. I told all this to Bernerd and it led to an invitation to lunch with Fisz.

It was then that I discovered why I had never been approached before about the Wembley deal. Irving Felt, an American businessman I had known for a number of years, had been a key player in the construction of the new Madison Square Garden in New York City, so much so that a part of it, the smaller annexe, the Felt Forum, was named after him. We had met many times in America and London and he told me that Fisz had approached him about the London project. I told him to forget it as I considered the proposition impractical. This, of course, was fed back to Fisz and he resented my advice to Felt and consequently excluded me from the talks. My view was borne out when the London Arena in Docklands turned out to be a disaster, costing its financiers over £30 million.

It seemed to me that Wembley was worth far more than the price being sought, probably double the £28 million needed. I felt that I could make a worthwhile contribution, so much so that I went out of my way to get to know the other members of the consortium. It quickly became clear that not only was Silkin the dominating figure, he was also the bullying kind, quick to put his former ministerial tank on the front lawn of anybody he did not get on with. There was a vivid example of this when he tried to intimidate my lawyer, Charles Randall. It left me distrusting Silkin even more than I had done in the early stages, and I was very wary of him and his motives. Oddly, when we met he could not have been nicer to me and at one stage told me we were going to be doing most of the running of Wembley together.

As a result of this unease, I asked Randall to draw up a list of vetoes, as many as possible, to be put before the shareholders and agreed by them. I did not want the consortium to borrow over a certain amount of money without consulting me. They couldn't issue more shares, nor could they alter the make-up of the board. Much to my amazement, all of these vetoes were accepted without question. It should have made me suspicious.

The deal started to splutter and though no-one would admit it, it was clear that the money from Silkin & Co just wasn't there. People came and went as potential members of the consortium and then Fisz introduced Louis Dolivet to it. He was of Romanian-French extraction and had been heavily involved in bankrolling films and producing them – for a while he had been Orson Welles' partner. Dolivet was a good talker, a man with a very sharp brain, and appeared to have large amounts of Swiss banking money. That made him a major player and he used to fly over from Paris to stay at the Berkeley Hotel through Monday to Friday to work on the deal. He and Silkin ended up as the leading figures in the consortium. By now Standard Chartered Bank, who were forwarding a considerable part of the loan to the consortium, were ready. But still the deal could not be landed.

BET extended their deadline and even went as far as agreeing to take only some of the money then and there, with an IOU for the outstanding balance. They were very keen for the business to be wrapped up. At that time the various businesses of BET were not exactly setting the world on fire and they were committed to wiping their balance sheet clean, and that included Wembley, regardless of the potential of the place. They had held on to it for too long because the chairman of the company, John Spencer Wills, had a soft spot for it. Then Wills died and his son Nicholas became the chief executive, and while this meant the sentimental links were cut, it also delayed matters.

It was not until July 1984 that it all came together. On the day of completion, my family trust's lawyer arrived with a banker's draft and Harry Goodman's lawyer came along with a cheque, while the Fisz and Silkin side of the consortium arrived with a cheque from Citibank made out for £3 million. It was a relief to see the cheque because I had seriously doubted it was going to turn up. However, when the truth emerged, only hours after the deal was completed, it proved to be a very different story.

The money from Citibank turned out to be a loan from Comfort Hotels and Fisz and Silkin were a front for Comfort, because they could not keep up the repayments to Citibank. When I stop and look back, I have to question why Citibank would lend £3 million on what looked a weirdly constructed contract with no security. It just didn't make sense. The way Silkin and Fisz had done it, they had put a delayed detonator in the loan which was primed to go off ten days after the contract had been signed. It was then that the money from Citibank was revealed to be a loan from Comfort Hotels.

How did a loan from Citibank become a loan from Comfort Hotels? The answer is it was always a loan from Comfort. Silkin and Co used Citibank as a catalyst, a conduit. Harry Goodman and the trust put their money in; Silkin and Co didn't put their money in, did not tell us they were not doing so, and what they did was cheating us, nothing less.

Their consideration for borrowing from Comfort Hotels, using Citibank as a conduit, was that Comfort Hotels would get the management contract of the Wembley Conference and Exhibition Centre. Comfort Hotels, then run by Henry Edwards, had weighed up the benefits of getting their hands on the Wembley Conference Centre. Edwards had become aware of the potential of the conference business and had wanted to come in on the deal at the outset, but would never have got away with it because I had my rights of veto. With the consortium struggling to raise the finance, Comfort Hotels provided a parachute to save them from all their troubles. The result was Silkin's group had imposed on Wembley a liability in favour of Comfort Hotels, completely without the approval of the board. Once they couldn't deliver the management contract of the Conference Centre and Exhibition Hall to Comfort Hotels, Comfort Hotels withdrew their support of the Citibank loan.

All this led to a court case being brought against Wembley Stadium plc, originally by Comfort Hotels. The case was continued by Hilton Hotels, a Ladbroke subsidiary, after it bought Comfort, much against the wishes of the then chairman of Hilton Hotels, John Jarvis, but insisted upon by the Ladbroke chairman, Cyril Stein.

Silkin & Co were out on a limb and they had to sell their shares to Abdul Shamji. He wanted to come on the board with his own people, Barclays Bank having given him an impeccable reference. Shamji, a Ugandan Asian, had previously owned the hotel at Wembley. During the time he was in control, he had developed a big interest in Wembley and went as far as to approach BET to do a deal, but they were not interested. BET had a big sense of heritage and would not have wanted complete control of the national stadium to fall into overseas hands. They just wouldn't deal with Shamji and even when Silkin proposed him as a member of the consortium, BET, who had the right of veto, were not having it and rejected Shamji again. Despite this Shamji, through Silkin and Co, had a toehold at Wembley and evidence came to light later which showed Dolivet had organised a deal with Shamji whereby he was going to take a large portion of the Wembley company via Switzerland.

The first I heard of Shamji's involvement was on the day we completed the deal. I had heard his name before and knew it had been rejected, but all of a sudden here he was in as a participant in the consortium, albeit in a minor role. I discussed his appearance with John Davy, the BET director and negotiator, who was aware of Shamji's presence. Wary, he inserted a last-minute clause which stated that Shamji could not increase his holding in Wembley without the permission of BET, who were retaining the other forty-nine per cent of the company.

My relationship with Shamji actually began very well. He invited me to lunch, the first time I had really sat down with him, and he was impressive – very smooth, very friendly and conciliatory. We agreed that we would co-operate to rescue the situation and together buy out Fisz, Silkin and Dolivet, who were obviously weak players and wanted some sort of quick return. I left Shamji outside Les Ambassadeurs Club with an agreement that we would talk more about it over the next few days. But less than forty-eight hours later I heard from Davy that Silkin, Fisz and Dolivet were meeting in Shamji's office and were about to sell out, obviously taking some sort of profit. I was mortified. I phoned Shamji immediately and said to him that I had received news about his impending deal and added that I was quite surprised by it because the two of us had an agreement. He immediately said we had no deal and from that point I felt that the less than flattering comments I had heard about him were absolutely justified. We had an understanding which, as far as I am concerned, should be valued and binding as any contract.

In spite of this double cross, I felt there was still a chance of hitting back. I knew that BET could veto this deal and I immediately went and saw Nicholas Wills. I told him the sequence of events, explained clearly about the lunch and the agreement and how Shamji had then gone behind my back, so much so that I only heard about it by absolute chance. I urged Wills to veto the deal, warning him of the troubles which would lie ahead if Shamji were to become a major figure at Wembley. Davy had also warned Wills, but Wills was having none of it. His attitude was that he was fed up with the whole business and he just said, 'It couldn't be worse than Silkin &

Co.' About Shamji he said, 'At least he's got money.' That was the impression Shamji had given and it proved how you can fool people, if only for a time.

So BET, with Wills running the show, let their veto go just for the sake of convenience and allowed Silkin & Co to sell to Shamji. There was nothing I could do about it. All this happened towards Christmas 1984 when I was due to go away to Florida for a holiday. I carried on with my holiday, which was due to run into the New Year. Just a short while after 1985 was ushered in, I received a phone call from my right hand man, Percy Davies, who informed me that a board meeting of Arena Holdings, the intermediate company in the Wembley deal, had been called to take place that day at noon. Arena Holdings wanted to know whether Davies would be representing me at the meeting. I immediately got in touch with Charles Randall, with the instruction to go along to the meeting and stop it happening. In the meantime, I arranged to come back to Britain a day early.

Davies went to the meeting, where he and Randall successfully blocked it. Randall also halted a plan of Shamji's to put more directors on the board. The minute I got back I went and saw Davies to be brought up to date. I found out that Shamji had suggested that he and I meet. A meeting was arranged between Davies, me and Shamji, who had his solicitor at hand. We went to his office and it was a very interesting get-together, so interesting in fact that I wished I had been in a position to videotape it.

As I went in, I noticed the solicitor was stationed by the fireplace. Shamji said to me, 'I promise you, I didn't know you were away when we called the meeting.' Was I ever going to believe that? He knew I was out of the country, he'd found out from someone and had then deliberately made his move. I wanted to say what I thought of him there and then, but no point would have been served by behaving like that, so while I thought to myself, 'Of course you knew', I actually said, 'Well, if you didn't know, okay, it doesn't matter. There was no harm done, as I had my vetoes.'

He again said that he wanted to work with me at Wembley and wanted me to suggest a way that this partnership could gel. He wanted to know what plans I had for the place. I went into a good twenty-minute detailed explanation of what I thought could be done and how it could work between us. He had apparently made some money out of property and knew about that side of the business, so as I saw it, he could be left to deal with that end. I wanted to take charge of the entertainments, the sport and the promotions. I knew all about that and had plenty of experience. That was the obvious way we could work together. All the time I was talking, Shamji was doodling. It was a habit of his, listening intently while drawing patterns on a piece of paper.

When I finished, he looked up at me: 'Is that all?' There was a pause and then he continued: 'I've got the shares and I'll tell you what you'll do at Wembley. Your shares are worthless, your vetoes don't mean a thing and don't forget my lawyer is here.'

I was furious. I clenched my fist knuckle-white tight and brought it crashing down on his desk.

'You told me that you were a football fan, keen on Liverpool. Well, remember this, the home team has an advantage and you are playing on my pitch. This is my pitch.'

He took exception to that, thinking I was making a racist comment, but I was referring to the legal situation. That, in effect, was the end of the meeting, but not my last word.

As I turned with Davies to leave the room, I said to Shamji's solicitor that if he was advising his client that my vetoes were worthless, and if he was recommending Shamji to act as if that were the case, then I would report him to the Law Society for inducing a client to breach a contract. It obviously hit home, because a short while later the solicitor resigned. As for Shamji, I told him we would meet again but only once he had learned to conduct himself in a proper manner. He proffered his hand but I ignored it: 'I only shake hands with people who know how to behave themselves and, until you learn to behave yourself, I cannot shake your hand.'

War was declared from that moment and for the rest of that year Shamji tried every possible move to change the board. But every time he tried to pull one of his stunts, he was informed by my lawyers that I would take out an injunction against him. Clearly he was advised about what he could not do, but despite such legal advice he would not stop trying.

At the meeting in Shamji's office, Davies had told him he was making a big mistake treating me the way he did, because I was a man who knew his way around and Davies had told him that if he stuck with me and co-operated, he would do very well. However, Shamji would not stop. He called in Harry Goodman, who had faith in me, and told him that his shares were worthless. That, of course, far from turning Goodman against me, worked the opposite way. It merely convinced him that Shamji was a very bad egg. And by now, it transpired, Shamji was in big trouble.

I distrusted him so much that I had made my own enquiries through a private investigator. I found out that Shamji was a man of straw. He owed a fortune to Johnson Matthey Bankers. The assets he had against collateral were nothing, relatively speaking. Shamji's lines of credit with Johnson Matthey were being squeezed and taking control of Wembley was going to be his life. He could have ended up in a position where he robbed Peter to pay Paul – Wembly is a very big cashflow business and would have been ideal for that purpose. He persisted in trying to squeeze me out, but in the process only succeeded in angering BET, who were still holding forty-nine per cent of the company. The ball landed back in Davy's court and he was instructed to try and rescue the situation and, as a consequence, we worked closely together.

The crunch came with Shamji forcing me into an injunction hearing which signalled the end for him. He was knocked silly by it. Not only did he lose – and Mr Justice Hoffman made it quite clear what he thought of Shamji's case – but Johnson Matthey, who had an observer in court, made careful plans to deal with him. Within seventy-two hours of Shamji losing the case, they foreclosed on him. Now it became quite obvious that he had gone into court with me and forced the injunction because Johnson Matthew were heavily breathing down his neck and about to bring the guillotine down on his head.

Shamji's defeat was total. Johnson Matthey foreclosed on him and his company, Gomba, ended up in liquidation. Shamji was finally jailed for fifteen months for perjury. By then Johnson Matthew's own problems largely as a result of lending to people like Shamji, had been revealed but the Bank of England had taken control, rescuing the bank in one hectic weekend.

The good book tells us we should never wish ill of anyone and in general it would give me no pleasure to say I was glad a man was jailed, but with Shamji it was the only punishment and one that was fully deserved. Of all the people I have ever met in business, and over the last fifty years there have been a lot of them, there have been some very strange, awkward, devious and off-the-wall characters. But Shamji was the most treacherous.

I was very fortunate in that my second wife Nadine was very supportive throughout this saga with Shamji, just as she had been in the ACC affair. This came about not long after we were married and I don't believe she had anticipated so many early morning and late night lengthy telephone calls. Phyllis, my first wife, had also been extremely loyal and supportive particularly during the Mappin and Webb problems and the conflicts with her brother, Henry Oppenheim. I was obviously blessed in having two intelligent wives and I recall Charles Clore used to tease me about Phyllis, who he admired, and would say to me about her, 'Now I know where the brains in your family are.'

Incidentally, in that fight with Shamji, apart from Charles Randall, I had the valuable assistance of Anthony Grabiner, a young QC, so young indeed that I had reservations about using him. But his conduct and control of the case, along with the advice he provided, belied his youthful appearance and he

has certainly deserved the successes that have since come to
him.

That same year, 1985, as I battled against Shamji, saw one
of the highlights of my involvement with Wembley. Bob
Geldof, the Irish rock singer who led the band, the Boomtown
Rats, conceived the famous Live Aid Concerts at Wembley
and Philadelphia which resulted in millions being raised for
the victims of the famine in Ethiopia and Geldof being given
an honorary knighthood.

Two days before the concert, I was at the stadium and was
asked to meet with Harvey Goldsmith, one of the promoters,
urgently. We met in the Stadium boardroom and Goldsmith
brought along Maurice Jones, another promoter, and Geldof.

Goldsmith proceeded to make a large number of complaints
about our staff and suggested that they were being less than
cooperative. My first inclination, not surprisingly, was to
defend our staff although, of course, I was going to investigate
the major complaints. My attitude brought forth a string of
four-letter expletives from Geldof, who accused me of not
listening to them and he banged his fist on the table very
forcibly.

I reacted by telling him that he could not stay in the meeting
unless he behaved himself and if he used that sort of language,
I suggest that he leave it to me and Goldsmith to sort it out
Geldof stayed quiet after that while Goldsmith, Jones and I
discussed the problems sensibly and, after spending about
twenty minutes appearing to study an advance copy of the
concert programme, Geldof took his leave and we shook hands.

On the day of the concert, the performers were all gathered
in the Stadium banqueting hall waiting to be presented to the
Prince and Princess of Wales when a young girl approached
my wife, Nadine, obviously thinking she was appearing in the
show, and asked her if a large security man who happened to
be standing next to her was her bodyguard. Nadine naturally
in her surprise said, 'Oh no!' and Geldof, who was standing
alongside, said, 'She doesn't need a bodyguard with her

husband,' and said to Nadine, 'Your old man is a tough one.'

There is an epilogue to the story that during the concert, Prince Charles told me that he would like to invite Geldof and his wife Paula Yates to a party he was giving at Buckingham Palace three days later, to which Nadine and I were already invited. I gave the Prince's detective Harvey Goldsmith's address and telephone number and suggested that route for the invitation.

When we drove up to the Palace entrance for the party, by coincidence we were in the car immediately behind the one bringing the Geldofs and when he saw me, he said, 'It's great that you are here, because I won't know anyone.'

I was amazed when during the evening some of the most distinguished people – and there were many, of course, present – came over to ask me to introduce them to Bob Geldof, who by then had become a huge celebrity and my friend. We still meet from time to time and I am pleased that after a bare patch in his career, he enjoyed great business success with his company's Big Breakfast television show.

THE Wembley story has moved on, although the final chapter is still being written. Shamji was forced to sell his shares to a group led by Brian Wolfson, who was no Shamji but neither was he quite the brilliant man in business he painted himself out to be. The company incurred unmanageable debt under his chairmanship and he suffered from a great deal of press criticism that did not seem to improve his judgement. He also seemed to love travelling long distances by plane and the general view of the staff at Heathrow Airport and Kennedy Airport in New York was that he was one of the most frequent travellers they knew.

He appeared to find it difficult to resist doing a deal and his many trips to the United States, and some to Japan, did not result in deals which turned out to be profitable for the company. In fact, on balance, the deals he did in these countries proved very costly indeed and things would have been worse had it not been for an 'ill wind' blowing us some good in Rhode Island, where our greyhound track had suffered badly as a result of casinos being opened in Connecticut only 50 miles away. To offset the dip in turnover and the resultant drop in State Betting Tax we were able to obtain permission to instal hundreds of slot machines at the track and these have proved far more lucrative than Greyhound Racing – which we still continue to run at the Rhode Island track – could possibly have been.

Wolfson left the company in an atmosphere of acrimony only to be replaced, at the behest of our merchant bankers, Charterhouse, by a Swedish business executive, Claes Hultman. In the meantime, other experienced businessmen joined the board. They were Clive Bastin, chairman of European Leisure, a public company; Roger Brooke, chairman of Candover Investments, a major capital venture company, and a director of Tarmac and Slough Estates, who was also chairman of the Government Audit Commission; and Peter Mead, chairman of Abbott Mead Vickers, the largest advertising agency in the United Kingdom.

Claes Hultman was, at the time, the chief executive of Eurotherm, a public company engaged in the manufacturing of thermostatic and process control equipment, but he had never been chairman of a company previously. This lack of chairmanship experience made itself apparent very quickly and it was not long before the rest of the board realized that Hultman had been a bad choice. Within a few months of his appointment, he upset company executives by saying in an interview, published in the press, that Wembley was a 'tin pot company', and this resulted in him having to make a written apology to all the staff, which was posted on the staff notice board at Wembley. He also told the managing director of our greyhound track company, Clive Feltham, that he had too expensive a company car. This did not go down too well with a man based in Birmingham who often travels to London three times a week and often to Manchester and Portsmouth.

Alan Coppin, now released from the shackles of Wolfson's

domination, emerged as a brilliant chief executive and exceeded all expectations. He realized very quickly the dangers presented by Hultman, particularly in relations with the company executives and customers, so he made a point of seeing to it that Hultman's exposure to those people was severely limited. Whenever there was a big match at Wembley Stadium, Hultman, with one or two exceptions, was consigned to the company box in the upper reaches of the Stadium, well away from our customers who, of course, included the Football Association and Rugby League officials together with their guests. In fact I, as deputy chairman of Wembley Stadium, represented the company at all those events.

Hultman played very little part in running the business and it was therefore no detriment to the company when he became embroiled in a dispute with the board of Eurotherm which resulted in him being sacked from that company. He took his sacking very badly and became terribly upset, losing a tremendous amount of weight in the process and thus spending nearly all of his time during that period of several months concentrating entirely on his Eurotherm problem. He returned to Eurotherm, at the instigation of institutional shareholders, and was reinstated as chief executive although not obtaining what he apparently most wanted, chairmanship of the company. In the event, as I have learned recently from one of those institutional Eurotherm shareholders, their faith in him appeared to be misplaced and there was a sharp decline in the fortunes of the company, which was sold early in 1998, signalling the departure of Hultman.

He continued, however, at every opportunity to claim credit for the success of Wembley since the financial reconstruction of the company in 1995, although Alan Coppin, with whom I enjoyed a close and friendly relationship until his departure from the company at the end of September 1998, was primarily responsible for the improvement in the company's fortunes. Alan was, unfortunately for us, head-hunted by Compass, a huge catering organisation where he has great prospects, and he deserves that opportunity. I say this despite the fact, as I have always made clear to him, that I disapproved very strongly with the way he conducted the negotiations with the Sports Council and the Football Association for the sale to them of Wembley Stadium.

In fairness to Alan, knowing that he was leaving the company for six months before his departure, it was wrong of Claes Hultman to insist upon Alan conducting the negotiations for the sale of the company's most important asset and, in fact, the largest deal in the company's history. I am sure that an experienced chairman, with leadership qualities, would not have countenanced such an arrangement, particularly one in which I believe Alan was to receive a bonus of £150,000 for completing the sale.

When Wembley was first selected, as a result of a two-year long process by the Sports Council, as the site for the new National Stadium, it was intended the new stadium would be created jointly by Wembley and the Sports Council. For that purpose a trust was formed by the Council and it was expected that there would be a limitation on Wembley's profits for its involvement with the scheme, with the basis of that limitation subject to negotiation and obviously related to the then current profits of the stadium. The Sports Council bureaucracy, and some of the totally unreasonable require-ments imposed by them, created something of an impasse which first of all resulted in an approach from Ken Bates, chairman of Chelsea, who had been appointed by the since discredited FA chairman, Keith Wiseman, and David Dein, vice-chairman of Arsenal and a great friend of mine. Bates and Dein at that time were joint chairmen of the FA committee appointed to deal with the Stadium and it appeared likely that we and the FA would develop a new Stadium without assistance from the Sports Council. In fact, Bates, at one of the meetings which Alan Coppin and I attended with him, said that Tony Banks, a recent surprise appointment as Minister for Sport, had asked him to 'destroy the Sports Council's proposal'. This did not surprise me because, apart from the fact that the Sports Council's requirements, as I have said, were unreasonable, I knew that Bates and Banks had a very close relationship.

Banks's appointment was particularly surprising as Tom Pendry appeared to have done a good job as shadow spokesman on sport and someone responsible seemed to have forgotten Banks' scandalous behaviour when Dennis Wise, the Chelsea captain, was given a prison sentence after being convicted of assaulting a cab driver. Banks said publicly on that day that the magistrate at Horseferry Court had only sent Wise to prison in order to draw attention to himself. I told Banks what I thought of this statement of his at Stamford Bridge on the same evening where a Chelsea game was taking place. He protested that he was entitled to his opinion but I pointed out, in no uncertain terms, that as an MP he was supposed to be a 'law maker' and not encouraging people to be law breakers. We were in the restaurant at the time and I asked what effect he thought remarks like the one he had made could have on 'hooligans' in the stadium at the time. I had started the conversation by saying he was a disgrace to the Labour Party at the end of our sharp exchange, the four or five men he was sitting with did not remonstrate with me or make any comment – and I thought their silence was significant.

The proposal for the joint deal with the FA foundered, largely I felt, because of a difference of opinion between Ken Bates and Graham Kelly – who was recently forced to resign as chief executive of the FA about the way in which these negotiations between us should be conducted. It seemed that Bates resented being dictated to by Kelly, who he, I suppose understandably, felt was an employee taking too much authority upon himself. In the event, I must say I formed the opinion that Kelly was too often inclined to adopt such an attitude which obviously brought about his demise.

The next step in this long drawn-out affair brought about an offer from the Sports Council to buy the Stadium from us for the sum of £103 million, and although I was not over impressed by that figure, I felt that Wembley could gain further by retaining an ongoing interest in the project by having a management contract which would provide us with income from a guaranteed sum plus a percentage of either the proceeds or profits. I was appalled when I heard that, in fact, the intention was that we would be selling the Stadium, under that deal, lock, stock and barrel, and that our company would be entirely losing its association with the Stadium. I considered this disastrous because I felt that the Stadium was the 'jewel in the crown' of our company and that it was a huge error to do a deal on those terms. I voiced my protest but was unable to persuade any of my colleagues, at that time, that my objections were valid.

I was, therefore, delighted when we were approached by Arsenal Football Club, who were having unfruitful negotiations with Islington Council in their attempts to obtain permission to increase the capacity at Highbury from the existing and totally inadequate 38,000. The idea was that Arsenal should move to Wembley in 2002, when our contract with the FA ended. Meetings were held between Alan Coppin and myself with various members of the Arsenal board – excluding David Dein, because of his FA position – as well as Arsenal's merchant bankers, Hambros. Everyone at Wembley, including Claes Hultman – who apparently had to be told by Alan Coppin who the Arsenal were – appeared to greet the Arsenal approach with open arms and the negotiations were proceeding at a steady pace. The principal difficulty which arose with Arsenal was their reluctance to enter into a contract which was not conditional upon planning approval for the extensive refurbishment of the Stadium, although they had been given the advice of planning experts that as long as they did not increase the height of the Stadium building, there was no reason why planning permission should be refused. They were prepared to offer £50 million in cash and the balance of £100 million upon planning permission being obtained. In a late stage of the negotiations, they also offered us approximately 10% of their company's shares, which at that point were valued at approximately £15 million but which have since doubled in value, probably as a result of Rupert Murdoch's approach to Manchester United and the approach Arsenal received to sell their company from Carlton Communications.

Eventually Arsenal came to the conclusion that they were being used by Wembley as a 'stalking horse' simply to obtain improved offers from the Sports Council, which by that time had, unbeknown to us, got together with the FA, which I thought was astonishing in view of what Bates had said about the Council and the views of Tony Banks that Bates had passed on to us. I subsequently learned, almost by accident from one of the trustees, that it was intended that when the Sports Council's trust acquired the Stadium they would pass it on to the FA for the sum of £1. I gather that, because that arrangement might have been too blatant a contravention of the Lotteries Act, there is an arrangement whereby the FA will have a 115-year lease rent free – and if that is not a contravention, or at least a circumvention, of the Lottery rules I wonder what would be.

The Arsenal, thoroughly fed up because of their 'stalking horse' suspicions, eventually withdrew from negotiations amidst a great deal of publicity which had been the case since they first came upon the scene. This at least was much to the relief of David Dein, who had been embarrassed by what appeared to be a conflict of interest and he found it necessary to stand down from the FA committee on which he served, losing his joint chairmanship of the National Stadium Committee. For me, the most unfortunate part of the whole Arsenal episode was that there appeared to be some resentment towards me on the part of David, who felt that I was partly to blame for the way they had been treated. Nothing could have been further from the truth, as I always hoped we would do a deal with Arsenal. I value my longtime friendship with David and his wife Barbara, who have been good friends of mine for many years.

I always felt that if we had done a deal with Arsenal, the FA would eventually have come into line and we would still have a number of international matches as well as the Cup Finals and Football League play-off matches played at Wembley, because it is so much more lucrative for the FA and the clubs to play at Wembley than at provincial grounds. That situation would not be dissimilar to every country where football is played throughout the world. For example, in Italy, most international matches are played at the Olympic Stadium in Rome, which is shared by Lazio and Roma, while in Germany, the Olympic Stadium in Munich is shared by Bayern and Munich 1860, and so on. We also had made it clear to Arsenal that we would want a contract for the management of the Stadium, which would have maintained our company's connection with it, contributed to our income and enabled us to retain our company's valuable identity.

Once it was known by the board that Alan Coppin was leaving, apart from the natural concern about the 'hole' he would be leaving in the company's management, there was the question of his replacement and Clive Bastin – who unfortunately suffered a stroke in mid 1998 while visiting Singapore and has since been incapacitated – was the first to say that he did not consider Nigel Potter, the then finance director, a suitable choice as chief executive. This view was shared by the other non-executive directors as well as by Alan Coppin himself, notwithstanding the fact that Potter had made it clear that he wished to be considered. It was felt that we needed to seek a replacement for Alan but in view of the fact that the Stadium was to be sold and there were no positive plans for the company's future, it was thought it would be extremely difficult to bring in a suitable chief executive at that time. The negotiations for the sale of the Stadium continued at a rather slow pace, primarily, we understood, because there were difficulties arising between the Sports Council, the

National Stadium Trust and the FA. These difficulties continued until after the New Year and only appeared to be finally resolved during the first week in January.

During the summer of 1998, following a couple of inept performances by Claes Hultman in chairing company board meetings, including two occasions when he had knowingly made misleading statements, the independent non-executive directors, Clive Bastin, Roger Brooke, Peter Mead and myself, arranged to meet. It was the unanimous view that for the benefit of the company, Hultman should be replaced. This view was conveyed to Alan Coppin, who agreed with it and volunteered to approach Hultman to ask him to resign. Alan did, however, make the point that it would be most opportune for Hultman to leave the Company immediately the sale of the Stadium had taken place, and the fact was also taken into account that following his departure from Eurotherm he was seeking another job. If and when he found such employment, that would also be an appropriate time for him to resign. I am afraid that our generosity to him has resulted in a substantial price to pay, when one considers recent events.

In any case, Alan Coppin left the company at the end of September and it was decided to instal Nigel Potter as chief executive, on what I understood was a caretaker basis – in fact, when Roger Brooke told me about the meeting, at which I was not present as I was unwell, he did tell me that he certainly regarded it as a temporary arrangement and that when we eventually asked Potter to stand down he would be given a bonus for doing so. At the same time Mark Elliott, who had been the assistant to Nigel Potter, was installed as finance director. During the time that Alan Coppin was on the board, he had persuaded the other directors that the sale of the stadium was the appropriate course to take, and in persuading them he put forward opinions which in my view one could drive a coach and horses through.

Quite dramatically, soon after Alan had left the company, Peter Mead, who had always been ambivalent about the sale, and Roger Brooke came to the conclusion that selling the Stadium on the then existing terms was a mistake. Roger's attitude was influenced greatly by his having an opportunity, for the first time, to see a draft copy of the sale contract. His considerable experience told him that the division of the management responsibility for the Complex, involving Wembley Arena, the Conference Centre and Exhibition Halls on the one hand and the Stadium on the other, was illogical and a recipe for continuous dispute. He, like Peter Mead, was also influenced by the considerable increases in the figures quoted in relation to football generally, including television fees and the offer in excess of £650 million made by BSkyB for Manchester United and the failed attempt by Carlton to buy Arsenal Football Club for £250 million.

Now that Messrs Brooke and Mead fully supported my view of the situation, there were heated discussions at several board meetings. Then at a meeting on 9 December another heated discussion ensued. Hultman insisted upon a vote being taken and used his casting vote to decide to proceed with the sale. Roger Brooke was obviously very annoyed and told Hultman that he had a great deal to answer for. Peter Mead was extremely angry, and blamed Hultman for his inept performance as chairman and for showing no leadership at all in attempting to settle the considerable dispute that existed and which had resulted in the board being totally split. Peter was so angry that he refused to stay at the meeting and left. For my part, I told Hultman he did not know what he was talking about and that his vote had been given without any real knowledge of the matter under discussion.

I thought, as I still do, that for a decision which drastically changed the fortunes of our company to rest upon a vote of Hultman was bordering on the farcical and made no sense at all. I also felt that the conduct of our merchant bank adviser, Paul Baines of Charterhouse, left a great deal to be desired and I told him, in no uncertain terms, that he was failing in his duty to the company if he was prepared to stand by and make no attempt to heal the breach among the directors, which had clearly arisen as a result of Hultman's casting vote.

Unfortunately, according to Alan Coppin, the day after that meeting was the first opportunity that he had to meet with Hultman to attempt to persuade him to resign, but Hultman was apparently so buoyed up by the fact that he had this power with his casting vote that he was not prepared to even consider resignation. The unfortunate delay in his approaching Hultman was brought about by the fact that immediately after Alan had left our company, he spent a number of weeks travelling in various parts of the world learning about the Compass Group's business, and when he was in London Claes Hultman was back in his homeland, Sweden.

There was a significant and dramatic change in the situation in October when ENIC, a public company engaged in the sports and leisure industries, came on the scene suggesting, in the first instance, that there should be a merger with Wembley plc on the basis that the Stock Market valuation of both companies was almost identical. ENIC, was a relatively new company formed by Joseph Lewis, who made a considerable amount of money by operating theme restaurants in London and then moved to the Bahamas, where he amassed a huge fortune principally by large currency dealings and property transactions. ENIC has a controlling interest in a number of European football clubs, Vicenza in Italy, Slavia Prague in Czechoslovakia, AEK Athens in Greece and FC Basel in Switzerland, and they also own twenty-five per cent of Glasgow Rangers. They have an eighty per cent holding in Warner Brothers merchandise stores in the UK and have an exclusive franchise to create and operate Warner Brothers theme restaurants around the world, with the first such restaurant opening soon in the 6,000-room Venetian Hotel in Las Vegas. Although Warner Brothers only hold five per cent of the shares in ENIC, their relationship with the company is obviously serious because, apart from the stores and the restaurants agreement, one of the Warner board, Dan

Romanelli, is on the ENIC board, which is chaired by Howard Stanton, a reputable and experienced City figure, and the chief executive is Daniel Levy, a bright young man in his early 30s who has a longstanding relationship with Joseph Lewis.

The initial approach from ENIC was understandably rejected by our merchant bankers on the grounds that ENIC was making very little profit and our current profits were almost £30 million. Furthermore, they were suggesting a merger on the basis of one ENIC share for each Wembley share.

Messrs Brooke, Mead and I were very keen to go forward and maintain ENIC's interest in Wembley because we thought that the concept of their company with its management had a future, while we were very pessimistic about the prospects of Wembley under Nigel Potter's management. The obvious reason for the pessimism was that our business is an entrepreneurial one and Potter, although a competent finance director, had never indicated in any way whatsoever that he had any entrepreneurial talent or flair.

ENIC did maintain their interest, in no uncertain manner, and finally made a bid of 412p per share (200p in cash and 212p value in shares in the new company – Wembley/ENIC), a substantial premium over the Stock Market price of 289p when ENIC first made their approach. Although Potter and Elliott went through the motions of looking in to ENIC's business and indicated that they were impressed, particularly with Daniel Levy, I had the feeling – which has since proved well justified – that they were 'going through the motions' with no real intention of accepting the ENIC bid. Even more importantly, Potter and Paul Baines of Charterhouse, the Wembley banking advisers, who had been, contrary to board instructions, to see two of the major institutional shareholders who control 37 per cent of Wembley's shares between them, came back to the board stating that those shareholders were not interested in taking ENIC shares and had said that we should proceed with the sale of the Stadium. Those same shareholders confirmed that view to me and Roger Brooke, although we did not feel their attitude was entirely justified because the shares being offered would not be simply ENIC shares but they would have been shares where at least 55 per cent of Wembley's current profits would have been freely available to the new company. ENIC eventually indicated they would offer 300p per share in cash plus 112½p in Wembley/ENIC shares, but Hultman, Potter and Elliott exhibited no interest whatsoever.

It seemed that we had interminable board meetings and Hultman, Potter and Elliott were implacably opposed to doing the ENIC deal. They were set on signing a contract, albeit conditional on shareholders' approval, for the sale of the Stadium to the FA. I could not help but come to the conclusion that their attitude was self-serving and that they were far happier remaining as big fish in the small pond that Wembley plc would be without the Stadium than being smaller fish in the big pond created by Wembley plus ENIC, retaining the interest in the Stadium.

This interest in the Stadium was regarded by us as essential from the company's point of view, as the identity of our company was almost entirely dependent upon the Stadium, the best known sports venue in the whole world – even in the United States, where they have come to know about Wembley through the televising of the NFL football games and the major pop concerts which have been held at the Stadium. The fact of American interest was borne out when I was contacted by Robert Sillerman, based in New York, who had amassed a large fortune through owning radio stations throughout the United States with his company SFX Entertainment. In the last few years SFX have sold their radio stations and have secured the control or ownership of 74 major entertainment venues in the United States, and Wembley appeared to be ideal for their first venture overseas. They also, being Americans, had no inhibitions about our gaming interests in Rhode Island. I first met Bob Sillerman in the early 90s when he owned the New York team in the American Football World League. He accompanied the team when it played at Wembley on two occasions and had obviously become impressed with the Stadium.

SFX engaged a heavyweight group of advisers, Lehman Brothers, bankers, Slaughter & May, a leading firm of solicitors, and Ernst & Young as accountants to assist them in formulating an offer of £4.50 per share which Charterhouse, the Wembley bankers, they said they could recommend as acceptable. They also sent Tom Benson, their chief financial officer, and Brian Becker, a senior vice president over to Wembley to make their own assessment. Our lawyers, Herbert Smith, whose team of David Gold, Patrick Mitchell, Alan Watts and Julia Pyke were absolutely brilliant in their handling of a difficult situation, revealed what was another strange development. There was a contract between Wembley and Charterhouse signed only on 4 January 1999 by Potter, agreeing to pay Charterhouse £500,000 primarily for advice on the sale of the Stadium, whether the sale was completed or not. This agreement was never put to the board for approval and this was certainly surprising in the then reigning circumstances.

We had been openly critical of Baines' conduct all through and I had told him to his face that I regarded his behaviour as completely one-sided and obviously biased. The revelation of the agreement certainly did nothing to reduce the strength of these feelings.

When considering the ENIC proposal, Baines' indifference to it was remarkable in view of the value per share in comparison with the price of £2.85p when ENIC first came on the scene. I pointed out to him more than once that he had never uttered one syllable in favour of any aspect of the ENIC deal. Not even, for example, suggesting that ENIC's tie-up with Warner Brothers was a favourable aspect to be considered, as it obviously was. This attitude was certainly shared by Hultman, Potter and Elliott, who had a glazed look in their eyes whenever I pointed out that Warners obviously had a favourable view of ENIC. It was a case of 'None are so deaf as those who will not hear.'

While all this was happening, with the date of the shareholders' meeting on 11 March looming ever nearer, some facts emerged which caused confusion. First a *Sunday Express* City column writer discovered that Potter and Elliott had service agreements which gave them capital sums of £400,000 and £180,000 respectively if 'control of the company changed hands'. Potter's agreement was dated 30 November and Elliott's 19 January 1999, both dates well after ENIC had met the directors and made their intentions known. These contracts were apparently similar to those given to executive directors previously, and in the case of Potter's agreement, only the amount of salary was changed from his previous contract as finance director. Elliott's, however, was something new and in his case certainly it would have been far more discreet for the question of his agreement to have been brought up before the full board. No doubt it would have been approved, if only on the casting vote of the chairman, but it certainly would have been better for it to have been discussed. Apparently there was a big fuss made by Clifford Chance, the company's solicitors, about the reference to the agreements in the *Sunday Express*, which resulted in a correction in the following issue.

The lack of enthusiasm for any bid for the company on the part of Paul Baines was certainly apparent when I attended a meeting to introduce Charles Alexander and Simon Costa of Lehman Brothers to him. Even when Alexander made it clear that SFX were considering an offer of £4.50 in cash, fifty-five per cent higher than the pre-ENIC price, Baines appeared likely to hedge until I pressed him to repeat his assertion of only two weeks previously that the figure was acceptable. Eventually, by 5 March, only six days before the Extraordinary General Meeting of shareholders was to be held to vote on the Stadium sale, SFX asked for a delay in that meeting of 30 days so that they could formulate a proper offer for the shares, with a minimum figure of 400p in cash and aiming possibly for a cash offer of 450p, the figure which both Baines and Potter had previously said would be acceptable.

This seemed to be a reasonable proposal from SFX, particularly as they were obviously people of substance, having engaged very expensive 'heavyweight' advisers to support them in their bid. They took the view, just as Peter, Roger and I had, that the terms of the proposed sale to the FA were so bad for Wembley that there was a need to renegotiate the deal with the FA and even suggested that the initial purchase price would be significantly reduced in exchange for an ongoing arrangement including a management agreement – which, of course, was something we had been campaigning for. Predictably, our two executive directors and Hultman rejected this proposal on the extremely weak grounds that the FA would walk away from the deal, which they were entitled to do if we passed the fateful date of 15 March without completing the sale. This was an unrealistic view, particularly as Wembley was the central feature in the FA's 2006 World Cup campaign. Abandoning Wembley would effectively have been abandoning the World Cup bid, which they would never have done.

I confirmed this view to the board members when I mentioned a conversation I had had the previous day with Bobby Charlton, a member of the World Cup Campaign Committee at Old Trafford, which supported this view. Despite the significance of what I had related, I couldn't have received less interest if I'd talked about the weather. Peter Mead then weighed in with a description of Tony Banks' appearance on David Frost's TV show the previous day when he said Wembley was an essential ingredient in the World Cup bid, but neither of our statements had any effect whatsoever and the response was one I would expect to get from a wall. More than ever it became obvious there was no way that these 'Turkeys' were going to vote for Christmas!

Incidentally, in the conversation with Bobby Charlton,

which he started by asking me about what was going to happen with the SFX proposal while making it clear that Wembley was an essential ingredient for the World Cup campaign, I found myself having to repeat to Bobby what I had told him on a previous occasion at Wembley: that I regarded our bid for the World Cup as extremely dubious. I reminded him that I had been present in December 1993 at Las Vegas at the time of the draw ceremony for the 1994 World Cup, when it was made clear to me by Bert Millichip, then chairman of the FA, and Egidius Braun, president of the German federation, that the FA would be supporting the German bid for the World Cup 2006 in return for Germany supporting us, when it was greatly needed, as hosts for Euro 96.

The day before my conversation with Millichip and Braun, Lennart Johannson, president of UEFA, the European football federation, said that there was a great deal of pressure for Euro 96 to be taken away from us but hopefully, with the essential support of the Germans, we would keep it. I remember distinctly telling Johannson how concerned I was, obviously on behalf of Wembley, and he said that he would like us to keep the tournament but our supporters were something of a liability. Only in January of this year, Johannson told the UEFA Conference in Lausanne that the European countries should support the German bid because of what was now described as a 'gentlemen's agreement' and he was amazed that 'the English denied any knowledge of it'. Bobby Charlton pointed out to me that the agreement between Millichip and Braun was never minuted by the FA, but as Bert Millichip told me recently, there were many arrangements he made during the time of his chairmanship which were never minuted yet the FA acted upon and benefited for them.

Remarkably, Tony Banks, chairman of the FA World Cup Campaign, only a matter of months before he was appointed, signed an Early Day Motion in the House of Commons, together with Ken Livingstone and a few other MPs, stating that, in their view, it was wrong for any country in Europe (obviously including England) to have the World Cup Finals in 2006 and it should go to South Africa.

Inevitably it appeared that the Stadium would be sold and this would eventually lead, in the not too distant future, to a break-up of Wembley plc, which I viewed with a great deal of sorrow, particularly having suffered through the Silkin, Shamji, Wolfson and Hultman eras. The meeting of shareholders was held on 11 March at Wembley Conference Centre and it was very stormy indeed, although only about fifty people turned up for 9.30am – an early start to get to Wembley. There were as many press and television people present, which was not surprising in view of the considerable publicity the whole issue and dispute had attracted. The press were not admitted to the meeting, with about twelve shareholders speaking. Ten of them spoke very strongly against the sale of the Stadium, with some being very critical of the executive directors and particularly the chairman.

All this was to no avail because the institutions had made up their mind, as I have related, and their proxies were sent to the chairman in advance of the meeting, despite a considerable amount of press criticism of the sale and with some papers commenting on the apparent reluctance by the chairman and executive directors to seriously consider the takeover approaches first from ENIC and subsequently from SFX. There was a show of hands vote with 30 voting against the sale and only 8 in favour. The poll, however, with the institutional shareholders' proxies included, resulted in 32 million for a surprisingly high minority vote of 8 million against. The vast majority of the 32 million, of course, were polled by only a handful of fund managers – similar to union bloc votes which were so severely criticised in the past – and I left the meeting feeling that I had attended the funeral of Wembley plc.

I travelled to New York that evening and two days later saw the Lewis v Holyfield heavyweight championship fight. It struck me that the decision in that fight was as much as misjudgment as had been made by our institutional shareholders.

14

Variety and Other Clubs

As a sportsman, Arnold Palmer was a man with ice water running through his veins. Whatever the pressure, however far the putt, regardless of a packed gallery, he was the man you would want playing for your life. His golfing success owed much to that coolness while others around him were losing their heads.

Yet here he was standing beside me, tears streaming down his face and totally unable to speak. It took more than two minutes before he could compose himself enough to address the crowd, telling them, 'I'm not ashamed to show my emotions.' Arnie had given $5 million of his own money and raised another $6 million to create a children's hospital in Florida, and was in Orlando at Disney World to receive from me the Variety Clubs International Humanitarian Award. We had just had a video presentation about the work of the hospital and been serenaded by the children's choir from the same hospital.

In many ways the story of my life and times which I have tried to tell in this book is full of such moments where I have had a glimpse of the great and the good in a way most other people do not see. That moment with Palmer came as the last act in my two-year term as president of Variety Clubs International between 1991 and 1993, during which I had gone round the world, met people I would otherwise never have come across and seen the work being done in a host of amazing projects throughout the world.

The Variety Clubs worldwide, with 70 branches from Australia to North America, provide children's hospitals, electric wheelchairs, artificial limbs, and buses known as Sunshine Coaches which transport underprivileged and handicapped children on trips. It is known as the 'Greatest Children's Charity in the World' and deserves the description. I first joined the Variety Club in 1954, being invited to do so by Monty Berman, the film and theatre costumier. I became involved in running race meetings at Sandown Park to raise funds for the organization and since then my association with it has often helped reshape and refocus my life. This was certainly true in 1976 when Trevor Chinn, an old friend, was asked to be the Chief Barker (President) of the Variety Club of Great Britain. He was a little unsure about accepting. I told him I thought he'd be a marvellous Chief Barker. We ended up with a deal – he'd accept the honour and I would join his Crew – the team which traditionally helps the Chief Barker organize events during his or her period in office.

It meant a lot of work but I was glad to be kept so busy. Two years earlier my wife Phyllis had died, my life seemed bereft and with time on my hands, despite my involvement with Dustin Hoffman, I was glad to throw myself into Variety Club work. This burst of activity led to other things and by 1983 I was myself elected Chief Barker of the Great Britain branch of Variety Clubs, which these days raises as much as £8 million annually.

It meant an incredibly busy year for me and my second wife Nadine, whose help was invaluable. I took up the position on 1st January 1983 and over the next three months I presented the annual televised Variety Club Showbusiness Awards, presided over a dinner at Caerphilly Castle organized by the South Wales Committee of the Variety Club and attended by the Prince and Princess of Wales, and went to Buckingham Palace to make a presentation to winners of the Duke of Edinburgh Awards. As summer rolled on, events became even more crowded. There was a lunch at the Guildhall with a children's party in the Courtyard, again attended by the Prince and Princess of Wales, a Royal Garden Party at Buckingham Palace, and in August a dinner for major benefactors of the Variety Club on board HMS Hermes, the aircraft carrier which had served in the Falklands War. Later that year the Woman of the Year Dinner was held by the Leeds Committee of the Variety Club and I presented the award to the author Barbara Taylor Bradford. In November there was a televised lunch at the Guildhall, where the guests of honour were the Archbishop of Canterbury Robert Runcie, Cardinal Basil Hume and the Chief Rabbi, Immanuel Jakobovitz. On that same day, the Chief Rabbi and I were inducted as Freemen of the City of London. It brought home to me just how much good and varied work the Variety Club does through the events it stages in order to raise funds for its all-important work.

If my year as Chief Barker was both hectic and fulfilling, another great honour was to follow when eight years later, at our International Convention in Vancouver in May 1991, I was elected President of Variety Clubs International. There were many highlights during my two years in office, but I particularly recall the dinner in honour of Joe Roth, chairman of 20th Century Fox, at the Century Plaza Hotel in Los Angeles. The gathering was star-studded, to say the least, and so was the cabaret, compered by Billy Crystal. He was as irreverent to the Hollywood establishment as he had been when compering the Academy Awards. The dinner raised $750,000 for Variety Club children's charities in California.

The grandeur of that event was more than matched by the one in January 1992, when Margaret Thatcher was the guest of honour at a dinner attended by 1,000 people at the Waldorf Astoria Hotel in New York. The guest list was quite simply a Who's Who of New York City and the speakers included Henry Kissinger and the actor Anthony Quinn. That night we raised $850,000 for the Variety Clubs' Lifeline Programme, which brings children from the Third World to the United States, Canada and Great Britain for life-saving operations. I was particularly grateful to Mrs Thatcher because she was well aware of my political affiliations, having been my local MP when I lived for twenty years near Hampstead Heath in her Finchley constituency, and we had had some disagreements in the past.

If those were the two great dinners during my two-year presidency, there were many other notable fundraising occasions. There was a football game in Dallas between the Cowboys and the Philadelphia Eagles, plus a ball in Memphis, Tennessee, which gave me the chance to visit Graceland, the home of Elvis Presley. To see how the guides showed people round this 'monument' was faintly amusing, because of their serious attitude. Yet the number of tourists lining up and arriving in buses was quite astounding and it seems that Elvis Presley's estate makes more money now than it did when he was alive.

One of my more unusual duties came when I took part in the famous Miss America Parade along several miles of the Boardwalk at Atlantic City in New Jersey. This meant me sitting on the back of a pink Cadillac convertible, with the roof down, of course, driven by a lady police lieutenant. I was riding in front of the Variety Club float and on the side of the Cadillac was a big poster saying 'Welcome to Jarvis Astaire – Variety Clubs International President'.

It was on Variety Club business on another occasion that I got to speak to my famous namesake. On a visit to Los Angeles I had been asked by the BBC to arrange interviews with appropriate celebrities for the Variety Club tribute to Gene Kelly which they were televising. I obviously wanted to include Fred Astaire and managed to get hold of his telephone number.

He came to the phone and to my amazement, when he heard my name he said, 'I have heard of you. You live in London, you are in the entertainment business and you breed racehorses,' a subject I knew he was interested in. He went on: 'I have been asked on a couple of occasions whether we are related, and of course we are not.'

I said, 'I am really surprised you have heard of me, but I want to thank you on behalf of my family for the good hotel rooms we have had all these years because of you.'

Incidentally, he refused to do the interview, saying he wasn't up to being filmed at the time and in any case he thought there were too many tributes being paid to too many people.

If that was America, Europe was not forgotten. I visited Prague, where there was a reception given in my honour by Madame Havlova, wife of the Czech President, and I presented two Sunshine Coaches to the Havel Foundation, named after him. I also particularly enjoyed being guest of honour at a dinner of the Israel Variety Club in Tel Aviv, when thirty-four Ambassadors to Israel were present.

Variety Clubs International is also the official beneficiary of the annual Miss World Contest, so I was twice invited to be a judge, firstly in Atlanta, where the winner was Miss Venezuela, and the following year at Sun City in South Africa, where the winner was Miss Russia. On that occasion I felt the judges were even more interesting than the girls because they included Joan Collins – a long-time friend with whom I had the pleasure of dining every evening – Gary Player, Ivana Trump and Alan Whicker. The show was compered by Jerry Hall as well as Debbie Shelton, the former Miss America.

I bowed out as International President at our Convention at Disney World in Orlando. The Disney Organization, long-time supporters of the Variety Clubs, really extended themselves and staged wonderful shows and various forms of entertainment, which for me rounded off my term of office in the finest possible style.

The Variety Club has played an enormous part in my life but there have been other associations, such as the Anglo-American Sporting Club. This was formed in 1964 under my chairmanship and was eventually merged with the National Sporting Club. I succeeded a great man, Lord Charles Forte, as chairman of the National Sporting Club and we staged many successful boxing and dinner evenings in London, helping to raise hundreds of thousands of pounds for various deserving causes. Our first President was the Marquess of Milford Haven, best man at the wedding of the Queen and Prince Philip. Some years later he unfortunately died suddenly and was succeeded as President by the Earl of Westmorland.

I particularly value my membership over the last twenty years of the Friars Club, which is the hub of showbusiness in New York City. Lunchtime at the Friars Club is where one will hear the best jokes and meet the most interesting people. During the time of my membership, the Deans of the Club have included William B Williams, a famous New York disc jockey who brought Ava Gardner to my home one evening, Jackie Green (yes, the agent involved with Sonny Liston) and, currently, the famous comedian Freddie Roman. The current officers include Milton Berle, Red Buttons, Billy Crystal, Paul Anka, Alan King, Sid Caesar, Tony Martin and Tom Jones, while until his recent death Frank Sinatra was 'The Abbot', which is the Friars version of president.

Some of those and other greats like Jack Benny, Bob Hope, George Burns, Jerry Lewis, Jackie Mason and particularly Henry Youngman, known as the King of the One Liners, have been a delight to meet and listen to.

Another involvement of which I am very proud is with the Royal Free Hospital, which came about by chance. I received a phone call the day after one of my closed-circuit Muhammad Ali fights from a man who introduced himself as Professor Kenneth Hill. He said he was a pathologist at the Royal Free Hospital and secretary to the London University Television Committee. Professor Hill said that he thought I could do for medicine what I had done for Muhammad Ali and boxing!

He meant relaying post-mortems carried out at the St Pancras mortuary by Professor Francis Camps, the senior Home Office pathologist, back to medical students at the Royal Free Hospital. This went on for several days and the students from various medical schools in London were invited to see them. This experiment was particularly important because when pathologists carry out post-mortems, they are not able to accommodate students around them as they would when performing regular surgery. Subsequently a symposium took place at the Royal Free Hospital – which by this time had moved from Grays Inn Road in Holborn to Hampstead – and was presided over by Dame Sheila Sherlock, a specialist in liver disease. Dame Sheila presented two of her cases in front of the cameras with all the necessary data and it was relayed to twelve medical schools around the country. Remarkably enough, with only the televised information available to them, the schools diagnosed the cases correctly. It seemed that such a service would be extremely beneficial to patients throughout the country. Alas, Government funding was not available at the time and the idea fell by the wayside.

However, because of my connections with the Royal Free Hospital, I became chairman of the Hospital and Medical School Appeal Trust and remained so for twelve years. During this time, among other projects we were able to purchase, through voluntary fund-raising, a body scanner and create an endowment fund for its continued operation. This cost £1 million and the fund-raising was greatly assisted by the Duke of Edinburgh kindly agreeing to be the guest of honour at a dinner launching the appeal.

I HAVE said how the death of my first wife in 1974 left a deep void in my life which was filled by activities such as the Variety Club and my involvement in the film business in America. Then, early in 1981, my life was uplifted by becoming romantically involved and subsequently married to Nadine Hyman. Nadine, a beautiful French lady, had come to England when she married her first husband. They were friendly with my brother and his wife and I used to meet them at my brother's place and other social gatherings. In 1980, after almost twenty-five years in this country, Nadine was divorced from her English husband and a year later, in February 1981, I was asked by a friend to take her to a party. I discovered she was a magistrate in the juvenile courts and a marriage guidance counsellor, who led a very active life. We had so much in common that falling in love was the easiest thing. Four weeks after that party, we decided to get married.

I had never thought I would find love after Phyllis, but with Nadine I did. If her beauty was something to behold, then just as wonderful was her very positive personality. There are many women who are beautiful but when you get to know them, you discover there is nothing beyond their beauty, nothing inside their hearts. That was not so with Nadine.

I was some years older than her, fifty-seven to her forty-four, and had every right to expect that we would have a long, happily married life together. But after five years and a good marriage, it was cut short by Nadine's tragic death from cancer, only five and a half weeks after it had been diagnosed. This, of course, was a tremendous blow to me, just as Phyllis's death had been twelve years earlier. However, I have, for as long as I can remember, held the philosophy that when someone young dies – and both my wives died in their forties – I feel sorry for them rather than the people left behind, who can remake their lives. They had so much opportunity and the good they could have done is gone. All that is left is the memory of them and among the many legacies I derived from my all too short marriage with Nadine was that she got me playing tennis again after an interval of many years. Subsequently, through the introduction of my Californian tennis friend Barry Murkin, I became a member of Queens Club in London. Queens is second only to the All England Club at Wimbledon and I have spent and continue to spend many enjoyable times at the club, where I have made many new friends. When she died Nadine had just been appointed chairman of the Juvenile Bench of magistrates and she was also chairman of the British Friends of the Art Museums of Israel. Today the rose garden at the Art Museum in Jerusalem is named in her honour. It is a fitting tribute.

I remain more than ever convinced in my thoughts about

those who die young after the death at a very young age of Diana, Princess of Wales. Yes, it is true that her two sons have a heavy burden to bear having lost their wonderful mother, but what we must mourn is that the life of such a remarkable woman was so tragically cut short. I was fortunate enough to meet her on several occasions, and what struck me about Diana was how thoughtful she was.

She attended the 1988 FA Cup Final, the one where Liverpool, in a big upset, lost 1-0 to Wimbledon. Before the Final, Sam Hammam, the Lebanese owner of Wimbledon, was very anxious about sitting in the Royal Box next to the Princess of Wales and invited me to lunch a couple of days before the match to ask me how he should conduct himself. I told him he only had to act naturally and immediately prior to the official lunch before the game, I mentioned his fears to the Princess. She said with a smile that he had nothing to worry about. 'I'll soon sort him out,' she said. I noticed that she did pay particular attention to Sam . This was typical of someone who, amidst all her work and troubles, bothered to look after Sam Hammam and make him feel at ease.

Diana used her royal position to aid many charitable causes, which will certainly miss her contribution to their fund-raising efforts. But I believe that this can be redressed by focusing attention on other members of the Royal Family, particularly Prince Charles, and in the not too distant future on her very attractive and appealing sons. I am afraid those causes will not be helped if the media continues to 'flog' Diana's memory almost to the extent of endowing her with a 'sainthood'.

My memories of the great, good and not so good could go on, but before I do conclude, I must reflect again on one significant event which took place on 1 May 1997. This was the election of the Labour Government, something many people had given up all hope of ever seeing again in this country. I never lost faith. I did not, it is true, anticipate such a spectacular result – I thought Labour would get about a 40-odd seat majority. In this election, as in previous ones, I did my bit canvassing in several constituencies. I tried hard to guess the mood but it was impossible to say, looking at people's faces, what they were thinking. I can only reflect that they had long ago made up their minds to get rid of the Tories, and this they duly did.

'Bliss it was to be born in that dawn,' wrote the poet, and many Labour people felt such bliss in 1997. I shall long remember the party on the night of 1 May at the Festival Hall when not only those who had always supported Labour came but so did David Puttnam, who had not surprisingly defected but now returned, and Richard Branson, who had not declared his hand during the election, but was now keen to join the victors. My great satisfaction was that I had never deserted Labour or even felt tempted to. I am, however, first and foremost a democrat and am concerned that we seem to have virtually no opposition to a Government with a huge majority.

The day before the election, I had gone to Wembley to attend the Soccerex exhibition, held just before England's World Cup qualifying match against Georgia. When I got there I was told the Prime Minister, John Major, had come for some publicity photographs with the FA Cup and to promote England's campaign to stage the World Cup finals in 2006. I went to welcome him but when I turned to leave to let Major get on with the photographers, he put an arm on my shoulder and said, 'Jarvis, in moments like this we need old friends.' I had originally come to know Major through our mutual interest in and membership of Surrey County Cricket Club.

I was touched by the gesture, the more so as he knew I am a Labour supporter. After the election, I wrote to Major expressing my personal appreciation of his demeanour at Wembley on that day, because he obviously knew he was staring defeat in the face. I was delighted to receive a letter back thanking me for my letter and particularly for my welcome at Wembley. I received the letter within a few days of one from Tony Blair thanking me for my efforts on behalf of Labour.

I did not like John Major's party or his government but had nothing against the man, a decent, fine human being, although an indecisive leader. Already there are signs that Tony Blair will be one of our great Prime Ministers, bringing back those qualities of humanity and decency that have made this country great. I count myself lucky that I was born here and, despite temptations, have never felt like leaving.

I am also lucky that despite the heartache of losing two wives, I have had two lovely children, Steven and Susan, who have given me five grandchildren.

Steven, who was a good athlete, became interested in horse riding in his late twenties and subsequently became an amateur jockey, riding under National Hunt and Jockey Club rules, as well as in many point-to-point races. He rode seven winners and finally retired only last year. He has also been an enthusiastic racehorse owner and serves on the Council of the Racehorse Owners' Association. He is the senior partner in a stockbroking firm which my brother originally founded and developed successfully over twenty years.

Susan, who obtained a Bachelor of Arts (Hons) in jewellery design at the Central School of Art, has been for some years a successful jewellery designer.

No man blessed with such wonderful children can say his life has been anything but fulfilled.

15

All the Way

When you met Sammy Cahn, you were confronted by a man who didn't appear to have a romantic bone in his body. He came across as a cynical being, full of biting, spontaneous wit, but that helped make him absolutely great fun. And for all this 'cynicism', Sammy wrote some of the loveliest, most romantic songs ever heard: 'Call Me Irresponsible', 'Time After Time' and 'Three Coins in a Fountain', which earned him one of his five Oscars.

The fact was that Sammy, the man whose acid tongue never missed a punchline, could also be the most lavish of hosts and the most generous of givers. He gave his talent to the world and shared his gifts with his friends. I was lucky to be a recipient.

My first meeting with him came some time in the early 1970s when he was a special guest at a Variety Club lunch in London. He had brought his show 'Words and Music' to London after it had enjoyed a very successful run in the United States. In London it was retitled 'The Sammy Cahn Songbook'.

The second run of the show some years later was at the Duke of York Theatre under the production banner of Bill Kenwright, who has become London's most prolific theatrical producer. Sammy was enjoying excellent critical reviews and receiving a standing ovation after every performance. On the third Saturday of the run came a wholly unscripted moment of high drama. After the show I took Sammy and his wife Tita, with whom he had a tempestuous relationship – marriage, divorce, remarriage – to dinner. It was quite late by the time I returned home and I was reading the early editions of the Sunday papers in bed, around about 1.30am, when the telephone rang. It was Tita. Her voice was anxious: 'What's Dr Dymond's number?'

Geoffrey Dymond is my doctor and for Tita to ask for him suggested something was seriously wrong. I asked her what the matter was and she said, 'It's Sammy, he can't breathe.'

I immediately went round to their hotel, which was only a few minutes away, and as soon as I saw Sammy I could tell it was congestive heart failure. A friend of mine had died from it, so I knew exactly what the symptoms were. Dr Dymond met me at the hotel and told me that my diagnosis was spot on. While it was pleasing to have my medical verdict endorsed, more important was that something was done to help Sammy, and quickly. There was no time to call an ambulance and wait for it to arrive, so we took Sammy down to my car and headed at breakneck speed for the Wellington Hospital. Dr Dymond had phoned ahead and the staff were ready with a wheelchair as soon as we arrived.

At the hospital, a young lady doctor took charge and Sammy was kept up all night, with the doctor draining fluid from him. Amazingly, by the middle of the next morning Sammy was feeling as right as rain, so much so that he wanted to get back on stage and continue the show, the old stage adage that 'the show must go on' being one of his golden sayings. But in the end medical advice prevailed and the rest of the run was postponed for three weeks. Sammy needed rest and monitoring and had to return to San Francisco to see his heart specialist.

Sammy went on to live for another five years after that. He died at the age of 79 in Los Angeles on 15 January 1993. About twelve hours before he died, Tita walked in and said to him, 'Come on Sammy, we're going to beat this.' He retorted: 'Tita, after all this time please don't get corny.'

It summed up the man totally.

Sammy Cahn came from an era of incredible music and there wasn't a person in showbusiness that he didn't know and couldn't tell a tale about, often quite cruel but always so very funny. He had a great talent in his ability to write songs and lyrics, or 'special material' as he would call it. He would adapt his words or write new lyrics to suit an occasion and nothing, however, complex the situation, seemed to be beyond him. He was quite happy to come up with parodies virtually off the top of his head. Typical examples of this were to the tune of 'The Girl that I Marry':

> *'The Girl that I Marry*
> *Will have to be*
> *A nympho who owns a distillery'*

or 'My First Affair':

> *'This is my first affair*
> *So what goes where?'*

He could produce endless such variations, almost at will. You could say, 'Sammy, I've got to give a speech at a wedding to toast the bride and bridegroom. There are going to be 350 guests, it is the third time the bridegroom has been married, the second time for the bride and they have been living together for seven years – could you come up with something appropriate?'

That is almost exactly what I told him when I was asked to give the toast at the wedding of Harry Goodman, tour operator and airline owner, to Yvonne, a former air stewardess. Sammy's response was immediate. Down the phone he started to sing, 'Come fly with me, come fly with me is how the story all began, up in the air . . .' My toast became Sammy's parody of 'Come Fly With Me', which I sang accompanied by the band.

And he could do that every time. He would be back to you inside twenty-four hours with a new set of words that fitted the occasion and the tune perfectly. Another time, I was asked to be in a Variety Club Pro-am show. The cream of British showbiz was in the performance, people like Anthony Andrews, Patricia Hodge and Joanna Lumley. They wanted me to sing 'Strangers in the Night' but though I'm proud of my singing voice, I'm not a public performer and I didn't want to stand before a full theatre and sing. If I had to sing, I wanted it to be something that was a little different.

I gave Sammy a call and he said, 'OK. If that's what you want, how about this? "Strangers in the night, tonight I'm viewing strangers in the night, who might start booing. Bet you're wondering why I even try to sing,"' and so on. The Variety Club audience had not expected anything like that and it quite brought the house down. Afterwards Prince Edward came up to me, amazed that I had got Sammy to write a new lyric. I explained how Sammy was a great friend and that he had done a lot of work for the Variety Club. What was astounding was the speed with which he could come up with his 'special material'. He once said to me, 'Don't tell anyone how quickly I do it – they won't want to pay me how much they do.'

Nothing was beyond him, as I discovered when we held a dinner in New York to honour Audrey Hepburn. She was receiving the Variety Clubs International Humanitarian Award for all her work for UNICEF helping children throughout the world. It was during my term as President of the Variety Clubs International and the evening before the event I went with Sammy, just in from Los Angeles, to Tribeca Grill, the New York restaurant owned by Robert de Niro.

'Sammy,' I said, 'it's a pity I did not know you were going to be in New York. I could have got you to do something special for Audrey Hepburn.'

He replied, 'It's not too late, you know.'

For Sammy, such short notice was a challenge and the next

night he presented a very special version of the song, 'I've Grown Accustomed To Her Face'. It was greeted by a standing ovation from the eight hundred people present.

That story – and there were numerous other occasions when he came up with these songs – just shows how generous Sammy was with his talent. He had the stories, he had the words and music and he was more than happy to share it with everyone.

And it was Sammy who paid me a great compliment one day at his New York apartment. We were there with his producer, Les Davies, when Sammy suddenly jumped up and said to Les, 'I'm going to play you a tape of two singers. I want you to tell me who they are.' The tape came on and I recognised the first voice as Frank Sinatra, as did Davies. The second singer started and I realized with some surprise that it was myself on a tape of songs I had made for charity. I was wondering what sort of verdict Davies was going to reach. The tape played through and he looked over to Sammy and said, 'It sounds like early Tony Bennett to me.'

I was knocked out and told him, 'Mr Davies, what a compliment you have just paid me.' The record had been made as a result of another party in Hollywood given by Earl and Marion Jorgensen, where people were singing around the piano. I have always fancied myself as a singer and the pianist started to play 'The Way We Were'. I was the only one who knew the words so I took the spotlight and was warmly applauded at the end. A lady there, whom I had asked to donate money towards the Royal Free Hospital, said she would give me $5,000 if I ever made a record. Shortly after this I was in London and discussing fundraising at a dinner. Sitting next to me was the head of Chappells Music, Stephen Gottlieb, and he offered me his studio free of charge for a day. The record was made and the many thousands of pounds raised from it were split between Variety Clubs, the Royal Free Hospital and the London Federation of Boys' Clubs. I started selling copies for 'donations' of £1,000 and after reducing the price to £500, sold some CDs at £100.

But there was another side to Sammy, when generosity and laughter turned to lacerating wit. I was present on one occasion when he was asked to entertain at a state dinner in Washington being given by George Shultz, President Reagan's Secretary of State, and this time Sammy performed a very biting and cynical lyric. He didn't approve of Republicans and was quite fearless when he came to showing it, although he was friendly with Reagan himself. They had got to know each other when they were both under contract to Warner Brothers, Reagan as an actor and Sammy as a songwriter. But for all his friendship with Reagan, he could not get to love the Republicans and did not care who knew about it or where he expressed it, even at the Reagan White House.

What I will remember Sammy for most are his parties and his stories. He used to say, 'Give me a name and I'll give you a story.' One of my favourites was about the time he went to see Frank Sinatra to sing a song called 'All the Way' which Sinatra was going to perform in the film 'The Joker Is Wild'. The film's producer invited Sammy over and said Sinatra would sing with him over breakfast. It was five o'clock in the afternoon when Sammy got there and the song was duly sung with Jimmy van Heusen on the piano. When they finished, Sinatra turned to Sammy and said: 'OK, now let's eat breakfast.'

Another such tale concerned Artie Shaw, a famous bandleader who played the clarinet. Shaw was not only a big star of the 1940s but as a human being was far ahead of his time. He even hired Billie Holliday at a time when black and white were totally segregated in America.

However, Shaw was very selfish in dealing with women. The story Sammy told about him concerned his love for Betty Grable and how he did not get her but ended up with someone quite different, thousands of miles away. When Shaw and Betty Grable fell for each other, they couldn't be together because she was married to Jackie Coogan. Shaw had to wait a year for that marriage to fall apart. Grable ended up on

Broadway doing a show, 'Du Barry Was A Lady', and for Betty and Artie life was like the movies, literally. After the show they would dance down Fifth Avenue as if they were re-enacting a scene from 'Singing in The Rain'.

In the middle of the run, Artie got a call from Louis B Mayer to go to California and make a film for MGM. Sammy said not to worry because Phil Silvers, another genius of the era destroyed, sadly, by gambling, would look after Artie when he arrived. Betty was all the more reassured as she received long, lovely letters from Artie proclaiming his love and pledging undying allegiance. Then one night, Sammy wandered out of the 46th Street Theatre to hear newsboys shouting, 'Artie Shaw marries Lana Turner. Read all about it!'

Artie Shaw had always said that if he could meet the girl of his dreams, he would throw it all in and go off to live on an island, and it seemed that now Lana Turner was the girl. The two of them had gone out on a date while in Hollywood and on that first outing, they had taken a plane to Las Vegas and got married. However, it did not last. The nuptials were proclaimed in February 1940 and by September 1940 it was all over. As Sammy told the story, Artie was the most remarkably talented but vainest and meanest of men, especially to women. He took Grable from Coogan and Ava Gardner from Mickey Rooney, but he neither made his women happy nor found happiness himself – not surprisingly, since he was married eight times.

To associate with Sammy Cahn was to be touched by magic and it could suddenly give you a celebrity status, as I once found out. The occasion was one of the legendary parties Sammy threw. He was a tremendous host and held some magnificent parties in his home, his magnetic personality making the guest list read like a Who's Who of Hollywood, including Gregory Peck, Jack Lemmon, Clint Eastwood, Dudley Moore, Angie Dickinson and the legendary director Billy Wilder.

This time I had just arrived in Los Angeles from London

and checked in at the Beverly Hills Hotel when I received a call from Tita Cahn. She was very keen for me to go to a birthday dinner that Angie Dickinson was holding for Richard Brooks, the film director whose credits included 'The Blackboard Jungle', 'Cat On A Hot Tin Roof' and 'Lord Jim'.

'Tita,' I said, 'it's been a long flight, I've only just checked in and really I need to go to sleep.'

Twenty minutes later, there was a call from the front door of the hotel and the doorman said that a lady had arrived and was asking for me. They put her on the phone and it was Angie Dickinson. She said, 'You've got to come to the Richard Brooks party. You can leave early if you want to.' I could not resist her and, having got dressed, went down to meet her.

On my way out, the hotel manager said to me, 'You're amazing, Mr Astaire. You have only been in the hotel for thirty minutes and you've got a beautiful star like Angie Dickinson stopping by to pick you up.'